MEDIA AND CLASS

Although the idea of class is again becoming politically and culturally charged, the relationship between media and class remains understudied. This diverse collection draws together prominent and emerging media scholars to offer readers a much-needed orientation within the wider categories of media, class, and politics in Britain, America, and beyond. Case studies address media representations and media participation in a variety of platforms, with attention to contemporary culture: from celetoids to selfies, *Downton Abbey* to *Duck Dynasty*, and royals to reality TV. These scholarly but accessible accounts draw on both theory and empirical research to demonstrate how different media navigate and negotiate, caricature and essentialize, or contain and regulate class.

June Deery is Professor of Media Studies at Rensselaer Polytechnic Institute and author of *Consuming Reality: The Commercialization of Factual Entertainment* (Palgrave, 2012) and *Reality TV* (Polity, 2015). Her latest work looks at reality TV and the campaign and early administration of Donald Trump.

Andrea Press is William R. Kenan, Jr. Professor of Media Studies and Sociology at the University of Virginia. She is the former Executive Editor of the Virginia Film Festival and Producer of the Roger Ebert Film Festival. She is the author or co-author of *The New Media Environment, Speaking of Abortion, Women Watching Television,* and the forthcoming volumes *Media-Ready Feminism and Everyday Sexism, Handbook of Contemporary Feminism,* and *Feminist Reception Studies in a Post-Audience Age.*

MEDIA AND CLASS

TV, Film, and Digital Culture

Edited by
June Deery and Andrea Press

Routledge
Taylor & Francis Group
NEW YORK AND LONDON

First published 2017
by Routledge
711 Third Avenue, New York, NY 10017

and by Routledge
2 Park Square, Milton Park, Abingdon, Oxon OX14 4RN

Routledge is an imprint of the Taylor & Francis Group, an informa business

Library of Congress Cataloging in Publication Data
A catalog record for this book has been requested

ISBN: 978-1-138-22978-5 (hbk)
ISBN: 978-1-138-22979-2 (pbk)
ISBN: 978-1-315-38798-7 (ebk)

Typeset in Bembo Std
by diacriTech, Chennai

CONTENTS

ACKNOWLEDGMENTS

June would like to thank Katya Haskins and Doug Scott for their valuable feedback on her essay and her co-editor Andrea Press for her unflappable good humor (a precious resource in these endeavors). At RPI, she is grateful to friends and colleagues for helping the department survive a very trying year, especially Ellen Esrock, Tamar Gordon, Katya Haskins, Rebecca Rouse, Pat Search, and Dean Mary Simoni. Thanks are also due to the School of HASS for a Flash Grant in support of this project. As always, June appreciates the love and encouragement of family and friends on both sides of the Atlantic, with a special shout-out to Alanna, Eoin, and Catherine Deery, John B. Scott, and Maggie McD. She dedicates this work to the memory of Gaby McDonough, a beloved uncle and man of infinite jest.

Andrea would like to thank above all her co-editor June Deery for her strong sense of organization and her theoretical acuity, which reflects in the introduction and the editing of this volume. Julia Adams and Marjorie Rosen deserve thanks for their continued support in the preparation of this volume. Tasha Oren provided valuable feedback on my essay, as did audiences at the Film History Conference and the Society for Cinema and Media Studies. The Media Studies Department at the University of Virginia provided a stable support group for ongoing scholarship, as did Deans Len Schoppa and Ian Baucom, and our Vice-Provost Kerry Abrams. My colleague Allison Pugh and my student Francesca Tripodi deserve special thanks for their critical responses to my scholarship over the past several years. I dedicate this work to my family, Bruce Williams, Jessie Press-Williams, and Josh Press-Williams, who have been a great support throughout.

At Routledge, we would both like to thank Erica Wetter for her strong encouragement of this project since its inception and Mia Moran for her always courteous guidance. We are also grateful to Brooke Dinsmore and Alicyn Zall for help with the manuscript submission.

1

INTRODUCTION: STUDYING MEDIA AND CLASS

June Deery and Andrea Press

The topic of class, having helped launch the fields of Media and Cultural Studies, has in recent decades been largely neglected, with scholars turning instead to individualization and identity politics,[1] and politicians to neoliberal visions of meritocratic marketization.[2] In Sociology, the topic also faded to an extent, even as—and perhaps because—the class configuration of contemporary societies has become more complex. An initial spur to studying popular media was understanding the class dynamics of production and representation, yet while this topic was fundamental to early research at the Birmingham Centre for Contemporary Cultural Studies (Richard Hoggart, Stuart Hall, Raymond Williams),[3] attention to gender and race began to overtake this original mission. In Britain, but more especially when British Cultural Studies crossed over the Atlantic, examinations of class largely subsided as a component of media analysis.[4]

Today, in both academic and non-academic circles, there is a renewed interest in class—due, at least in part, to recent and somewhat shocking political events. In decades past, a few scholars and many more politicians floated the idea that advanced democracies were approaching a post-class era: in Britain it was a sentiment voiced by both the Right (Thatcher) and the New Left (Blair). Whereas today, scholars, politicians, and ordinary people alike are more convinced that if we want to understand contemporary society we cannot dismiss class as a meaningful category. Furthermore, there is an understanding that the media has a vital role to play in forming and understanding class identities, and that we need to know more about its impact. As both cultural expression and industrial product, the media represent and shape class; and in particular, the new media environment has enabled the rise of isolated opinion nodes which have fostered the rise of class-specific discourse. How and to what degree the media reflect or construct class are matters of debate, but certainly those who finance, produce, compose, distribute, those who receive, interpret, use, and modify, all occupy classed positions whether consciously or not.

Popular Consciousness

Today, the nexus of class, media, and, ultimately, politics is much more a part of public consciousness in America and Britain than even a few years ago when this collection was first conceived. The frequency with which popular and political discourse now acknowledges class differences is, in fact, a significant trend. This used to not be the case. In fact, in American culture class was for a long time something of a taboo and its mention deemed rude or even unpatriotic. However, the patricians' rejection of class discussion as objectionable "class warfare" has receded since the Bush era and now there is unapologetic probing of class division. Increasingly people are naming it, characterizing it, and discussing it as a problem.

Some people have even taken to the streets—all over the world. Protest against a neoliberal wealth disparity was brewing in the Seattle WTO protests in 1999. A similar outrage over economic injustice figured in the overthrow of plutocratic regimes in the Arab Spring of 2010, in the English working-class riots in August 2011, and in the Occupy movement in the autumn of 2011 (with largely bourgeois supporters). Anxieties about economic divisions also figure in the rise of a recent right-wing populism in Europe, often with lower-class support (Judis, 2016; also Frank, 2004). But for Britain and America the great explosion came in 2016 with Brexit (June referendum) and Trump (November election). Both cultures shared the shock of these two events, and in both nations these populist eruptions not only foregrounded class but also demonstrated the apparent failure of the media, particularly news organizations, to understand festering class conflicts and dissent. At the same time, candidate Trump was a creature of the media who, as he exploited and condemned its coverage with equal enthusiasm, highlighted a disturbing link between media profitability (ratings) and a weakening of democracy.

The Brexit referendum and Trump's victory were immediately attributed to protest votes on the part of the White working class whose jobs are threatened by de-industrialization, immigration, and globalization. It seemed, therefore, that the elite had neglected the pains and injustices of class division at their peril—except that in actuality the oligarchic Trump administration successfully co-opted this working-class revolt and in Britain, too, the Conservative government remained in place. Nevertheless, intellectuals and others have since been scrambling to understand the disaffected working class and books that foreground class and economic distribution are now in high demand, from Thomas Piketty's erudite *Capital in the Twenty-First Century* (2014) to ethnographic or personal accounts like *Strangers in Their Own Land* (Hochschild, 2016) and *Hillbilly Elegy* (Vance, 2016), both best-sellers that examine poor White cultures in the American South.

Similarly, in Britain, there has been considerable interest in negative stereotyping of working-class Whites, for example, *Chavs: The Demonization of the Working Class* (Jones, 2011).

It is once again recognized that class matters because, quite simply, it still marks and consolidates power, which means that it also affects the fundamentals of life and death. For each of us, our class position affects *how* we will live and how *long* we will live, how we will be cared for and educated, how we will interact with the law, and what experiences and pleasures are open to us. To a large degree, class still determines geographic and social location: where we live, where we go to college, where we go on vacation. It affects how we speak and who listens.

Certainly, there is some class flexibility and movement in both Britain and America, but not as much as people think, or used to think.[5] Socioeconomic mobility is statistically less evident today in both countries and this can be attributed to many factors: the loss of skilled manufacturing jobs (due to automation and outsourcing), the rising cost of higher education, stagnant middle-class incomes, tax codes, global trade, and other legislation that favors the very wealthy.[6] Now multigenerational socioeconomic inequality is increasingly a subject of inquiry. Both the extent of the chasm, as captured in widespread debate about the ascent of the "1%," and how difficult it is to cross, are topics of continuing public debate. From President Obama to Pope Francis, international leaders have urged nations to address this issue as a matter of some urgency. In the United States, more people now dispute that upward social mobility—a moral imperative that many Americans believe is enshrined in the constitution—is a fair representation of how things work (if it ever was). If building a classless society was a raison d'être for the new nation, it is now feared that the vision has soured. And there is some finger pointing at the media, since its output has for some time helped perpetuate a hegemonic narrative that masked unequal opportunities and persuaded people to vote against their own economic interests. This, of course, is encapsulated in "the American Dream," the almost trademarked ideology of frictionless social advancement that popular media have frequently endorsed, whether by selling the immediate thrill of a meteoric rise or by relying disproportionately on portraits of the highly successful for audiences to admire, envy, or vicariously live through and identify with, emotionally and politically.

Scholarship on Class

The Concept

Few ideas are more contested in the social sciences than the concept of class. However, most scholars would agree that class refers to one's position within a social structure of unequal access to available resources (material, social, political). The concept is therefore relativistic and involves categorization within systems of stratification. There is also agreement that while in any human society some form of differentiation may be inevitable, the particulars are not universal but are orchestrated through sociopolitical means. Therefore, relative wealth or poverty may be expected, but the range is constructed and variable. Beyond this, there are disputes about what criteria ought to be used to determine class ranks, and how cohesive these groups are. Within academic literature, there are theories about class formation in general, about how to categorize class, and accounts of class relations within a particular culture or historical moment. Some accounts are descriptive and others are explanatory. But whatever the approach taken, there is some agreement that the major theorists are Karl Marx, Max Weber, and Pierre Bourdieu, with E.O. Wright essentially continuing the tradition of Marx and John Goldthorpe of Weber, though of course there is considerable overlap. See, for instance, Weber (1978), Bourdieu (1984), Wright (1997) and Goldthorpe (1987). Marx (1818–1883) was a scholar and a political advocate whose work encompassed both explanations and future projections of class relations. In the context of early industrial society, he regarded class differences as hinging on the relationship to the means of production, and his approach stressed the exploitation of the working class (labor) by the upper class (owners), although Marx's brilliant early writings contained the seeds of a more cultural theory of social class. Above all, Marx established that understanding class relations was fundamental to understanding how society functions. Later, in a more bureaucratic and service economy, Max Weber (1864–1920) emphasized that class assessment also involves cultural status or social prestige indicated by lifestyle and associational groupings. Weber took a less purely economistic approach than Marx, but he didn't deny that economic rank and social status are often correlated. While he also critiqued capitalist systems, he was not so critical of modern economic arrangements and their rational bureaucratic implementation as was Marx in his observations of industrialization.

Following Weber, and as Sociology continued to grow as a discipline, there was a prime period of stratification research from the 1940s to the 1970s. After that there was a relative falloff in attention to class, although, particularly in Britain, socioeconomic categorization continued to be used as an administrative instrument by governments and bureaucracies. By the 1990s, some scholars proposed that in high-consumerist, service economies class is no longer a useful explanatory tool for understanding social behavior (Pahl, 1989; Pakulski & Waters, 1996; Kingston, 2000). The rise in importance of theories of individualization such as those of Giddens (1991), Beck (1992), Bauman (2001), and Beck and Beck-Gernsheim (2002), and the transformation of Marxist Sociology with the fall of the Soviet Union, meant that social class analyses became less prominent in Western social science.

Yet a major shift was already occurring when the writings of Pierre Bourdieu became more widely distributed among scholars in Britain and America in the last decade of the twentieth century. The French theorist placed more emphasis on what he termed cultural and social capital, and looked closely at taste and everyday behavior to demonstrate how culture is a mechanism through which class relations are constituted and perpetuated (Bourdieu, 1984). Bourdieu's dual focus on material and cultural assets is now increasingly popular among scholars and has inspired a new cultural approach to class in Sociology, particularly among those writing in the tradition of the Birmingham School for whom Marxist class analyses were always primary even as advanced economies have changed and social class categories have become more complex. Among sociological and interdisciplinary studies that focus on class are Giddens (1973, 1991), Dahrendorf (1976), Sennett and Cobb (1977), Willis (1981), Katznelson (1982), Burawoy and Skocpol (Eds.) (1983), Scott (1996), Skeggs (1997), Reay (1998), Lamont (2000), Savage (2000, 2015), Sayer (2005), Devine, Savage, Scott, and Crompton (2005), Crompton (2008), Biressi and Nunn (2013), Milkman (2016), and Standing (2016). Areas of interest include social stratification and inequality, mobility, cultural identity (lifestyle, education, race, gender), capitalism, and neoliberalism. Also well regarded are historical accounts like Cannadine (1999) and Rose (2010). Sociologists who are interested in media, in addition to authors in this collection, include Bennett et al. (2009), Couldry (2011), Skeggs and Wood (2012), and Couldry and Hepp (2016).

More specifically, a variety of scholars, including media sociologists, have of late tried to revive the concept of class in Media Studies. This constitutes a relatively small portion of media research but has produced several titles. In addition to contributors to this collection, who represent some of the most important research in this area, there are, for example, works by Morley (1980), Hill (1986), Stead (1989), Ross (1998), Walkerdine (1998), Rowbotham and Beynon (2001), Horne (2001), Grindstaff (2002), Beach (2002), Bodnar (2003), Gillett (2003), Heider (2004), Vineberg (2005), Foster (2005), Dave (2006), Gandal (2007), Nystrom (2009), Kendall (2011), Wood and Skeggs (Eds.) (2011), Tyler (2013), Henderson (2013), Ross (Ed.) (2014), Cloarec, Haigron, and Letort (Eds.) (2016), and Sharot (2016). As feminist Media Studies, and feminist scholarship more generally, have taken intersectionality seriously, studies targeting the importance of race, gender, sexuality, and often social class have become central to feminist Media Studies (McRobbie, 1991, 2004; Steedman, 1987; Press, 1991; Skeggs, 1997; Press & Cole, 1999; Walkerdine & Lucey, 2001).

Categorization

The basic questions that arise when categorizing class include, what are the criteria, boundaries, fluidity, mobility, and number of class categories? Each of these refers to dynamic and changing patterns, and no one claims they have understood and predicted them for all time. Fluidity here refers to broader changes in class formations and criteria over time, not to individual mobility between ranks.[7] In addition to establishing classifications, scholars typically have to consider how does class operate, what effects does it produce, and how is it perceived by outside observers or by individuals as their own personal experience. There are a variety of methods in use today and some disagreement about their relative effectiveness, for example, smaller focus groups for qualitative research versus large statistical surveys, and self-reporting versus ethnographic observation. Some scholarship focuses on taxonomies or data collection and others on large social causes and consequences.

Despite this variegation, there is some consensus that class membership is based on a combination of economic (income, wealth) and social factors (family background, education, occupation, social prestige), these of course being frequently interdependent (e.g., education is correlated with occupation and wealth). These different life experiences are then expressed in lifestyle, values, behavior, manners, etc. Some of this data is more easily discovered than others. But further complications arise given that even reasonably objective and verifiable data, such as income, education, or occupation, have to be weighted, interpreted, and operationalized, as in, where do scholars seeking to establish class categories set the boundaries on income levels, or what is the relative weight of new wealth over family background, and do Americans prioritize wealth more than the British do? Then there is the matter of what subjects *think* is their class rank, or the degree to which they are conscious of class at all or are informed when making class distinctions; again, this varies between the US and Great Britain. In either case, how one judges other people's class could conceivably depend upon one's own position and experience—all of which raises the question of whether scholars should identify and write consciously from their own class background and current position.

The assessment of class faces both intellectual and political pressures and constraints. For many purposes, observers of Western industrialized nations settle on three basic class ranks: upper, middle, and lower. But beyond this Goldilocks approach, there is some debate about whether the middle class is best understood as differentiated into two or three subdivisions (especially in Britain), or whether a distinction between working and non-working underclass is significant. A recent major and well-publicized study defined seven class categories in contemporary Britain: elite, established middle class, technical middle class, new affluent workers, traditional working class, emergent service workers, and precariat (the precarious proletariat) (Savage, 2015).[8] Others distinguish five or six relative levels (upper, upper-middle, middle, lower-middle, working, and underclass), or simply two classes, in Marxist fashion, recently revived as the 1% versus 99%. Whatever the number chosen, a reasonable approach might be to say that the granularity of the categorization should depend on why it is being applied. Another area of investigation—and, again, disagreement—is how much conformity and homogeneity there is within each class category. This could take the form of exploring how much race, gender, age, religion, or region/nation can affect behavior and status within the same class (e.g., there may be similarities and alliances between men of different ranks or White people of different ranks).[9] Another variance is the degree to which scholars identify conflict between different levels of society. Most agree that the advantages of some are predicated on the disadvantages of others; but the perceived level of exploitation varies.

Class Relations

Over the last century, in both the UK and the US, the middle class expanded after World War II, but then lost ground after the 1970s when the gap between those in the top and bottom income brackets began to grow increasingly large. With de-industrialization, the working class suffered decades of depressed wages and underemployment, with previously well-paid manufacturing jobs being replaced by less well-paid, less secure, and less unionized service positions. In addition, this same service economy has sharply squeezed the middle class and, along with large corporations reducing "mom and pop" operations and a heavy burden of taxation, post-industrialism has made the socioeconomic distinctions between the middle and the working class less clear. Some upper-middle-class professionals have managed to hold their own, but even here there has been some proletarianization (i.e., micro-management or corporatization) and loss of autonomy in their working conditions, not unlike Marx's predictions.[10]

The most striking trend, especially in America but also in Britain, is the significant redistribution of wealth *upwards* since the 1990s. Recently, this has been much remarked on in popular journalism. Under the banner of "free trade" and neoliberalism—with its deregulation, privatization, and narratives of meritocracy—the very wealthy have secured ever more advantages: through legislation on taxation, regulation, government oversight, public service expenditure, and private ownership. Moreover, since more inequality means less intergenerational mobility, and since money increasingly buys political influence, there appears to be little to stop this trend.

Class in Media Studies

Class Focus

When it comes to considerations of intersectionality, including gender, race, sexuality, and class, the latter is generally the least discussed amongst them. Typically, the topic will appear in textbooks as one minor section or be apportioned a few essays in large anthologies. Often class merits attention only as intersecting with race or gender (sexuality, less so). Indeed, in both scholarship and common speech, "diversity" tends to refer not to class but to the other three terms. Media advocacy groups monitor race and gender representations but there is not the same attention to class. Therefore, while recognizing that an intersectional approach is indisputably valid, this collection aims to give class its due by focusing on this concept and its shaping of media production.

Class can be used as a way to examine both agency and purpose in all stages of mediation: how media content is produced, distributed, received, interpreted, and used. Much of the focus in the humanities is on class *representation*, but there is also scholarship on class matters in production and reception. For production, industry, and class see, for example, Horne (2001), Grindstaff (2002), Bodnar (2003), Mayer,

Banks, and Caldwell (2009), Hesmondhalgh and Baker (2011), Mayer (2011, 2017), and Hesmondhalgh (Ed.) (2013). A broader approach is to study the relationship between text production/ownership and audience in Marxist terms and identify the audience as a commodity, as in Williams (1980 [1973]), Garnham (1979), Smythe (2012 [1981]), Golding and Murdock (2000), and Andrejevic (2003). On issues of reception and class see, for example, Morley (1980), Press (1991), Press and Cole (1999), Skeggs and Wood (2012), and Livingstone and Sefton-Green (2016). In each of these areas, adopting the perspective of class brings up fundamental ethical and political issues such as fairness, equity, discrimination, prejudice, tolerance, and respect.

Class Representation: Variables and Expectations

When it comes to media representation, there are different degrees to which its producers can intentionally *point to* class, and different degrees to which any given viewer will *notice* class and *activate* these cues; for instance—as any of the essayists that follow can attest—class cues become more evident in popular entertainment when one is looking for them. Since it is not physically expressed in an obvious way, class is generally less noticeable than gender or race and therefore more dependent on the judgment of the observer. But, as this collection will illustrate, class representation is demonstrably present in a wide range of media production.

Beyond identifying specific references, scholars differ about the role and purpose of media representations, whether with regard to class or any other variable. Many of these implicit stances are unstated but assumed. One position would be that the media should fairly—meaning "accurately"—reflect real-life experience, however interpreted or measured. This might involve assessing if, within a representation, there is a quantifiable reflection of actual social demographics (an exact ratio of contemporary class relations). Or it might lead to a scholarly judgment as to how positive or negative these portrayals are. Others could argue that the media have a right to select what they represent, with no obligation to mirror society or provide a one-to-one mapping. In any case, since media companies don't work as a collective, how would an accurate reflection of class relations be accomplished, or even assessed, they might ask. Does every program need to reflect the whole in some fractal fashion? A more activist position might be the belief that of course media products can't simply reflect social arrangements, nor should they try, but that they can instead provide better models and nudge society toward change.

Media Influence

All of this leads to a rather large issue, which is the question of the social impact of media representations, concern for which motivates virtually all of the scholarship presented here. Scholars vary in their estimation of how substantially media representations influence culture, or, crucially, how influence can be proven. Underlying assumptions and goals that are not always articulated, and the distinction between correlation and causality, often remain unexamined. Different terms have been used to describe media impact—framing, priming, agenda-setting, cultivation—all suggesting some considerable but limited effect on the audience. Many see the relationship between media and society as mutually influential but difficult to determine; for example, if we dwell in a media saturated environment can we easily separate media *from* society? There is also the question of ascertaining the best methods for assessing impact, be they surveys, self-reports, or ethnographic and situated knowledge, etc. Scholars of reception take different approaches to this kind of study.

Nevertheless, it seems reasonable to suggest that the media play some role in the formation of societal beliefs and attitudes and that representation therefore has significant repercussions. Class is a particularly interesting case because of a probable gap between mediated and unmediated knowledge. Given increased socioeconomic segregation—people occupying different neighborhoods, different schools, different shopping areas—the role of the media will be all the more acute and influential when there is a lack of personal contact in everyday life, as has been demonstrated for race (Darden, 1986; Hochschild, 1995). To be sure, social media can dampen or amplify communication across these different life situations, but broadcast media still have some burden to represent the "Other" and portray, in an intimate way to a large audience, the experience of another class, as well as contribute to the formation of an individual's own class identity. Even simple presence or absence can have political consequences, as has been demonstrated in the case of gender absence in popular media; for example, Tuchman argued this vis-à-vis the symbolic annihilation of women in the media (2000). A relative absence of classed portrayals could shore up the idea that this reflects a classless society, or at least a society where class is not a strong determinant. Or when one class such as the poor is under-represented, this could mean that voters will see less need for providing public welfare. When, instead, there is a larger representation of the affluent, this could be internalized by less wealthy viewers as indicating that something is defective about their own ability and effort. Or if, as is often the case in both television and film, the focus is on the middle class, this could bolster the idea that more people occupy this class position than a sociologist would recognize.

Chapter Overview

Despite the widespread—even standard—declaration in many academic fields that gender and race cannot be understood without also considering class, the intersection between media and class remains a relatively understudied topic. Given this scholarly deficit and the renewed popular awareness of class and its presence in media productions, we invited a variety of key scholars in both the humanities and social sciences to share their thoughts on this topic. Contributors include both established scholars and emerging voices who take a variety of approaches to both fictional and non-fictional content across a range of platforms. Whether engaging in broad theoretical discussion or specific empirical studies, they explore how different media navigate and negotiate, caricature and essentialize, or police and regulate class. In some instances, the content under consideration is explicitly classed, and in others the class dimensions are drawn out by the essayist. A major strength of this collection is that it analyzes both British and American media, with almost equal attention to each. It should therefore interest readers who are curious not only about their own culture but also about similar yet distinct others. Early American attitudes to class were an offshoot of British culture but were also defined in contrast to it. The focus on these two systems is deliberate and it is our belief that trying to encompass a wider range of cultures is beyond the scope of this volume.

In the first section, "Class Representation as Entertainment," each contributor focuses on a genre or area of entertainment and unpacks what is most often the underlying and unarticulated class dimension of the phenomenon they discuss. Here we see how social class themes remain implicit or marginalized, or, if more overt, how they are distanced and contained. David Hesmondhalgh's major overview essay delves deeply into the sociological literature about class to theorize precisely why we have such inaccurate representation of social class in entertainment media. While the common-sense response to this question might be that media narratives reflect the social class background of those who create them, it turns out the truth is more complex, although certainly it is connected to the undeniable fact that working-class people have largely been denied access to the means of "symbol-making," and these are the skills necessary to contribute in a visible way to the stories media make available to us. Richard Butsch provides an extended overview of representations in popular television to illustrate how, for seven decades from the beginning of television in the US, working-class families were basically erased. In the few instances in which they appeared, working-class men were represented as fools, in contrast to their wives and children, and in contrast to the representation of husbands and fathers in the middle-class sitcoms that predominated. These stereotypes, and the erasure of the authority and dignity of the working-class male, remained in place until the recent plethora of alternative sexualities and family types.

June Deery, in "Television Screening: The Entertainment Value of Poverty and Wealth," examines techniques that turn economic disparity and the injuries of class into forms of entertainment. Focusing on lower-class and upper-class portraits in contemporary American television, she illustrates how the comic mode of reality TV "rednecks" and the melodrama of *Downton Abbey* employ different forms of spatial, temporal, and social distancing to reduce potential ethical and political discomfort through a process of *affective displacement*. An analysis of comdocs (reality sitcoms), docusoaps, and costume drama demonstrates how different types of audience recognition and producer engagement in fictional and non-fictional modes allow distinct forms of class containment. Andrea Press and Marjoire Rosen in "Sex, Class, and Trash: Money, Status, and Classed 'Dreams' in Classical Hollywood Cinema" draw from theories of intersectionality to unpack the interconnection between social classed, gendered, and sexualized identities in post-war Hollywood cinema. They argue that the social class dimension of identities has historically been overlooked by film scholars who have focused on issues of gender and sexuality, and that, in addition, social class has always been an important dimension of the identities seen in important post-war films, and an integral dimension of major Hollywood star personae. They speculate as to the impact this incorporation of lower-class "trash" sexuality into popular highly sexualized images might have on our popular perceptions of what makes a woman sexually desirable.

The next section, "Documenting Class," includes essays that examine the subtle ways social class is defined, implicitly, in various media representations, in particular those that assume the aura of documentary "realism." The first piece by John Corner, "Performing Class and Taste through the Documentary Lens," probes in depth the implicit definition of social class and of the class–taste relationship as exhibited in a popular three-part British television series, entitled *All in the Best Possible Taste*. Placing the series in the long history of British documentary treatments of class, Corner finds that ideas of social class, and in particular class mobility, are today subtle and shifting and dependent upon the class fragment the researcher or journalist is sampling. Laurie Ouellette, in "How the Other Half Lives: The Will to Document from Poverty to Precarity," offers a close reading of recent American documentaries about the poor. She notes how the poor, and the financially insecure, are "othered" in these post-welfare programs, and how few systemic solutions, beyond crowdsourced GoFundMe sites, are offered. Both Corner's and Ouellette's pieces contextualize recent programming within national traditions of documenting the poor and highlight the continued relevance of the concept of class in contemporary neoliberal societies.

Essays in the "Media Leisure/Labor" section explore the classed dimension of those whose non-professional labor helps create media products, thereby reproducing our media system. This includes labor located in the interstices between audiences and producers in a new media environment characterized by reality genres and new forms of interactivity—labor which is often defined as "leisure." Helen Wood, Jilly Boyce Kay, and Mark Banks, in "The Working Class, Ordinary Celebrity, and Illegitimate Cultural Work," describe how the production of ordinary celebrity, such as that produced on reality television, is a type of labor engaged in primarily by working-class citizens that remains uncredited as such. They suggest that its devaluation plays into the overall devaluing of working-class labor in our society. Their piece highlights how the new culture of reality celebrity thereby supports and reproduces existing class hierarchies. Its authors call for more empirical research into the embodied and gendered experiences of ordinary celebrity workers.

Anita Biressi, in "Idols of Self-Production: Selfies, Career Success and Social Class," uncovers the continuing importance of social class in what she terms "selfie culture." Selfies, the "calling cards of neoliberalism," function to mask the reality of class–capital relations, not least due to the virtually invisible nature of the labor involved in their production. They are a stark instance of the construction of the valuable self, which is the subject of much contemporary scholarship describing neoliberalism. Jo Littler and Milly Williamson, in "Rich TV, Poor TV: Work, Leisure, and the Construction of 'Deserved Inequality' in Contemporary Britain," illustrate another facet of neoliberal discourse as they unpack the way those who are prosperous and successful are assumed to deserve their success due to their "hard work," while those who are poor are often seen to be deservedly so. They document how the moral outrage that accompanies the alleged "failures" of the poor is balanced by the ironic idea, turning Veblen's idea of conspicuous leisure on its head, that the leisured class deserves its allegedly "hard-earned" leisure. Once again, this essay indicates that the neoliberal assumptions of the current age validate and rationalize social class inequality as resulting from differences in individual initiative and talent.

Finally, essays in "Digital Cultures" explore the meaning of the new media environment for continued social class inequity. Robert Wilkie takes on software studies in "When Left Theory 'Leaves behind the Dream of a Revolution': Class and the Software Economy" and he challenges the notion that the immaterial labor of code eliminates traditional class divisions between owners and workers. Reading software through a materialist framework, he shows why a class analysis of the "code" economy must start with the exploitation of wage-labor at the point of production. Sonia Livingstone and Julian Sefton-Green's "Class in 'The Class': Conservative, Competitive, and (Dis)connected" draws out the social class implications of their important recent book *The Class: Living and Learning in the Digital Age* (2016). Their year-long ethnography of media use amongst a class of 13–14-year-olds illustrates that mediated disconnection reproduces boundaries of social class distinction, as well as other forms of difference. Vicki Mayer and Aline Maia, in "For Themselves and for Their Communities: Alternative Mediations of Digital Natives," demonstrate the subtle and complex ways in which young adults represent themselves through online media as members of African diasporas in the US and Brazil. Their essay presents a close reading of the *Favela em Danca* and *Noirlinians* online social projects, which combine digital media with popular performances of specific ethnic subcultures in the US and Brazil. They illustrate the continuity of the new media environment with earlier media forms by drawing on traditional media theories concerning the way ethnic, racial, and class worldviews are expressed in media generally, using these theories to help us understand more recent digital expressions. In the final essay, "Big Data Is Too Small: Research Implications of Class Inequality for Online Data Collection," Jen Schradie illustrates the ongoing digital divide as measured by unequal access and competency in the new world of Big Data. Her work illustrates that this divide persists when measured according to social class, as well as according to race and gender. Schradie's methodological commentary on the current state of digital data scholarship, and the methods used for its collection, disentangles the hype from the reality of digitally produced data for sociological research. In the process, she offers strategies to address the weaknesses of data that are derived from the Internet vis-à-vis its ability to represent marginalized populations.

In conclusion, it is our hope that each of these essays will inform and inspire further research on class and media by making the case for the continued importance of analyzing the interconnections between the two in an era of increasing social inequality.

Notes

1. Identity politics has tended to focus on gender, race, and sexuality over class.
2. Clearly, any overview of this sort will not be able to do justice to the many nuances and exceptions that occur within such a large topic as class, but it is hoped that it will provide a useful initial orientation.
3. See, for example, Hoggart (2009 [1957]), Williams (1980 [1973]), Hall (2016a, 2016b), and many others not cited here. These scholars drew their inspiration from Marx's works, in particular the "Economic and Philosophic Manuscripts of 1844," the "Communist Manifesto" (Marx and Engels, 2009 [1848]), and "The Eighteenth Brumaire of Louis Bonaparte" (Marx, 1994 [1852]). See also the updated discussion and interpretation in Burawoy and Wright (2010).
4. For a good overview of the waxing and waning of class as a topic in Sociology see Atkinson (2015). It should be noted that the Birmingham School developed, in the work of McRobbie and Morley, an early intersectionality with regard to class and gender. This work influenced others such as Press (1991) and Press and Cole (1999).
5. For a recent and detailed study of mobility in the UK see Chapter 6 in Savage (2015). For recent trends in America see Swanson (2016) and Pinsker (2015).
6. For details on the economic decline of the American middle class see Pew Research (2015). Some scholars disagree on the rates of mobility depending on the main criterion selected: e.g., whether income or occupation or lifestyle (see Atkinson, 2015, pp. 110–14).
7. Sometimes overlooked is the micro mobility of an individual possibly occupying different class positions in a short time period: e.g., work position versus family status, or country of origin versus current residence (the ex-surgeon taxi driver).
8. The Great British Class Survey (GBCS) of 2011 included over 160,000 participants (on a BBC website), making it the largest study of social class ever undertaken in Britain. The results showed increased polarization between a prosperous elite and a poor "precariat," a fragmenting middle class, and changing but still powerful class divisions overall.
9. One complication in governmental surveys is the evolution of gender roles and employment: increasingly it is limiting to categorize a family's class position according to the occupation of the father/male, although couples do tend to marry within their class rank.
10. Academics will be familiar with the top-down administration of increasingly corporate educational environments.

Works Cited

Andrejevic, M. (2003). *Reality TV: The work of being watched*. Lanham, MD: Rowman & Littlefield.

Atkinson, W. (2015). *Class*. Cambridge, UK: Polity.

Bauman, Z. (2001). *The individualized society*. Cambridge, UK: Polity.

Beach, C. (2002). *Class, language, and American film comedy*. Cambridge, UK: Cambridge University Press.

Beck, U. (1992). *Risk society*. London, UK: Sage.

Beck, U., & Beck-Gernsheim, E. (2002). *Individualization*. London, UK: Sage.

Bennett, T., Savage, M., Silva, E., Warde, A., Gayo-Cal, M., & Wright, D. (2009). *Culture, class, distinction*. London, UK: Routledge.

Biressi, A., & Nunn, H. (2013). *Class and contemporary British culture*. New York, NY: Palgrave Macmillan.

Bodnar, J. (2003). *Blue-collar Hollywood: Liberalism, democracy, and working people in American film*. Baltimore, MD: Johns Hopkins University Press.

Bourdieu, P. (1984 [1979]). *Distinction: A social critique of the judgment of taste* (R. Nice, Trans.). London, UK: Routledge.

Burawoy, M., & Skocpol, T. (Eds.) (1983). *Marxist inquiries: Studies of labor, class, and states*. Chicago, IL: University of Chicago Press Journals.

Burawoy, M., & Wright, E.O. (2010). Sociological marxism. In J.H. Turner (Ed.), *Handbook of sociological theory* (pp. 459–486). New York, NY: Springer.

Cannadine, D. (1999). *The rise and fall of class in Britain*. New York, NY: Columbia University Press.

Cloarec, N., Haigron, D., & Letort, D. (Eds.) (2016). *Social class on British and American screens: Essays on cinema and television*. Jefferson, NC: McFarland.

Couldry, N. (2011). Class and contemporary forms of 'reality' production, or hidden injuries of class. In H. Wood & B. Skeggs (Eds.), *Reality television and class* (pp. 33–44). Basingstoke, UK: Palgrave Macmillan.

Couldry, N., & Hepp, A. (2016). *The mediated construction of reality*. Cambridge, UK: Polity.

Crompton, R. (2008). *Class and stratification* (3rd ed.). Cambridge, UK: Polity.

Dahrendorf, R. (1976). *Class and class conflict in industrial society*. London, UK: Routledge and Kegan Paul.

Darden, J.T. (1986). The significance of race and class in residential segregation. *Journal of Urban Affairs*, *8*(1), 49–56.

Dave, P. (2006). *Visions of England: Class and culture in contemporary cinema*. Oxford, UK: Berg.

Devine, F., Savage, M., Scott, J., & Crompton, R. (Eds.) (2005). *Rethinking class: Culture, identities and lifestyle*. New York, NY: Palgrave Macmillan.

Foster, G. (2005). *Class passing: Social mobility in film and popular culture*. Carbondale, IL: Southern Illinois University Press.

Frank, T. (2004). *What's the matter with Kansas? How conservatives won the heart of America*. New York, NY: Henry Holt.

Gandal, K. (2007). *Class representation in modern fiction and film*. New York, NY: Palgrave Macmillan.

Garnham, N. (1979). Contribution to a political economy of mass-communication. *Media, Culture & Society*, *1*(2), 123–146.

Giddens, A. (1973). *The class structure of advanced societies*. London, UK: Hutchinson.

Giddens, A. (1991) *Modernity and self-identity: Self and society in the late modern age*. Stanford, CA: Stanford University Press.

Gillett, P. (2003). *The British working class in postwar film*. Manchester, UK: Manchester University Press.
Golding, P., & Murdock, G. (2000). Culture, communications and political economy. *Mass Media and Society*, *3*, 70–92.
Goldthorpe, J. (1987). *Social mobility and class structure in modern Britain* (2nd ed.). Oxford, UK: Clarendon Press.
Grindstaff, L. (2002). *The money shot: Trash, class, and the making of TV talk shows*. Chicago, IL: University of Chicago Press.
Hall, S. (2001 [1980]). Encoding/decoding. In M.G. Durham & D.M. Kellner (Eds.), *Media and cultural studies: Keyworks* (pp. 166–176). London, UK: Wiley-Blackwell.
Hall, S. (2016a). *Cultural studies 1983: A theoretical history*. Slack, J.D., & Grossberg, L. (Eds.) Durham, NC: Duke University Press.
Hall, S. (2016b). *Selected political writings: The great moving right show and other essays*. Davison, S., Featherstone, D., Rustin, M., & Schwartz, B. (Eds.) Durham, NC: Duke University Press.
Heider, D. (Ed.) (2004). *Class and news*. Lanham, MD: Rowman & Littleman.
Henderson, L. (2013). *Love and money: Queers, class, and cultural production*. New York, NY: New York University Press.
Hesmondhalgh, D. (2013). *The cultural industries* (3rd ed.). London, UK: Sage.
Hesmondhalgh, D., & Baker, S. (2011). *Creative labour: Media work in three cultural industries*. London, UK: Routledge.
Hill, J. (1986). *Sex, class and realism: British cinema 1956–63*. London, UK: BFI.
Hochschild, A.R. (2016). *Strangers in their own land: Anger and mourning on the American right*. New York, NY: The New Press.
Hochschild, J.L. (1995). *Facing up to the American dream: Race, class, and the soul of the nation*. Princeton, NJ: Princeton University Press.
Hoggart, R. (2009 [1957]). *The uses of literacy: Aspects of working-class life*. London, UK: Penguin.
Horne, G. (2001). *Class struggle in Hollywood 1930–1950*. Austin, TX: University of Texas Press.
Jones, O. (2011). *Chavs: The demonization of the working class*. London, UK: Verso.
Judis, J.B. (2016). *The populist explosion: How the Great Recession transformed American and European politics*. New York, NY: Columbia Global Reports.
Katznelson, I. (1982). *City trenches: Urban politics and the patterning of class in the US*. Chicago, IL: University of Chicago Press.
Kendall, D. (2011). *Framing class: Media representations of wealth and poverty in America* (2nd ed.). Lanham, MD: Rowman & Littlefield.
Kingston, P. (2000). *The classless society*. Stanford, CA: Stanford University Press.
Lamont, M. (2000). *The dignity of working men*. New York, NY: Russell Sage Foundation.
Livingstone, S., & Sefton-Green, J. (2016). *The class: Living and learning in the digital age*. New York, NY: New York University Press.
Mayer, V. (2011). *Below the line: Producers and production studies in the new television economy*. Durham, NC: Duke University Press.
Mayer, V. (2017). *Almost Hollywood, nearly New Orleans: The lure of the local film economy*. Berkeley and Los Angeles, CA: University of California Press.
Mayer, V., Banks, M., & Caldwell, J.T. (Eds.) (2009). *Production studies: Cultural studies of media industries*. London, UK: Routledge.
Marx, K. (1994 [1852]). *The eighteenth brumaire of Louis Bonaparte* (E. Paul & C. Paul, Trans.). New York, NY: International Publishers.

Marx, K., & Engels, F. (2009 [1844 and 1848]). *The economic and philosophic manuscripts of 1844 and the communist manifesto* (M. Milligan, Trans.). New York, NY: Prometheus Books.
McRobbie, A. (1991). Feminism and youth culture. New York, NY: Routledge.
McRobbie, A. (2004). Notes on "What Not to Wear" and post-feminist symbolic violence. *The Sociological Review, 52*(2), 97–109.
Milkman, R. (2016). *On gender, labor, and inequality*. Urbana, IL: University of Illinois Press.
Morley. D. (1980). *The nationwide audience: Structure and decoding*. London, UK: BFI.
Nystrom, D. (2009). *Hard hats, rednecks, and macho men: Class in 1970s American cinema*. Oxford, UK: Oxford University Press.
Pahl, R.E. (1989). Is the emperor naked? Some questions on the adequacy of sociological theory in urban and regional research. *International Journal of Urban and Regional Research, 13*(4), 709–720.
Pakulski, J., & Waters, M. (1996). *The death of class*. London, UK: Sage.
Pew Research Center (2015, December 9). The American middle class is losing ground. Washington, DC. Retrieved from http://www.pewsocialtrends.org
Piketty, T. (2014). *Capital in the twenty-first century* (A. Goldhammer, Trans.). Cambridge, MA: Harvard University Press.
Pinsker, J. (2015, July 23). America is even less socially mobile than most economists thought. *The Atlantic*. Retrieved from https://www.theatlantic.com
Press, A. (1991). *Women watching television: Gender, class, and generation in the American television experience*. Philadelphia, PA: University of Pennsylvania Press.
Press, A., & Cole, E. (1999). *Speaking of abortion: Television and authority in the lives of women*. Chicago, IL: University of Chicago Press.
Reay, D. (1998). *Class work*. London, UK: UCL Press.
Rose, J. (2010). *The intellectual life of the British working classes* (2nd ed.). New Haven, CT: Yale University Press.
Ross, S. (1998). *Working-class Hollywood: Silent film and the shaping of class in America*. Princeton, NJ: Princeton University Press.
Ross, S. (Ed.) (2014). *Movies and American society* (2nd ed.). Chichester, UK: Wiley-Blackwell.
Rowbotham, S., & Benyon, H. (Eds.). (2001). *Looking at class: Film, television and the working class in Britain*. London, UK: Rivers Oram Press.
Savage, M. (2000). *Class analysis and social transformation*. Philadelphia, PA: Open University Press.
Savage, M. (2015). *Social class in the 21st century*. London, UK: Pelican Books.
Sayer, A. (2005). *The moral significance of class*. Cambridge, UK: Cambridge University Press.
Scott, J. (1996). *Stratification and power: Structures of class, status and domination*, Cambridge, UK: Polity.
Sennett, R., & Cobb, J. (1977). *The hidden injuries of class*. Cambridge, UK: Cambridge University Press.
Sharot, S. (2016). *Love and marriage across social classes in American cinema*. New York, NY: Palgrave Macmillan.
Skeggs, B. (1997). *Formations of class & gender: Becoming respectable*. London, UK: Sage.
Skeggs, B. (2004). *Class, self, culture*. London, UK: Routledge.
Skeggs, B., & Wood, H. (2012). *Reacting to reality television: Performance, audience and value*. New York, NY: Routledge.
Smythe, D.W. (2012 [1981]). On the audience commodity and its work. In M.G. Durham and D.M. Kellner (Eds.), *Media and cultural studies: Keyworks* (pp. 230–256). London, UK: Wiley-Blackwell.

Standing, G. (2016). *The precariat: The new dangerous class*. London, UK: Bloomsbury Academic.

Stead, P. (1989). *Film and the working class: The feature film in British and American society*. London, UK: Routledge.

Steedman, C. (1987). *Landscape for a good woman: A story of two lives*. New Brunswick, NJ: Rutgers University Press.

Swanson, A. (2016, October 6). Striking new research on inequality: "Whatever you thought, it's worse." *The Washington Post*. Retrieved from https://www.washingtonpost.com

Tuchman, G. (2000). The symbolic annihilation of women by the mass media. In L. Crothers and C. Lockhart (Eds.), *Culture and politics: A reader* (pp. 150–174). London, UK: Palgrave Macmillan.

Tyler, I. (2013). *Revolting subjects: Social abjection and resistance in neoliberal Britain*. London, UK: Zed Books.

Vance, J.D. (2016). *Hillbilly elegy: A memoir of a family and culture in crisis*. New York, NY: HarperCollins.

Vineberg, S. (2005). *High comedy in American movies: Class and humor from the 1920s to the present*. Lanham, MD: Rowman & Littlefield.

Walkerdine, V. (1998). *Daddy's girls: Young girls and popular culture*. Cambridge, MA: Harvard University Press.

Walkerdine, V., & Lucey, H. (2001). *Growing up girl: Psycho-social explorations of class and gender*. New York, NY: New York University Press.

Weber, M. (1978 [1924]). *Economy and society* (G. Roth and C. Wittich, Eds.) (G. Roth, Trans.). Berkeley, CA: University of California Press.

Williams, R. (1980 [1973]). Base and superstructure in Marxist cultural theory. In R. Williams, *Problems in materialism and culture* (pp. 1–49). London. UK: Verso.

Willis, P. (1981). *Learning to labor: How working class kids get working class jobs*. New York, NY: Columbia University Press.

Wood, H., & Skeggs, B. (Eds.) (2011). *Reality television and class*. New York, NY: Palgrave Macmillan.

Wright, E.O. (1997). *Class counts*. Cambridge, UK: Cambridge University Press.

PART I

Class Representation as Entertainment

2

THE MEDIA'S FAILURE TO REPRESENT THE WORKING CLASS: EXPLANATIONS FROM MEDIA PRODUCTION AND BEYOND[1]

David Hesmondhalgh

Introduction: The Media's Failure to Represent Working-Class People

There are many serious problems concerning media and class in contemporary societies. One of them is as follows: *the media have contributed to the immiseration and marginalisation of working-class people by failing to adequately represent the complexity, diversity, and richness of their lives and values.* This includes a failure to convey adequately the particular ways in which working-class people flourish and suffer, why they do so, and in what circumstances. Sometimes this failure is a result of a lack of attention to working-class people, to their attitudes and values: a failure of *under*representation. Sometimes it derives from other causes such as stigmatisation, sensationalism and even demonization: a failure of *mis*representation.

A much-discussed example of the latter is reality television. Many analysts have plausibly argued, sometimes using textual analysis, that sub-genres of reality television, notably its "makeover" (Lewis, 2009) and "poverty porn" (Jensen, 2014) variants, employ and amplify a number of representational tropes that construct working-class people in problematic ways, for example as in need of moral and aesthetic reform (Skeggs & Wood, 2011).

But the problem goes far beyond reality television. Biressi and Nunn (2013) show how, across a range of media and genres, "an often comical disgust is publicly expressed for the working class, and especially for those who seem to be rising above their social station" (p. 23) and they also recount the history of changing ways in which some working-class people with certain characteristics have been labelled as a dangerous, criminal "underclass" (pp. 44–68). There are huge problems too in journalistic representations, such as the remarkably prevalent use of images of "welfare mothers" in news coverage of US welfare reform (Kelly, 2010) or the virtual "eradication" of the working class from news and actual programming on Swedish television between 1982 and 2015 (Stiernstedt & Jakobsson, 2017). In many of these cases, class inequality and misrepresentation are often closely linked to gender and ethnic inequality, and to racist and sexist stereotypes (Gilens, 1999).

Such representational problems are likely to have damaging consequences. They may well, for example, make the lives of poor and vulnerable working-class people more difficult by helping to legitimise political actions that reduce various kinds of systematic support for them (Jensen & Tyler, 2015). The reinforcement of stereotypes about working-class dress and behaviour might work together with existing institutional practices to make it even more difficult for working-class people to gain access to prestigious universities, socially valued and/or well-rewarded professional jobs, and so on. What's more, the results of such media failure are likely to be bad for *everyone*, not just those groups under- or misrepresented, because of the misunderstandings, suspicion, misery, and violence that are likely to ensue in a situation of pronounced and worsening inequality such as the ones that currently prevail.[2]

My goal in this chapter is not to elaborate or evaluate studies of problematic representations of the working class (some of which are more rigorous and convincing than others).[3] Instead, I aim to consider what the study of media *production*, or media production analysis (MPA), might contribute to understanding such a representational failure.[4] But there is a problem. There seems to be remarkably little research that seeks to use MPA to explain why class is generally represented so poorly in the media. In fact, MPA seems to have paid very little attention to class at all, with some exceptions in studies of media labour (Mayer, 2011), where the production of class representations has not really been a central concern.[5]

So in the first part of this chapter, rather than draw on existing studies, I'll mainly discuss some *potential* ways of researching via MPA how the failure of representation has come about, focusing on the fact that media production workforces are overwhelmingly composed of people from middle- and upper-class backgrounds—but moving beyond reductive or excessively compressed explanations based on this fact. These potential routes of MPA might, I suggest: (a) seek to gather and analyse new empirical data on issues such as the class composition, practices, and values of media producers; (b) show how organisational processes and human judgement interact to shape content; and (c) analyse how cultural ideas and values shape occupational and organisational understandings of how to do things. However, I argue that MPA in general, and specifically when explaining a phenomenon such as the failure of class representation, needs to pay attention to a wider set of factors. These would include (d) the degree to which political-economic systems and government policy might push producers to pursue commercial goals rather than producing content that might have more general social and cultural benefits, and (e) the contemporary political status of the working class.

I then go on to argue that the general field of media and cultural studies and, within it, the specific field of MPA, needs to go beyond even this wider set of economic, political, and cultural contexts to consider *how the subjective experience of class shapes production.* Here the sociology of Pierre Bourdieu offers important though potentially problematic resources. I close by briefly discussing three potential solutions (education, digitalisation, and "class mobility") to the problems outlined and what the sociology of class might tell us about the obstacles facing efforts based on these factors.

For the sake of simplicity, I'm going to use the lay distinction between three class groups: the upper class, the middle class, and the working class. There are serious sociological studies which provide much more rigorous and systematic differentiations (e.g., Savage, 2015) and draw attention to important problems concerning boundaries between, and variability within, any class categories. I will draw on some of the most relevant and helpful aspects of such contributions below (notably the work of Erik Olin Wright). I recognize of course that the simplified tripartite conception I use here is haunted by ambiguities and fuzzy boundaries, further complicated by different national usages. In the USA, for example, the lay term "middle class" seems to suggest "ordinary people who are not upper class," and I am told that the term "working class" hardly exists as a lay concept, whereas in Britain, "middle class" tends to connote a certain degree of privilege (though not as much as "upper class").

How to define "working class"? This is notoriously tricky territory, but Erik Olin Wright's (1997) definition helps: those people (and their dependents) who do not own the means of production (p. 17) and who lack the official workplace authority and/or scarce skills that would make them middle class (p. 19). But of course the *experience* of being working class (see below) goes beyond workplaces, as complex cultural formations emerge, hugely inflected by ethnic, gender, and other dynamics.

For all the problems of definition and boundaries, "working class" remains a necessary concept in any egalitarian and progressive political project, and *some* kind of distinction between working class and other classes is vital for understanding inequality and injustice in modern societies.

Explaining Representational Failure 1: Organisational and Cultural Factors

I want to begin my discussion from a particular way of thinking about the relationship between media production and class: an explanation for the media failure to represent working-class people adequately that is sometimes offered by friends and colleagues of mine, whether they work in the academic realm of media studies or not. It is certainly not a hypothesis in the scientific (positivist) sense. Nor is it a theory, in the sense of a systematic set of connected ideas used to make sense of some aspect of the world. Instead I think of it as a lay explanation for a media phenomenon common on the political left. It might be expressed in the following form: *most people involved in media production are from "higher" social classes and media's failure to represent working-class lives adequately stems from this mismatch or asymmetry between media producers on the one hand, and the working-class people they are representing on the other.* I'm going to call this the "class asymmetry explanation" (although admittedly the word "asymmetry" does not quite capture the inequality involved). To put the explanation at its most simple: the media misrepresent the working class because media producers are mainly from the upper and middle class, and therefore have different sets of interests, experiences, and values than working-class people. Even though I have often encountered this lay explanation among (academic and non-academic) friends and colleagues, it is, as far as I can tell, almost never discussed explicitly in academic publications. Here, though, is one articulation of it from the English journalist Owen Jones' passionate book on "the demonization of the working class":

> Like Westminster, our media and entertainment are dominated by the most privileged sectors. They have been all too ready to put working-class people down in the crudest possible ways. (Jones, 2011, p. 108)

I do not think that the class asymmetry explanation is entirely mistaken. Like many everyday explanations of complex and important phenomena, it is based on something fundamentally true, but only gets us so far. So we need to go further, and I want now to go through various ways in which media production analysis (MPA) might use and yet go beyond the class asymmetry explanation. I do so in order not only to comprehend the problem of bad media representation of the working class but also to demonstrate the potential contributions of MPA to understanding media and class as a whole.

One contribution of MPA to testing the class asymmetry explanation would be to gather new data or seek out and interpret existing data on the class backgrounds of media producers. Generally, by contrast with the wide availability of statistics on ethnic and gender inequality in media industries there is a dearth of data on class inequality (O'Brien & Oakley, 2015). There are occasional references in studies (Weaver & Wilhoit, 1996, pp. 48–49; Marchetti, 2005, pp. 72–73) and rather sketchy surveys of the super-elite of journalists (Sutton Trust, 2006), but not much systematic data.

More recently, research on the "cultural and creative industries" (or CCIs for short, a policy category that includes the media industries but which goes considerably beyond them to include other sectors such as performing arts and even computer software) has at last attempted to provide systematic data on the class background of employees. O'Brien, Laurison, Miles, and Friedman have shown that in spite of "dominant policy narratives of openness and meritocracy,"

> there is a significant under-representation of people from working-class origins in creative occupations. While 34.7 percent of the UK population

> aged 23–69 had a parent employed in a routine or semi-routine working-class occupation, the figure among those working in the CCIs is only 18 percent. (O'Brien, Laurison, Miles & Friedman, 2016, p. 123)

Conversely, of course, those with parents in higher professional and management occupations are overrepresented in the CCIs, especially in the higher-grade jobs (Sutton Trust, 2006). O'Brien et al. name media sectors such as publishing and advertising as having especially high concentrations of people from professional and managerial backgrounds.

However, we need to seek reasonable *causal connections*, rather than just correlations, between, on the one hand, the relatively privileged social background of producers, and, on the other, recurring practices and values on the part of producers that lead to underrepresentation and misrepresentation. How do the class backgrounds of producers come to manifest themselves in terms of poor representation of working-class people? We need to look for possible mediating factors.

One potential mediating factor in explaining poor class representation that arises from the MPA literature as a whole is *organisational and occupational norms and practices*, often crystallised into histories of aesthetic and genre-based conventions and understandings within particular media industries concerning how to go about media production. Summarising a huge swathe of media sociology, James Curran (2002) has claimed that MPA studies have shown "the view that news reporting is *merely* the expression of personal views and backgrounds of journalists—whether they be conceived as being biased as a consequence of being mainly left-wing or right-wing, men or middle class—is partly misleading" (p. 128). This is because other major factors are at play beyond producer views and backgrounds, the most important of which, according to Curran's summary of MPA studies, is the "interaction of organisational processes and human judgement," for example the way in which "the need of news organizations to secure regular, predictable and usable copy" results in some journalists being assigned to particular specialisms, where they become locked into complex interactions with key sources, inhibiting the degree to which journalists really act independently of key institutions in society (Curran, 2002, p. 128).

However, a rigorous approach to MPA needs to go beyond merely tracking organisational and occupational norms. For those norms are of course in turn influenced by ideas, images, and assumptions embedded in cultural traditions of the society or communities to which media producers belong, and by the history of conventions and understandings within that industry. This of course applies to media production beyond the news media content discussed by Curran—in a whole range of television entertainment genres for example. Addressing such genres, Havens (2013) discusses an "industry lore" that emerged in the 1980s international television trade about the "universal" appeal of some programmes, "which supposedly tapped into shared human themes that audiences everywhere could relate to" (p. 6). Havens (2013) points out that such discourse had a negative effect on international understandings of "race" (and in particular African-Americans) because the "anti-mainstream" African American popular culture that shaped African-American television programmes meant that white executives could not recognise the programmes as potentially universal—and therefore as potentially sellable on the international market.

I am using an example from a critical MPA study of the role of "race" in media production because of the problem I noted above, a severe lack of studies of class in MPA. However, in Georgina Born's vast ethnographic study (2005) of the BBC can be found an example of the potential fruitfulness of empirical MPA for studying class representations. At one point, Born discusses her observations of the BBC's nightly current affairs flagship *Newsnight* and the production of an item on the issue of poverty shortly before the UK general election of 1997 (pp. 423–428). Some of Born's account is damning. The production team struggled to find anyone who might speak first-hand about the experience of poverty in a studio discussion—reflecting, perhaps, the way in which the production team inhabited social milieux cut off from working-class lives. But Born registers the producers' own "self-parodic" awareness of that gap: "We've had a poor person on before, haven't we?" jokes one producer. Born also shows that ultimately the final programme involved powerful images of poverty and interviews with people who were experiencing such poverty, and the studio discussion ends with a working-class woman saying, "If you want to know why your policies don't work, come to the people who'll tell you, the people at the brunt of it" (p. 427).

Born does not deny a problem in representations of the working class, but suggests that, in certain circumstances, the professional duties of journalists can—if only occasionally and temporarily—overcome the gulf between their class location and those of working-class people. This points to the fact that sometimes the limitations of producer background can be overcome if producers have a sufficient professional commitment to respectfully and thoughtfully representing a broader range of people, experiences, and voices. If that is right, then it suggests that producer background—whether race, gender, nationality, or class—may have an important role to play (after all, in the earlier quotation, Curran writes that the attribution of causality to personal background is only *partly* misleading) but that role might best be understood as shaping rather than fixing what is possible in representational terms. It makes certain outcomes more likely, rather than inevitable. In other words, MPA suggests that producer background is *mediated* through other factors, for example via organisational, cultural, and occupational discourses, conventions, and values. Nevertheless, it is vital not to overstate the significance of professionalism (as some journalists and journalism educators do). The general failure of media representation discussed suggests that such professional commitment is not currently sufficient to counter the problems that derive from class asymmetry. The positive consequences of professionalism have been rather limited (Curran, 2002, pp. 30–32).

Explaining Representational Failure 2: Systemic and Structural Influences on Production

I have been arguing that MPA can provide tools to help explain dubious media representations of class beyond the class asymmetry explanation. The main research methods that have been used by MPA to analyse the factors discussed above are interviews and observation. But it is important to be aware of the limitations of such empirical methods, and therefore of research based too much on them. When people are interviewed by visiting researchers about their work they may be guarded in their answers regarding their own practices and those of their colleagues. They may feel obliged (whether through loyalty, anxiety, or even fear of repercussions) to present a generally positive account of the organisation for which they work.

These limitations are particularly apparent in the case of interview methods, and the use of the method known as *participant observation* might overcome them. But participant observation requires considerable access, and if critical researchers are frank about their concerns, it might be extremely difficult to obtain permission to observe closely media organisations, especially those that are anxious about scrutiny or public exposure (such as Hollywood studios; see Ortner, 2011). A different problem is that, if they do succeed in gaining access, researchers using participant observation might come to share some of the values of the organisation they are working within. One route is that they may come to form warm personal relations with people working there. While it is still possible in such situations to achieve a critical distance, researchers may, consciously or unconsciously, feel inhibited in making public a rigorously honest account of production dynamics.

There is another even more serious problem for interview- and observation-based research. Even if researchers were permitted to carry out detailed observations and interviews, historically shaped "systemic" factors such as the degree of commercialism in a medium (television, or film, or popular music) or a genre (reality television, romantic comedy, or hip hop) are unlikely to be sufficiently analysed by these observational and interview means alone. Indeed, such factors might be so taken for granted by those involved in media organisations that they are hardly noticed at all, or are deemed not worthy of consideration.

This could certainly apply to the topic of this chapter: potential causes of poor representation. One example of such an all-pervasive (and therefore difficult to notice or articulate) cause of poor representation could be the fact that most media products are made as part of commercial businesses, oriented towards making a profit for private owners or shareholders. The types of pressure this exerts on media producers will vary hugely from industry to industry, and from organisation to organisation, depending, among other things, on attitudes towards commercial goals embedded within organisational cultures. Sometimes, certain groups of media producers will be relatively protected from commercial imperatives, even within commercial, for-profit businesses, while others will be exposed to unrelenting pressure to produce short-term profits. Such variations might even be found within the *same* organisation, depending on organisational division, or on the particular projects being undertaken. Some genres (genres are often the basis of organisational structure in media industries) might be more protected than others, perhaps because there might be a history of a particular division producing content that has achieved critical acclaim—such as a noted literary fiction department in a large publisher.

Now these different factors can certainly be investigated through the interview and observational methods discussed above. But other factors regarding what some writers conceive as an "art-commerce dialectic" (Ryan, 1992), and others frame as "creativity-commerce tensions," might evade researchers who depend excessively on primary empirical methods. For example, there are longstanding conventions concerning how the relations between creativity and commerce are negotiated, which might help to explain recurring patterns, including the way in which certain romantic notions of artistic freedom keep commercial imperatives relatively at bay, or, alternatively, entrench exploitation by encouraging people to think that it is fine to work for very little, or for free, as money does not matter ("sacrificial labor" as Ross [2000] calls it).

In other words, in explaining any problematic set of representations, there is a need to examine *structural and historical forces shaping relevant practices, values, and discourses*. History is necessary, even when studying contemporary media. For example, at certain historical junctures, entire industries might shift towards new sets of relations between commerce and creativity as a result of political, cultural, and regulatory change. There are reasons to think that since the 1980s some contemporary media systems have become significantly more commercialised—that is, they have become more oriented towards a maximisation of sales and/or profits rather than towards providing rich, revealing, or truthful representations in the service of democracy and/or quality of life. The direction of government policy in most countries around the world has been towards a proliferation of media outlets, channels, and texts, in the name of competition, though often with little attempt to challenge the emergence of powerful corporate oligopolies (Hesmondhalgh, 2013, chapter 4). Those medium-term histories, going back decades, are vital to understanding what is happening *now*.

How might a broad, historically informed MPA connect such systemic, institutional changes to media content? In the highly commercialised contexts created by the developments just outlined, in order to stand out from the competition, producers might well—whether they are aware of it or not—be pressured towards negative, sensationalist, or inadequate representations of (for example) working-class lives. Television programme makers are, other things being equal, more likely in such a situation to create "factually based" content in which the lives of working-class people are held up as objects of amazement, wonder, and disgust, rather than to make programmes that seek to dig beneath working-class experience, and that allow working-class people to speak for themselves on something like their own terms. There is certainly nothing wrong with producing strong emotion. But if producers fall back on simplification and distortions of people's lives to produce those emotions, something is wrong.

Nor is this a matter of making sociological documentaries rather than entertainment. I am referring to what might be achieved through a vast range of imaginative and skilfully made media content: it applies to comedy and drama as much as documentary (and in fact documentary can be deeply enthralling as well as world-revealing; check out the sad depiction of brutalised working-class lives in *Making a Murderer* if you haven't seen it). British soaps at their best, for example, have been provided a rich mixture of representations of working-class (and middle-class) life for decades. And although I am using the example of television here, it also applies to other media. Working-class sensibilities can and have been imaginatively articulated in music and video games as well as in feature films or "quality" television.

A problem though is that such careful and/or imaginative and/or powerful content, based on a more profound engagement with working-class experience, is likely to be expensive to make. What's more, it may struggle to find audiences in a contemporary media context in which many audience members have little time to sift carefully though the massive amounts of content on offer to them. Conversely, in a situation of marketization and of intense (though oligopolistic) competition between many different television channels, and many other leisure opportunities, television executives and producers seek to produce and market content that they feel is likely to generate rapid and widespread attention. This quest for attention may partly help to explain the recent surge in British TV programming that seems deliberately to seek out unsympathetic and damaged benefits claimants and to portray them negatively and sensationally, implying that most or all benefits claimants are "feckless scroungers" thereby contributing to significant public misunderstandings of the scale of welfare fraud (Jones, 2014).

My point is that systemic factors such as commercialism need to be analysed, explained, and understood, as part of MPA, when explaining certain media phenomena, including inadequate representation of working-class people. Such an enhanced MPA would minimally require contextual analysis of how media policies have changed, and some consideration of how "macro" level systemic factors might interact with the more situational "micro" factors observable by ethnographic researchers.[6] Government policies shape media systems in vital ways. They can provide incentives to produce truthful, thoughtful, inquiring content by stipulating that certain funding or licensing might only be available if a certain amount of such content is made available. Obviously there are limits to how tightly content can or should be controlled. But any serious analysis would need to move beyond the naïve position that *any* democratic government regulation of content represents a version of "censorship." The general tendency in government regulation of media has been towards reducing measures aimed at providing high-quality content in the interests of social well-being. The key point for this chapter is that MPA could—and indeed should—draw our attention to such potential systemic causal factors regarding public policy, marketization, and commercialism and provide plausible accounts of how such systemic contexts have effects in terms of "on the ground" production and content, even if it might be difficult finally and conclusively to prove a clear set of causal links.

How Sociologies of Class Might Enhance MPA's Understanding of How Bad Class Representation Happens

The factors discussed in the previous section might further enhance the class asymmetry explanation by identifying other factors, alongside that asymmetry, which might explain why representations take the form they do—such as political-economic and policy factors. But there is another missing link in the class asymmetry explanation. How can we explain and understand the tendency for middle-class and upper-class people to fail to represent working-class people, beyond just saying that they are different, and therefore must fail? To put it another way, how does the "middle-classness" (or "upper-classness") of media producers get *into* media representations? To answer this, we need more than MPA. Or, rather, MPA needs to go beyond its own boundaries into other areas of social science and humanities.

A vitally important contribution to thinking about these issues has come from Pierre Bourdieu. For Bourdieu, the statuses accorded to certain objects, practices, and ways of being (and in the realm of culture, to certain texts, genres, and artists) are not arbitrary, but are shaped by the shared sets of bodily and intellectual dispositions ingrained into people during their upbringing; Bourdieu's term for such a set of dispositions is "habitus."[7] So, for example, in his book on cultural consumption, *Distinction*, Bourdieu (1984, pp. 53–54) discussed how the "distance from necessity" of the various factions of the dominant class (analysed via surveys of different occupational groups) adopt, to different degrees, an aesthetic disposition that allows them to bracket off content and function—such as not being interested in feeling "horror at the horrible"—and focus on questions of "style," form, and the skill of the artist. By contrast, according to Bourdieu (1984), the dominated class (essentially, his term for the working class) tends, because of the difficulties of achieving the "distance from necessity" of the dominant class, to refuse artistic experimentation (p. 44), to strictly self-police any "pretension" (p. 38), and to value works of art not in terms of their style or artistic accomplishment, but in terms of the aesthetic features of what is represented (for example, commenting on the beauty of the landscape or a person in a photograph, not the photographic technique itself).

What Bourdieu provides, then, is a way of understanding and *explaining* the very different practices, tastes, and values of different classes. There is potential here for understanding why at least some "middle-class" media producers might inadequately represent working-class people.[8] However, Bourdieu's sociology of culture (see, e.g., Bourdieu, 1996) is not at all concerned with explaining recurring patterns of representation, of the kind we have been discussing here, involving deeply "ideological" representations of class. Instead, his work on cultural production was based on a historical examination of how some cultural producers gained a degree of autonomy from the state and from religious and business imperatives.[9]

Even more importantly in the present context, Bourdieu's structuralist approach shares a problem with the class asymmetry explanation: it seems to rely on an excessively homogeneous notion of how class identities manifest themselves in people's lives, downplaying agency and individual variability (Lahire, 2003). Here the concept of "contradictory class locations" developed by the US sociologist Erik Olin Wright may be of help. Wright (1997) shows that the very broad lay category of the middle class involves a large range of class locations, in terms of authority and skills, from expert managers to "nonskilled," non-management workers and many intermediate points (non-managing experts, skilled supervisors) in between. This is relevant to media production because in the media industries many of the workers involved in developing ideas for and executing media products, such as television programmes (i.e., those most responsible for representations), are in non-management roles but with quite high levels of scarce skills and even expertise (Hesmondhalgh & Baker, 2011, pp. 67–70; Ryan, 1992). In fact, such media producers can be thought of as intellectuals—not in the everyday sense of a very clever person, or a very bookish person, but in the sociological sense (famously associated with the Italian Marxist writer Gramsci) of "people whose activity is primarily that of elaborating and disseminating ideas" (Wright, 1979, p. 192).

While there is no space here to summarise his arguments fully, essentially Wright shows that intellectuals, such as teachers and, although he does not name them, artists, journalists, and media producers, tend to occupy particularly contradictory locations within class relations. This is so, first, in terms of their *economic* position: in some ways they are closer to the working class in terms of being employed and often exploited, in some ways they are like the bourgeoisie in terms of engaging in mental not manual labour. Second, it is true in terms of their *ideological* position: sometimes they reproduce the core values of the most powerful groups in society, sometimes they challenge them. What's more, as Bourdieu's sociology of cultural *production* (as opposed to his rather deterministic sociology of consumption) shows, intellectuals such as teachers and media producers are, depending on circumstances, and with considerable variation in different societies, granted varying degrees of autonomy that allows them to stand apart from the general class interests of the "dominant class"—and this allows class-divided societies to show that they still preserve some (currently rather vulnerable) liberal values.

Bourdieu's concept of habitus, leavened by Wright's attention to variability within the middle class, might help us understand how media producers' "middle-classness" gets translated into poor representations of the working class. As Andrew Sayer notes, Bourdieu's in-depth consideration of cultural and educational differences between classes enables him to "provide unparalleled insights into symbolic domination, and hence into the subjective experience and sense of class, which is always far more than an awareness of differences in material wealth" (Sayer, 2005, p. 77). Bourdieu's efforts to identify correspondences between background and upbringing, on the one hand, and tastes, behaviours, and practices, on the other, via the concept of habitus offers the possibility for MPA of identifying what it is in working-class lives, practices, and values that mainly middle-class media producers fail to understand and appreciate as a result of their different habitus and how this might lead to inadequate representation.

This is, as far as I am aware, a challenge yet to be undertaken by MPA, and certainly not undertaken by Bourdieu in his slender work on media. But a number of avenues of investigation of media production based on Bourdieu's way of thinking about class might be possible, three of which I briefly outline here (see also Randle, Forson & Calveley, 2015). One would be observing interactions between working-class people and producers as media production takes place. In their work on education, Bourdieu and his collaborator Passeron discussed how teachers assumed that students knew the underlying codes of their talk (Bourdieu & Passeron, 1977 [1970]), and educational researchers have identified on the basis of observation in schools how such assumptions operate as an obstacle, for example, in encounters between teachers and working-class parents (Weininger & Lareau, 2003). This might be extended into interactions between media producers and working-class subjects in researching, planning, and filming documentaries, reality television, and other "factual" media content.

A second avenue of research might be to focus on issues such as why media production companies might find it difficult to recognise skills and talents in working-class people (or people from working-class backgrounds) who apply to work in their organisations, because they do not understand how and why working-class communities value certain modes of talking, doing, and being.

A third potential research route would be to focus on the transitions from education to the workplace, examining over time how people from different class groups respond differently to the challenge of gaining access to media production. It is possible, for example, that middle-class graduates might have gained knowledge and information about how best to approach potential employers, and just as crucially, they might have greater confidence in putting to work such knowledge and information than students from working-class backgrounds.

However, in explaining inadequate media representations, there is a further factor that we need to consider, drawing on sociological and other accounts of changing class relations, and this in fact might be the most important factor of all. This takes us back to the importance of understanding historical and structural forces, but here not in terms of their effects on media production and the media industries, but on the social realm that the media represent and mediate. For we have seen in many countries a serious worsening of the condition of the working class, a devastation of their institutions (such as trade unions), and an erosion of working-class people's belief in their own ability to bring about positive change for themselves. This is probably the biggest factor of all influencing the way media producers represent the working class. We need to take into account the other factors I have discussed above, but any explanation that did not recognise the more general political and economic attacks on the working class of the last forty years would be failing to see the wood for the trees. Any MPA account that did not pay significant attention to this factor would be in danger of a disabling media-centrism.

What Can Be Done?

In this chapter, I have tried to lay out what MPA might contribute to understanding the causes of the media's general failure to represent working-class people adequately. I have done so via an attempt to build on, and yet go beyond, a partially correct but potentially simplistic explanation (the "class asymmetry explanation") based on the undeniable fact that media producers occupy upper- and middle-class locations. I have shown how, even though MPA has mostly neglected class analysis, some of its existing empirical methods, techniques, and achievements might be fruitfully adapted to explain poor media representations of class, as long as they are combined with (a) an understanding of political-economic and policy factors that might lie "behind" or above the situational contexts that might be observed, or discovered through interviews; (b) an understanding of the subjective experience of class, based on a combination of Bourdieusian theories of class habitus and symbolic domination, with Wright's Marxian-Weberian analysis of contradictory locations in class relations; and (c) a sense of the actual political status of the working class and how it might shape media producers' choices of representation. This needs to be combined with discussion of what would constitute better representations of working-class people and rigorous inquiry into the actual and potential needs of working-class people themselves.

But of course academic analysis can only play a very small part in improving the conditions of working-class people. What can be done to reduce the gap between existing systems of media production and adequate representations of the working class? One commonly proposed solution to the problem of class inequality is education. But education tends to "remove" working-class people from the working class—and often not without psychic cost to those who make that move.

Faced with this problem, some commentators have seen the cure for media ills in digitalisation and the internet, supposedly offering the means for marginalised groups to represent themselves, overcoming boundaries formed by professional groups protecting their own class privileges. It is not at all clear that digitalisation offers a really meaningful enfranchisement of working-class people. Many years of research have shown a strong link between, on the one hand, inequalities in income and education (which, other studies suggest, tend to be strongly correlated with class) and, on the other, inequalities in access to digital communication. Analysts have noted the emergence of a "digital underclass" (Helsper & Reinsdorf, 2016) even in relatively equal countries such as Sweden, put off by costs and a lack of skills, with especially low levels of participation among the less educated, elderly, and socially isolated. Putting aside the question of massive inequalities in access to the means of digital communication, the evidence of inadequate representation of working-class people cited at the beginning of this chapter also suggests that digitalisation and the internet are having rather limited positive effects. Digitalisation and the internet have been present in some societies for some time now, and there does not seem to have been a significant improvement in the way that working-class people are represented in those societies.

The standard mainstream political response to class inequality, from left and right, is the pursuit of, or at least lip-service to, greater social mobility (see Milburn, 2012). But Bourdieu's sociology, with its emphasis on the highly ingrained (though not immutable) nature of class dispositions, suggests that class mobility might not be so easily achieved. Why is this so? One problem is that meeting the challenge of representing marginalised and often oppressed groups such as the working class needs a particular set of skills, which might broadly be defined as "symbol-making": using words, images, sounds, etc. to convey meaning. Although it is vital to remember that the media and cultural industries depend on the labour of many people, including working-class occupations involved in construction, manufacture, cleaning, and so on (Mayer, 2011; Ross, 2015), the fundamental tools at the centre of cultural production involve such symbol-making. In societies such as the UK and the USA, and many others too, a number of factors have led to these skills being dominated by middle-class people. Schools tend to value ways of manifesting symbol-making skills, especially involving written language, that tend to prosper among more privileged class groups (see Bernstein, 1971).[10]

Surely, then, the solution lies in untying class from education and skills so that working-class people are given the symbol-making skills and education necessary to represent themselves. That would certainly be my view—though education policy, including teacher training, has moved far away from the goal of truly understanding and appreciating the class cultures of school students over the last thirty years (Reay, 2006).

More fundamentally, working-class belief in working-class cultural production has been seriously undermined. Social histories by writers such as Michael Denning (1996) and Jonathan Rose (2001) have highlighted the capacity of working-class people and institutions to engage with symbols and ideas and to achieve distinctive forms of cultural production. There is nothing natural or inevitable about the way in which mental and manual labour, and different ways of speaking, are distributed between classes. But these unequal distributions will be hard to shift. The inspiring achievements recorded by Denning and Rose were founded in the period when the labour movement provided, for a century or so up until the 1970s, a focus for an unprecedented degree of proletarian class consciousness, pride, and self-belief. Restoring such political confidence is the main way in which dubious representations will be overcome, but it will be a supremely challenging task.

Notes

1. My thanks to Carly O'Neill for research assistance on this chapter, and to June Deery, Lisa Henderson, Kate Oakley, Dave O'Brien, and Fredrik Stiernstedt for their thoughtful and helpful comments.
2. See Wilkinson and Pickett (2009) for an important analysis of the negative consequences of inequality for entire societies, not just for the losers.
3. Some studies pay insufficient attention to the existence of thoughtful, compelling, and entertaining media products that engage with working-class life, some of them produced by people from working-class backgrounds.
4. Media production studies, or MPA as I prefer it here, is now an established area or field of media and communication studies research and teaching. As is often the case for fields and sub-fields of research, it gets labelled in different ways. Some prefer the formulation "media industry studies." Many people erroneously equate MPA with "critical political economy of media," when the two are separate but overlapping and sometimes mutually reinforcing areas of inquiry. For my efforts at overviews, see Hesmondhalgh (2010, 2013).
5. Critical political economy of media (see note 3) has paid attention to media and class (Mosco & Wasko, 1982) but, again, with little or no reference to representation.
6. Such an investigation of commercialism would be aided by more sophisticated contributions to the political economy of media (e.g., Hardy, 2014) and by historical accounts of the rise of commercial cultural production (such as Williams, 1981).
7. Bourdieu sees class relations in terms of competition and differentiation; he does not put the emphasis on exploitation, as some Marxists do (see Sayer, 2005, p. 80).
8. Bourdieu's way of analysing how habitus manifests itself in culture, based on an account of French culture in the 1960s and 1970s, undoubtedly requires adaptation to different national contexts and different times. Some efforts have been made in this direction (see Weininger and Lareau, 2003), though few of the studies seem to have been oriented towards understanding working-class experience.
9. Bourdieu provided some brief, polemical, and rather underdeveloped analysis of journalism and television, and others have made admirable efforts to apply his ideas to journalism (e.g., Benson & Neveu, 2005).

Works Cited

Benson, R., & Neveu, E. (2005). *Bourdieu and the journalistic field.* Cambridge, UK: Polity.
Bernstein, B. (1971). *Class, codes and control.* London. UK: Routledge & Kegan Paul.
Biressi, A., & Nunn, H. (2013). *Class and contemporary British culture.* Basingstoke, UK: Palgrave Macmillan.

Born, G. (2005). *Uncertain vision: Birt, Dyke and the reinvention of the BBC*. London, UK: Secker & Warburg.

Bourdieu, P. (1984 [1979]). *Distinction: A social critique of the judgment of taste* (R. Nice, Trans.). London, UK: Routledge.

Bourdieu, P. (1996). *The rules of art*. Cambridge, UK: Polity.

Bourdieu, P., & Passeron, J-C. (1977) *Reproduction in education, society and culture*. London, UK: Sage.

Curran, J. (2002). *The media and power*. London, UK: Routledge.

Denning, M. (1996). *The cultural front: The laboring of American culture in the twentieth century*. London, UK: Verso.

Gilens, M. (1999). *Why Americans hate welfare: Race, media, and the politics of antipoverty policy*. Chicago, IL: University Of Chicago Press.

Hardy, J. (2014). *Critical political economy of the media: An introduction*. London, UK: Routledge.

Havens, T. (2013). *Black television travels: African-American media around the globe*. New York, NY: NYU Press.

Helsper, E.J., & Reisdorf, B.C. (2016). The emergence of a "digital underclass" in Great Britain and Sweden: Changing reasons for digital exclusion. *New Media & Society*. Retrieved from http://journals.sagepub.com/doi/abs/10.1177/1461444816634676 (accessed 7 April 2017).

Hesmondhalgh, D. (2010). Media industry studies, media production studies. In J. Curran (Ed.), *Media and society* (5th ed.) (pp. 145–163). London, UK: Bloomsbury.

Hesmondhalgh, D. (2013). *The cultural industries* (3rd ed.). London, UK: Sage.

Hesmondhalgh, D., & Baker, S. (2011). *Creative labour: Media work in three cultural industries*. London, UK: Routledge.

Jensen, T. (2014). Welfare commonsense, poverty porn and doxosophy. *Sociological Research Online, 19*(3). Retrieved from http://www.socresonline.org.uk/19/3/3.html

Jensen, T., & Tyler, I. (2015). "Benefits broods": The cultural and political crafting of anti-welfare commonsense. *Critical Social Policy, 35*(4), 470–491.

Jones, O. (2011). *Chavs: The demonization of the working class*. London, UK: Verso.

Jones, O. (2014, January 8). Benefits Street: A healthy media would stand up to the powerful and wealthy. Ours targets the poor and voiceless. *Independent*. Retrieved from http://www.independent.co.uk/voices/comment/benefits-street-a-healthy-media-would-stand-up-to-the-powerful-and-wealthy-ours-targets-the-poor-and-9046773.html

Kelly, M. (2010). Regulating the reproduction and mothering of poor women: The controlling image of the welfare mother in television news coverage of welfare reform. *Journal of Poverty, 14*(1), 76–96.

Lahire, B. (2003) *The plural actor*. Cambridge, UK: Polity.

Lewis, T. (2009). *TV transformations: Revealing the makeover show*. London, UK: Routledge.

Marchetti, D. (2005). Subfields of specialized journalism. In R. Benson & E. Neveu (Eds.), *Bourdieu and the journalistic field* (pp. 64–84). Cambridge, UK: Polity.

Mayer, V. (2011). *Below the line: Producers and production studies in the new television economy*. Durham, NC: Duke University Press.

Milburn, A. (2012). *Fair access to professional careers. A progress report by the independent reviewer on social mobility and child poverty*. Retrieved from https://www.gov.uk/government/publications/fair-access-to-professional-careers-a-progress-report

Mosco, V., & Wasko, J. (Eds.). (1982). *The critical communications review: Vol. 1: Labour, the working class and the media*. New York, NY: Ablex.

O'Brien, D., Laurison, D., Miles, A., & Friedman, S. (2016). Are the creative industries meritocratic? An analysis of the 2014 British Labour Force Survey. *Cultural Trends, 25*(2), 116–31.

O'Brien, D., & Oakley, K. (2015). *Cultural value and inequality: A literature review.* Swindon, UK: Arts and Humanities Research Council.

Ortner, S.B. (2011). Studying sideways: Ethnographic access in Hollywood. In V. Mayer (Ed.), *Production studies: Cultural studies of media industries* (pp. 175–189). New York, NY: Routledge.

Randle, K., Forson, C., & Calveley, M. (2015) Towards a Bourdieusian analysis of the social composition of the UK film and television workforce. *Work, Employment and Society, 29*(4), 590–606.

Reay, D. (2006). The zombie stalking English schools: Social class and educational inequality. *British Journal of Educational Studies, 54*(3), 288–307.

Rose, J. (2001). *The intellectual life of the British working classes.* New Haven, CT: Yale University Press.

Ross, A. (2000) The mental labor problem. *Social Text, 18*(2), 1–32.

Ross, A. (2015). *The gulf: High culture/hard labour.* New York, NY: OR Books.

Ryan, B. (1992). *Making capital from culture: The corporate form of capitalist cultural production.* Berlin, Germany: Walter de Gruyter.

Savage, M. (2015). *Social class in the 21st century.* London, UK: Penguin Books.

Sayer, A. (2005). *The moral significance of class.* Cambridge, UK: Cambridge University Press.

Skeggs, B., & Wood, H. (2011). *Reality television and class.* London, UK: BFI.

Stiernstedt, F., & Jakobsson, P. (2017). Ghettos and gated communities in the social landscape of television: Representations of class in 1982 and 2015. In M. Wayne & D. O'Neill (Eds.), *Considering class: Theory, culture and media in the 21st century.* Leiden, the Netherlands: Brill.

Sutton Trust (2006). *The educational backgrounds of leading journalists.* Retrived from http://www.suttontrust.com/researcharchive/educational-backgrounds-leading-journalists/

Weaver, D.H., & Wilhoit, G.C. (1996) *The American journalist in the 1990s.* Mahwah, NJ: Lawrence Erlbaum.

Weininger, E.B., & Lareau, A. (2003). Translating Bourdieu into the American context: The question of social class and family-school relations. *Poetics, 31*(5), 375–402.

Wilkinson, R., & Pickett, K. (2009). *The spirit level.* London, UK: Penguin.

Williams, R. (1981). *Culture.* London, UK: Fontana.

Wright, E.O. (1979). Intellectuals and the class structure of capitalist society. In P. Walker (Ed.), *Between labor and capital* (pp. 191–211). Boston, MA: South End Press.

Wright, E.O. (1997). *Class counts: Comparative studies in class analysis.* Cambridge, UK: Cambridge University Press.

3

CLASS AND GENDER THROUGH SEVEN DECADES OF AMERICAN TELEVISION SITCOMS

Richard Butsch

The Middle is a successful domestic situation comedy of the 2010s, beginning its seventh season in Fall 2016, with over a hundred episodes and primed for syndication. Much of the story, as the title signals, revolves around difficulties the parents have paying the bills of their family of three children on a middle income. Hollywood, as with most Americans, has a vocabulary and conceptual deficit when it comes to class. For this show, class is measured by income: one is rich, poor, or in the middle.[1] That is how most Americans think of class as well. Like most Americans, the show—and its reviewers—is vague and perhaps confused about class. The father works at a quarry, but it's not clear whether he is a manual worker or a manager. The show also reflects the shifting reality and representations of social class in America in recent decades, from clear class boundaries to mixed images.

This vagueness, even confusion, reflects the recent landscape of class in America. At the dawn of commercial television American manufacturing was at its peak and the center of the economy. Blue-collar manual workers were numerous. Unionization too was at its peak and a widely accepted fact of life. Metropolitan daily newspapers typically had at least one reporter assigned to labor news. When commercial television began in the US after World War II, class lines were easier to see because occupational distinctions were in common parlance. Then everyone understood the difference between blue collar and white collar. Blue collar was manual labor in a factory, farm, mine, or in construction; white collar was mental labor as a professional or manager in an office. Education and income differed accordingly. Blue collar was working-class, often unionized, wage

---

This chapter extends research reported in previous publications, including Butsch (1992, 2005, 2016), Butsch and Glennon (1983) and Glennon and Butsch (1982).

work; white collar was salaried and above middle income. Clerical staffs, almost entirely women, were pink collar.

What changed was de-industrialization, the disappearance of tens of millions of blue-collar jobs in the 1970s through the 1990s. By the new millennium, there were few blue-collar jobs, so that the widely understood category of working class had few visible correlates in everyday life for most people.[2] Instead, millions more now worked in the service sector, a few with high salaries, but most in low wage, non-unionized, dead-end, essentially still manual labor, jobs with few benefits—jobs like those pink-collar jobs that women used to be confined to, but now many men as well.

Hollywood and Americans have become more adrift than ever about class without the old class categories. Google Ngrams for American English books show a substantial decline in usage of "working class," "blue collar," "proletariat," and "industrial worker" from the 1970s on. During this same period, "construction worker" increases, suggesting that the image of the working class shifted from industrial to construction workers.[3] Lost in the confusion is the fact that much lower wage service work also involves manual labor under close supervision, a new working class—but most Americans don't have a collar or a class name for them.

Implicit in studies of representation is the assumption that media representations are persuasive, that they affect people's thinking and acting. Effective persuasion arises from pervasive and persistent repetition, the sedimentation of representations in the dominant culture and its incorporation and naturalization in everyday thinking taken for granted (Lasswell, 1927; Stouffer, Suchman, DeVinney, Star & Williams, 1949; Hovland, Janis & Kelley, 1953). Repetition of representations (Hall, 1997; Dyer, 2013), often as stereotypes, maintains their pervasiveness and persistence. It is their persistence and pervasiveness that is the subject of this chapter. Television has been and continues to be the most pervasive and widely consumed representational medium, and thus ideal for documenting repetitive representation. I focus on the remarkable persistence and stability of stereotypes over seven decades about the working class. During these seven decades the most widely disseminated representations reaching the largest portion of the population were those on prime-time network television, making these the most pervasive representations as well. Within television I have further focused on the most pervasive and persistent genre in those seven decades, domestic situation comedy series.

More broadly, the subject here is culture. The pervasiveness and persistence indicates that these representations are not incidental, but integral to the dominant culture. Aesthetics of a cultural work can be enjoyed/understood at the level of individual works. But to ascertain social importance requires more than inquiry into individual works. Representations become social when they are sufficiently pervasive and persistent so that they sediment into the culture and thus become naturalized and enduring, and are reproduced through further representations and everyday discourse.

In what *particular* ways they are important depends on their content. I have researched how images of class are consistent and may support class inequality in the US. My purpose is not to provide a deep analysis of a particular text, but rather to document the representation of the working class across the broad television landscape to reveal how American television sitcoms, watched by tens of millions every night, reproduce and reinforce stereotypes of social class. They have repeatedly presented the same image of working-class men, which have become taken for granted as real, which dovetail with similar assumptions about class in other institutions and discourses that "discipline and punish," and which comfort higher classes by confirming their superiority, and shame lower classes for their inadequacies and failures.

To search for repetitious representations, I researched over 400 prime-time American domestic situation comedy series, 68 years of television from 1948 to 2016.[4] This has revealed durable patterns despite significant industry, genre, and audience changes. In this chapter I can only discuss a tiny portion of this data, and therefore concentrate on the more persistent, longest-running series as examples of the overall patterns revealed in the complete oeuvre. Last, I focus on the representations of two classes, a working class of manual labor occupations with little work autonomy, and an upper-middle class with managerial and professional occupations. These two constitute about ninety percent of all domestic sitcoms.

Why *domestic* sitcoms? First, domestic situation comedy series are numerous and have been a mainstay of American prime-time television since its earliest days. Other genres come and go, but domestic sitcoms have been the most reliable moneymakers for television networks for seven decades. Periodically, the trade magazine *Variety* has declared the sitcom dead only to witness a renaissance a few seasons later. Moreover, their formula has been fairly stable, despite some considerable variation and, recently, some hybridization. The longevity of TV sitcoms also has the advantage of allowing me to track the history of representation without shifting genres.

Second, their focus on family life does not predetermine the social class represented, unlike law or medical dramas for example, so producers can choose characters of any class, sex, or age. This openness of choice reveals that the representations are not due to individual prejudices, but rather to how industry structure and culture shape representations and reproduce stereotypes (Butsch, 2014). As an additional and unplanned bonus, the spouses and children in domestic settings capture gender and age relations as facets used to reinforce class representations.

Representation of class in domestic sitcoms begins with the relative frequency and visibility of different classes. Overall through the seven decades, upper-middle-class sitcoms were far more numerous, over-representing that class. On the other hand, working-class families were relatively scarce—roughly ten percent of all domestic sitcoms—even though manual workers constituted over half the labor force. The proportion of working-class sitcoms ebbed and flowed, but until recently were no more than a small percent of sitcoms.

Gerbner and Gross (1976) called such absences, especially the contrast, a form of symbolic annihilation. Invisibility implies that such people are not worthy of representation, uninteresting, boring, etc. At the same time, the over-representation of the upper-middle class normalized it as the universal American family experience. Illustrating this normalization, colleagues from working-class backgrounds have recounted to me how they, as children, watched and wished that their family were like those middle-class sitcom families. Even when working-class shows did multiply, the characterizations did not affirm the capability, admirability, or respectability of working-class men, but quite the contrary. In the small percent of sitcom series that depicted working-class families, there has been a striking consistency, especially in representing working-class men.

The nature of humor also has differed, depending on the class characterized in the sitcom. Drama historian David Grote (1983) identified three types of comic characters: the Innocent, the Fool, and the Scoundrel. Scripts intend audiences to sympathize with the Innocent and smile amusedly but protectively *about* their mistakes; *laugh with* the Scoundrel as he outsmarts Authority; and *laugh at* the Fool, so the Fool is diminished. Scoundrels rarely appeared in American sitcoms. One notable example is the *Phil Silvers Show* in the 1950s, about an Army sergeant that outwitted his superiors. Those under his command admired and aided him. A host of middle-class domestic sitcoms, like *The Brady Bunch*, focused on innocent children making mistakes with model parents guiding them. A few middle-class sitcoms feature a Fool, almost always the woman, usually a housewife. *I Love Lucy* was the classic. In rare instances the middle-class fool was a racial minority, as in *The Jeffersons*. In these few shows, the Fool is not working class, but is another lower status, a woman or racial/ethnic minority.

In *almost all* working-class sitcoms, however, comedy centers on a Fool, and he is almost always the male breadwinner. He is a buffoon or bungler, often well-meaning and warm-hearted, but incompetent, immature, ignorant, irresponsible. They are the opposites of models for their children to emulate. He is played against his wife and children, who typically are more sensible, competent, mature, and intelligent. The children will not follow his footsteps into a manual labor job, but will go to college and rise into the professional/managerial upper-middle class. The comedy of these shows is based on laughing *at* the man. These patterns shift over time and in some cases characterizations become more three dimensional and less stereotypic. But the stock characters of the working-class male buffoon and the middle-class super-parents continued for the most part unaltered. The overall effect is a consistent and unfavorable contrast between working-class men and their wives and children, and between them and middle-class men.

The contrasting portrayal of working-class and middle-class men is strikingly evident in the visual appearance, the figure, posture, and dress of the characters. Diana Crane's (2012) study focuses on fashion as a statement of class. Here we see dress combined with posture and figure to make a statement *about* class.

Figure 3.1 is a composite of the lead male characters of working-class domestic sitcoms from the 1950s into the 2010s. Note they are consistently overweight and beer-bellied and have poor muscle tone.[5] The animated characters are slump-shouldered and the two most famous are perpetually unshaven. Their dress is sloppy casual. The consistency over decades is striking. So is the contrast to the upper-middle-class men (Figure 3.2), who are slim, with flat stomachs, upright posture, and shoulders back.

While dress style changed over the decades from formal to casual, all the middle-class male characters remained well dressed, often in business attire that marked their occupational class. Taken together, the contrasting appearance of working-class and middle-class men affirms and elucidates contrasting valuations of class, so that physique becomes a symbol of the personal character of such men in real life.

Next, compare the contrasting working- and middle-class sitcom men to the remarkably similar physical appearance of wives *across* classes (Figure 3.3).

FIGURE 3.1 Working-class men: Chester Riley and Ralph Kramden (1950s), Fred Flintstone (1960s), Archie Bunker (1970s), Dan Conner (1980s), Homer Simpson (1990s), Doug Heffernan and Peter Griffin (2000s), Cleveland Brown (2010s). All images composed by Janet Duffy.

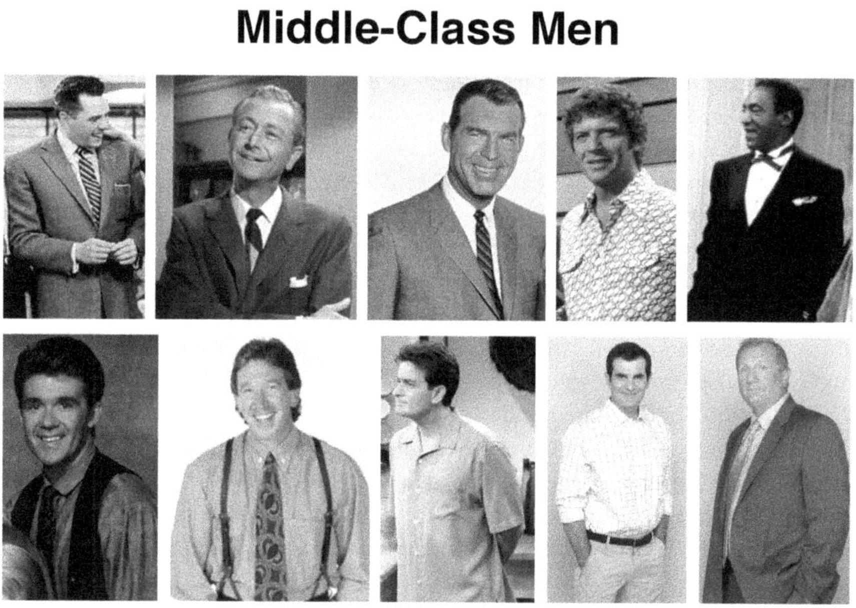

FIGURE 3.2 Middle-class men: Rickie Ricardo and Jim Anderson (1950s), Steve Douglas (1960s), Mike Brady (1970s), Cliff Huxtable and Jason Seaver (1980s), Tim Taylor (1990s), Charlie Harper (2000s), Phil Dunphy and Jay Pritchett (2010s).

FIGURE 3.3 Middle- and working-class wives: Peg Riley, Lucy Ricardo, Wilma Flintstone, Carol Brady, Edith Bunker, Clair Huxtable, Roseanne Conner, Marge Simpson, Carol Foster, Carrie Heffernan, Jill Taylor, Lois Griffin, Annie Camden, Debra Barone.

It is difficult to distinguish the differences between the two classes of women intermixed in this figure. Working-class and middle-class wives generally adhere to a middle-class norm, slim and trim figures with a narrow waist, shoulders straight and erect posture, as with the middle-class men. (One exception is Roseanne, as will be discussed later.) They are dressed neatly at home, usually with a freshly pressed dress and often a necklace or other jewelry. The similarity implies that the working-class women identify and express middle-class values rather than their own husband's working-class status. (This is often thematized in the stories, as wives aspire to the prestige and privilege of middle-class status and culture.) The physical depiction of working-class women thus stands as contrast and chastisement to their men, while the middle-class wives' appearance affirms the success and pride/respect of the middle-class men.[6]

The contrast between men and women has the effect of affirming class difference. Not all women are drawn in contrast to all men; rather the contrast depends upon class. Wives of both classes appear compatible with the middle class and contrast with the slovenly working-class men. Among shows built around a Fool, in working-class sitcoms the man is the Fool, inverting traditional sex status to diminish the man. In middle-class sitcoms the woman is the fool (the stereotyped ditzy woman), affirming traditional sex status to enhance the man. Thus the representation of women is used in two ways as a mechanism for contrasting men of different classes.

These stereotypic representations of class held sway on television, nearly unchallenged, for over a half-century. In the last decade, as we will see, even as the same old types have been repeated in new shows, a wider range of character and family types have appeared in many other shows, tipping the numerical balance and outnumbering the shows with the long-standing pattern.

Let us now briefly review a few sitcoms and their characters from the 1950s into the new millennium (further explanations are given in Butsch & Glennon, 1983; Butsch, 1992, 2005, 2016). Then we will look more closely at the most recent decade, when a wide variety of family types seems to suggest change. I mention only the most successful domestic sitcoms, but similar themes appear in many less successful, less well-known sitcoms. In particular, constructing the working-class man in the role of fool is most consistent across sitcoms and most persistent over time, even as characterizations have grown more diverse and complicated.

In the post-war baby-boom era, from the late 1940s into the mid-1960s, sitcom characterizations were quite simple and contrasts quite clear. Sitcoms were intended for family viewing and could easily be understood by young children. The basic formulas and characters already discussed were established in this era. Through later eras, these formulas and characterizations gradually tone down the one-dimensional stereotypes and complicate the stories, even while perpetuating much of the original contrasts between classes, and between men, women, and children.

Television comedy in the 1950s was often slapstick and drew more from vaudeville, filtered through radio sitcoms, than from theater or novels. Radio relied on sound effects, such as the tumble and clatter when Fibber McGee opened his closet door. TV reintroduced visual slapstick, pratfalls, and frozen facial expressions. Both radio and TV sitcoms were modeled on the vaudeville skit: standard two-dimensional characters repeating the same lines in each performance. Sitcoms relied on widely recognized and accepted stereotypes and caricatures that exaggerated the differences in class representation. The 1950s sitcom became a template used again and again.

A cluster of successful working-class sitcoms, *The Life of Riley* (1953–1958), *Mama* (1949–1957), *The Honeymooners* (1955–1956), and *The Goldbergs* (1949–1956), established the formula for working-class families. They were replaced during the 1960s by only one working-class sitcom, *The Flintstones* (1960–1965), which continued the old formula in animation, with father Fred modeled on Chester Riley and Ralph Kramden.

A version of this same formula was used in very few middle-class sitcoms, e.g., *Burns and Allen* (1950–1958) and *I Love Lucy* (1951–1957), but with the sex roles inverted. The wife was the fool and the husband successful, mature, and sensible. Most middle-class sitcoms of this era, however, were little homilies about parenting, with father and mother as ideal parents. The title of *Father Knows Best* (1954–1960) captures the message of these shows, broadcast in the same years as *Mama* declared mother knows best in the working-class home. *My Three Sons* (1960–1972) continued this formula through the 1960s. The sitcom landscape of these two decades leaves an impression that working-class men are inadequate, even embarrassing, while upper-middle-class men are successful at home as well as in business, to be admired and respected.

The 1970s and 1980s began with the winding down of the Vietnam War and the strife of the 1960s. Television's response to this was to finally include some of these issues in sitcoms. Yet, despite the progressive social messages of these shows, male leads representing subordinate groups continued the television stereotypes of the 1950s. The most well known of these was Archie of *All in the Family* (1970–1979), loud and angry, like Ralph Kramden, and vociferously prejudiced. *Sanford and Son* (1972–1977) was the black version of *All in the Family*. Fred was a junkyard owner-operator, a distinctly lower-class small businessman, loud-mouthed and prejudiced like Archie. Applying the same formula, *The Jeffersons* (1975–1985) features George and Fred. George appears to contradict the class pattern, since breadwinner George is a successful black businessman, but still a fool like Archie, meant to be laughed at. In this case the same formula was applied to race rather than class, just as it was applied to women in a few upper-middle-class sitcoms.

Other sitcoms continued the tradition of the idealized middle-class family. *The Brady Bunch* (1969–74) upheld the tradition of *Father Knows Best*. Even *Happy Days* (1974–1984), in which a working-class biker, the Fonz, unexpectedly became the audience favorite, offered a father of the male teen lead, a hardware store owner, whom the teens respected: even the Fonz urges the boys to listen to the father. However, for the first time, three middle-class sitcoms depicted a few professional and executive men as dumb and incompetent: *Maude* (1972–1978, an MD), *Newhart* (1972–1978, a therapist, dentist, and airline pilot), and *Benson* (1979–1986, governor), perhaps reflecting the unusually high levels of professional and managerial unemployment during 1970s recessions. Nevertheless, the working-class male stereotype and the middle-class super-parent formulas remained firm.

Two more shows carried the middle-class super-parent formula through the 1980s. *The Cosby Show* (1984–1992) reversed the black sitcoms of the 1970s, presenting instead ideal parents skillfully helping their children through modern difficulties of growing up. *Growing Pains* (1985–1992) featured dual career parents whose professional careers never interfere with their superb parenting. In the 1990s the sitcom class formulas persisted, even while some shows complicated the picture. *Roseanne* (1988–1997) contradicted the traditional representations in working-class family sitcoms, depicting the lifestyle and difficulties of the de-industrialized American working class. Roseanne is volatile and angry like Ralph and Archie, while the father, Dan, is the sensible and solid one. Yet, at the same time, the familiar formula survived in the animated sitcom *The Simpsons* (1990–2014). The father Homer is a carbon copy of Fred Flintstone, beard, beer belly, and all, while wife Marge is ditzy but relatively sensible, reminiscent of Edith Bunker, and the children are smarter than their father.

Three ostensibly middle-class sitcoms bend the class formulas. *Step by Step* (1991–1998) continued the super-parent formula, but the father, Frank Lambert, is variously depicted as a self-employed construction worker and then as owner of a company bidding on a multimillion-dollar contract. His wife is a beauty parlor owner/operator. He is physically fit in the middle-class mode, but wear flannel shirts, à la construction workers.

Home Improvement (1991–1999) introduced a new twist on the middle-class man. Husband Tim Taylor is the star of his own home improvement television show. He jokes around on the show as well as at home. However, he is not a buffoon; we don't laugh *at* him, but rather with him. He is a variant on the Scoundrel, willfully adolescent and macho.

The husband in *Everybody Loves Raymond* (1996–2005) is part Tim and part Fred Flintstone. Raymond is a successful sports writer, but is intimidated by his wife Debra and his own parents. He wants to have fun with his friends, like Tim and Fred, but unlike Tim and more like Fred, he is worried that his wife will be cross with him for it. Similarly, he is unable to stand up to his parents, who are loud and angry in the stereotype mode of the working class from earlier sitcoms. Perhaps the uncertainty of class distinctions in these shows is a reflection of the fading presence of blue-collar work in de-industrialized America.

The old stereotype remained and thrived in the 2000s. In the animated *Family Guy* (1999–present), Peter Griffin holds a miscellany of unskilled jobs and is Fred Flintstone all over again with wacky schemes to have fun. His wife Lois is a new Wilma, patient and tolerant with Peter. The *King of Queens* (1998–2007), too, is a revival of the Flintstones. Doug is a UPS truck driver. He's overweight and schlumpy like Fred. He concocts schemes to have fun and hides them from his wife. *According to Jim* (2001–2009) features the owner of a vaguely defined small construction business, as in *Step by Step*, so his class is a bit blurred. But his appearance and characterization are much the same as Doug's in *The King of Queens*.

Two and Half Men (2003–2015) stars Charlie, a fun-loving single guy, a modern twist on *Bachelor Father* (1957–1962) and *Courtship of Eddie's Father* (1969–1972). Charlie is a very successful jingle writer. The humor arises from his cluelessness about taking care of his brother's child. He is an upper-middle-class male lead, slim and trim, successful, but irresponsible and self-indulgent like Tim.

TV critics have noted a trend of de-masculinized male leads as child/men in film and television series. What they haven't noted is that this type differs with class. The fun-loving type appears in *Home Improvement, Family Guy, King of Queens*, and *Two and a Half Men*. However, the middle-class men are successful, affluent, slim, and trim. The working-class fun-lovers are just getting by, overweight and flabby, and apologetic to their wives when they get caught.

At the same time, the middle-class super-parent formula has continued alive and well.[7] *My Wife and Kids* (2001–2005) was black comedian Damon Wayans' homage to *The Cosby Show*. The father, Michael, is a self-made business success who works at home in a plush Connecticut suburb. Wife Janet is a housewife who also "works" at home, day-trading stocks. As in *The Cosby Show,* they are ideal parents.

In the 2010s, the dismantling of the traditional fall season debut of new series, along with more frequent series cancellations and replacements and the proliferation of cable networks and streaming services offering original series, have made it increasingly difficult to accurately enumerate all new sitcoms, particularly as these trends accelerated in the mid-2010s.

Also, shows have become more complicated. They blur lines between domestic sitcoms and those focusing on singles and workplaces. Households include aunts, uncles, cousins, ex-spouses, adult children, and gay couples, in addition to mom, dad, kids, and grandparents. Occupational class has become increasingly confused, blurring lower-middle, worker or manager, and mixed-class occupations. At the same time, of 36 shows with identifiable social class, 11 were working class, historically a high proportion.

Modern Family (2009–present) has been a big success, featuring an extended family living in three households, but spending all their time together. Patriarch Jay, a retired successful businessman with a sexy housewife, advises everyone and makes philosophical statements about families at the end of the episode. Jay's son Mitchell is a lawyer, gay, and married to schoolteacher, Cameron. Daughter Clair is a controlling, competitive, and attractive housewife to Phil Dunphy, a real estate agent and fun-loving, but inept husband. Phil is a bit geeky in his un-macho fun and apologizes to his wife when he messes up. In one show, Jay continues respectful representation of the upper-middle-class businessman, Phil plays a bit of the fool, usually reserved for working-class male characters, and Mitchell and Cameron introduce a relatively new dimension in prime-time television as the stereotypic gay couple. Jay's success and level-headedness are highlighted by contrast to the other male leads, as well as to his own wife and to both his children. Overall, the middle-class theme is sustained.

The Middle (2009–present) muddies class representation even while attempting to thematize it. A recurring situation in the series is their difficulties paying their bills. But the dad, Mike Heck, who works at a rock quarry, does not wear workman's clothes, nor those obviously managerial or professional. TV critic Emily Nussbaum (2013, 2016) identifies him as a manager, then calls the family, alternately, lower-middle class and working class. Mike does have the erect posture, shoulders back, and no beer belly that is standard for sitcom's middle-class men. The mom, Frankie, is alternately a used car saleswoman and a dental assistant, suggesting marginally working-class occupational ambitions. She is wound a bit too tight and easily upset, whereas Mike is the calm, sensible one, a bit like Dan and Roseanne in the 1990s reversing the working-class sitcom tradition. Their pre-adolescent boy and teen girl are smart, mature, and reflective, the ones who do the voice-over commentaries.

Mike and Molly (2010–2016) presents a working-class couple—a police patrolman and a fourth-grade teacher turned writer—both plus-sizes. The two bicker over relationship issues but resolve their differences. Mike has some of the Ralph anger and is often the butt of a joke, but both of these are softer versions of the traditional pattern. He often is at a loss for a retort to Molly and to his black police partner. But again repeating the old formula, both traditional sex and race statuses are used to undercut Mike's masculinity that, in contrast to affirmations of middle-class masculinity in the overall pattern, becomes a statement about class.

Offering another twist on the working-class man, two shows feature a twenty-something single man caring for a baby, like *Bachelor Father* without the playboy money. *Raising Hope* (2010–2014) seems like a mash-up of an innocent young-adult child, Jimmy, the only sane and considerate member of his family, contrasted to his stupid and callus parents and grandmother reminiscent of *Married with Children*. Jimmy works with his father as a pool maintenance crewmember, and later becomes a supermarket employee. In *Baby Daddy* (2012–2016) Ben is a bartender (later an owner) rooming with his brother and a friend. Both involve the good-hearted bachelor struggling with childcare. There are no wives or children to contrast to an inept husband, and the fathers are too young to be confirmed failures. *Man with a Plan* (2016–) is similar; a "contractor," a bit older and married, does childcare while his wife returns to work. All three are physically fit with good posture.

However, lest the tradition be lost, *The Cleveland Show* (2009–2013), another animated spinoff from *Family Guy*, continued the old working-class stereotype. Cleveland Brown is variously a cable installer and a cold-call salesman. His wife,

Donna, is an assistant to a school principal, a waitress, and an airport ground crewmember. He engages in the usual inept schemes, à la Fred Flintstone, while she is the sensible one, another Wilma, but a bit more annoyed and judgmental, reminiscent of Louise Jefferson. The tradition lives also through *Kevin Can Wait* (2016–), a remake of *King of Queens* starring the same lead actor.

The middle-class *The Goldbergs* (2013–) is a package of Jewish stereotypes. The father and grandfather own and operate a successful furniture store. The smothering mom intrudes to help but often it backfires, shades of Lucy. The father is a bit more sensible, but no Desi. He's overweight, loud, and sometimes inarticulate. The show foregrounds ethnicity rather than social class. The stereotypes muddle the traditional class formulas. Middle-class *Fresh Off the Boat* (2015–) and *Dr. Ken* (2015–) also draw on ethnic stereotypes for situations and laughs, muddling the formula for middle-class sitcoms.

But again, upholding tradition, *Fuller House* (2016–) revives the super-parent mold from *Full House* (1987–95). *Black-ish* (2014–) continues the line from *Father Knows Best* to *The Cosby Show*, showing us how to raise children. Solidly upper-middle class in a white suburb, a successful black ad executive and his biracial MD wife help their four kids deal with the many social issues facing the nation as well as African-Americans in particular. *Marlon* (2016–), a sitcom about a successful black comedian and loving, but immature, father co-parenting with his "very together" ex-wife, seems to follow the working-class formula, but in a black, middle-class home. *Black-ish* and *Marlon* address the intersection of race and class, perhaps a tonic for a TV land in which blacks are overwhelmingly represented as lower class, and whites overrepresented as middle class, engendering public conflation of class into race, as shown by Jhally and Lewis (1992) in their study of audiences for *The Cosby Show*.

Conclusion

In sum, for five to six decades, while there was a variety of exceptions to the formula, the contrasting representations of the working class and the middle class in domestic sitcoms held steady. The exceptions were more blips than trends. Beginning in the mid- to late-2000s, while the working-class male and the middle-class super-parents still were used as the template for a number of sitcoms, some larger changes were taking place. Non-traditional families seemed to become the norm rather than the exception, and a wide range of previously verboten LBGT characters and relationships peppered this new mix. This may be a temporary fashion—public discourse since the 2016 election has forcefully returned to the topic of class and may portend another shift in sitcoms in Fall 2017. (All the sitcoms discussed in this chapter pre-date the election.) Whether this period represents a trend or a fashion, its effect in part is to cloud the representation of class. If there is a trend in all this, it is likely due to exceptions and diversions from the previous formula accumulating to form a critical mass that is producing a post-modern deconstruction of categories—of families, sex, and sexuality—that probably has blurred or veiled the straightforward contrast of classes in the past.

The persistence and pervasiveness of these representations for decades helped to reproduce American class cultures and structure. They undercut respect for working-class men, the working class generally, and the manual labor by which they earn a living, contributing to their hidden injuries of class (Sennett & Cobb, 1972). Their representation as ineffectual and immature effectively justified close supervision of their work. It characterized them as offering meager human capital to employers and thus deserving of low wages. It remains to be seen how recent changes may alter this.

Notes

1. While income is an important factor, it alone does not capture class and class relationships. Nor does it address a far more important money matter: whether income is produced by one's wealth or by one's labor. That is the difference between a life dictated by the need for a job and one free of that necessity.
2. Manual labor is still essential to the operation of society. Yet, over the past forty years, median wages and benefits for unskilled and semi-skilled manual labor have dropped substantially. Shrunken apprenticeship programs and vocational education have limited paths for training in skilled manual work (Lerman, 2008; Olinsky & Ayres, 2013; Rosenbaum, 2001).
3. Google Ngram searches for terms in eight language categories in hundreds of thousands of books on Google Books to reveal patterns. See https://books.google.com/ngrams. Ngram shows a rise in use of the term "working class" from the start of the century to a plateau from the 1930s to the mid-1950s. It rises again to the mid-1970s, and then declines thereafter. Other terms referring to working class occur far less frequently, but show similar patterns of decline after the 1960s. It also shows a rise in use of "collar" terms through the 1960s, then steady decline after that. Similarly, "industrial worker" reversed course after the 1960s, but surprisingly "construction worker" increased as "industrial worker" declined. Use of "manual labor" rose from the start of the twentieth century to 1940, sharply declined until the 1960s when there was a small increase, then steadily declined thereafter.
4. Research was based on television viewings of shows; original TV scripts at the University of Pennsylvania Annenberg School Library and the Writers Guild Foundation Archive, Los Angeles; *TV Guide* (1953–1975) archived in the Theater Art Collection of New York Public Library at Lincoln Center; Brooks and Marsh (2007); and websites epguides.com, imbd.com, tvguide.com, and thewrap.com.
5. Interestingly, and indicating the continuing significance of these visuals, a full-size statue of Ralph Kramden now stands in front of the déclassé Port Authority Bus Terminal in New York City, memorializing his occupation as a bus driver and also his paunchy figure.
6. Before television, a strikingly different representation of working-class men and women was created in public art (Dabakis, 2011; Marstine, 1993). From the late nineteenth century, images of manual labor in public spaces celebrated the value of manual work and dedication of the workers, granting respectability to manual labor and laborers. Women too, from pioneer farmers to Rosie the Riveter, were depicted as well-muscled.

The most widespread contributions were made in the 1930s and 1940s by the Federal Arts Project (Melish, 1991; Park & Markowitz, 1984). A fairly common theme before the Great Depression was a narrative of national progress and glory, from pioneering and agriculture to industrialization as the pinnacle. Each of these was depicted through manual labor and muscle. Public art (sculptures, bas reliefs, and murals) through these eras was predominantly top-down, planned, designed and built under the careful eye of local officials and elites. Recently there has been a bottom-up public art movement, rooted mostly in poorer urban neighborhoods and often celebrating identity politics rather than manual labor (e.g., Cartiere & Zebracki, 2016).

7. *Seventh Heaven* (1996–2007), like *Eight Is Enough* (1977-1981), was one of a small genre of hour-long family dramas that occasionally appeared and repeated the super-parent pattern.

Works Cited

Brooks, T., & Marsh, E.F. (2007). *The complete directory to prime time network and cable tv shows, 1946-present*. New York, NY: Ballantine Books.

Butsch, R. (1992). Class and gender in four decades of television situation comedies: Plus ça change plus c'est le meme chose. *Critical Studies in Mass Communication*, *9*, 387–399.

Butsch, R. (2005). Five decades and three hundred sitcoms about class and gender. In G. Edgerton & B. Rose (Eds.), *Thinking outside the box: Television genres in transition* (pp. 111–135). Louisville, KY: University of Kentucky Press.

Butsch, R. (2014). Ralph, Fred, Archie, Homer, Family Guy and Cleveland: Re-creating the male working-class buffoon, 1950s to 2010s. In G. Dines & J. M. Humez (Eds.), *Gender, race and class in media* (4th ed.). Thousand Oaks, CA: Sage Publications.

Butsch, R. (2016). Six decades of social class in American sitcoms. In N. Cloarec, D. Haigron & D. Letort (Eds.), *Social class on British and American screens: Essays on cinema and television* (pp. 18–33). Jefferson, NC: MacFarland.

Butsch, R., & Glennon, L. M. (1983). Social class: Trends in prime time, 1946–78. *Journal of Broadcasting*, *27*(1), 77–81.

Cartiere, C., & Zebracki. M. (Eds.). (2016). *The everyday practice of public art: Art, Space and social inclusion*. New York, NY: Routledge.

Crane, D. (2012). *Fashion and its social agendas: Class, gender, and identity in clothing*. Chicago, IL: University of Chicago Press.

Dabakis, M. (2011). *Visualizing labor in American sculpture: Monuments, manliness, and the work ethic, 1880–1935*. Cambridge, UK: Cambridge University Press.

Dyer, R. (2013). *The matter of images: Essays on representations* (2nd ed.). New York, NY: Routledge.

Gerbner, G., & Gross, L. (1976). Living with television: The violence profile. *Journal of Communication*, *26*, 172–199.

Glennon, L. M., & Butsch, R. (1982). The family as portrayed on television. In D. Pearl, L. Bouthilet & J. Lazar (Eds.), *Television and behavior: Ten years of scientific progress and implications for the eighties* (Vol. 2, pp. 264–271). Washington, DC: U.S. Department of Health and Human Services, NIMH.

Grote, D. (1983). *The end of comedy*. Brooklyn, NY: Shoestring Press.

Hall, S. (1997). *Representation: Cultural representations and signifying practices*. London, UK: Sage Publications.

Hovland, C., Janis, I., & H. Kelley. (1953). *Communication and persuasion: Psychological studies of opinion change*. New Haven, CT: Yale University Press.

Jhally, S., & Lewis, J. (1992). *Enlightened racism: The Cosby Show, audiences & the myth of the American dream*. Boulder, CO: Westview Press.

Lasswell, H. (1927). *Propaganda technique in the World War*. New York, NY: Knopf.

Lerman, R. (2008). Are skills the problem? Reforming the education and training system in the United States. In T. J. Bartik & S. Houseman (Eds.), *A future of good jobs? America's challenge in the global economy* (pp. 17–80). Kalamazoo, MI: Upjohn Institute.

Marstine, J. C. (1993). *Working history: Images of labor and industry in American mural painting 1893–1903* (doctoral dissertation). University of Pittsburgh, Pittsburgh, PA.

Melish, B. (1991). *Engendering culture: Manhood and womanhood in New Deal public art and theater*. Washington, DC: Smithsonian Press.

Nussbaum, E. (2013, March 11). Moving on down. *New Yorker*, 78–79.

Nussbaum, E. (2016, March 21). Swing states. *New Yorker*, 102–103.

Olinsky, B., & Ayres, S. (2013). Training for success: A policy to expand apprenticeships in the United States. Washington, DC: Center for American Progress. Retrieved from http://www.americanprogress.org/issues/economy/reports/2013/12/02/79991/training-for-success-a-policy-to-expand-apprenticeships-in-the-united-states/.

Park, M., & Markowitz, G.E. (1984). *Democratic vistas: Post offices and public art in the New Deal*. Philadelphia, PA: Temple University Press.

Rosenbaum, J. (2001). *Beyond college for all: Career paths for the forgotten half*. New York, NY: Russell Sage Foundation.

Sennett, R., & Cobb, J. (1972). *The hidden injuries of class*. New York, NY: Knopf.

Stouffer, S., Suchman, E., DeVinney, L., Star, S., & Williams, R. (1949). *The American soldier*. Princeton, NJ: Princeton University Press.

4

TV SCREENING: THE ENTERTAINMENT VALUE OF POVERTY AND WEALTH

June Deery

As disparities in the wealth and opportunities of different social groups have become more apparent in recent years, so has the attention to classed behavior. This interest extends to popular entertainment and so gives rise to the question I explore here, which is: if pronounced inequality has become more widely recognized, and recognized as serious and injurious, how is this difficult matter transformed into entertainment? In other words, how do you make the pains and deprivations of what many recognize as unfair social arrangements amusing or pleasurable? Differences in classed behavior have long been a subject of drama, whether under the exquisitely sharp but ultimately sentimental scrutiny of Austen or the broader comic strokes of Chaucer or Aristophanes. This chapter examines contemporary forms of television drama that thematize class identities and in which people self-consciously perform class. Focusing on two modes, comedy and melodrama, and two ontological states, fiction and non-fiction, it identifies forms and techniques that subdue potentially radical impulses and, by producing different types of audience recognition and producer engagement, result in distinct forms of class containment.

There are both ideological and commercial reasons why media producers ordinarily focus on a broad, unmarked middle class: among them, maximizing audience reach, accommodating advertising needs, and intentional or unconscious political evasion from producers who are themselves mostly middle class. This chapter will instead focus on television programming that features those at the top and bottom of the hierarchy[1] in order to demonstrate how contemporary dramas capitalize on the emotional charge generated by strong class attribution—whether it be hostile, as in much comedy, or sympathetic, as in most melodrama—yet through various forms of spatial, temporal, and social distancing that reduces potential ethical discomfort and political angst in a process I term *affective displacement*. I illustrate this process with reference to two enormously popular forms of programming: reality television and costume drama, the one providing examples of comedic containment and the other of sentimental appeasement.

Class as a concept is both abstract and deeply felt. It is a categorization with powerful emotional, ethical, and political dimensions, which is why its attribution works for dramatic purposes but why it also requires careful handling. If the topic does appear in entertainment formats, the structural forces that generate class differentiations are generally ignored—which is not the same thing as avoiding the *individualized generalizations* of stereotyping and scapegoating. These become especially potent when a portrait is not from the normalized middle class and instead carries a great burden of representation (Shohat & Stam, 1994, pp. 182–188). This chapter does not probe how much representation can or ought to be representative—in the sense of reflecting actual demographics. Its goal is not to legislate principle but to examine practice.

Comedy

Comedy is a dramatic mode that typically involves a good deal of distance. My examination of comic treatments is informed by the incongruity and superiority theories of comedy, which in class comedy I suggest are conjoined. The first is the idea that comedy is due to the recognition of something being discordant, inappropriate, contradictory, and therefore ridiculous. This theory was promoted in the eighteenth century by, for example, the Scots-Irish philosopher Francis Hutcheson and later Kant and Schopenhauer (Stott, 2014, pp.176–182). Certainly, class comedy relies heavily on something being seen as inappropriate or discrepant or "out of place": class distinctions being described often in spatial terms (as when censure of a lower rank employs British colonial maps in the phrase "beyond the pale").[2] The other theory, that of comedy being generated by a feeling of superiority toward others, has been discussed by numerous thinkers from Plato to Hobbes and of course describes much class comedy and its affective displacement. Comedy distances and provides a socially sanctioned way to portray others as flawed and inferior and undeserving of pity or reform. Its energy comes from a power differential between superior (laughing) subject and inferior (laughed at) object and offers the schadenfreude of watching inferior others proving their inferiority. One could argue that this, too, boils down to a form of incongruity where the object is regarded as out of place in the world of the intended viewer. Akin to this is irony which, whether on the level of sentence or scene, is also a form of both incongruity and superiority that together feed comedy, including the often-ironic observations of class behavior.

Also popular is the idea that comedy can be a release mechanism when it exposes and thereby relieves pent up areas of discomfort and taboo. Hence, if recognizing class disparities makes a viewer uncomfortable or even prone to guilt, outing this and making stigma appear comic may relieve some of this moral discomfort. It is clear that comedy can be subversive—especially in the form of satire or parody—but while it exploits tension, comic drama typically and ultimately supports the status quo and therefore functions as a distraction that diffuses political energy, as in the temporary release achieved by Saturnalian and Carnival class inversions (Bakhtin, 2009 [1968]). After negativity has been released, comedies typically settle on a happy ending, usually in some form of compromise or social reparation (a wedding or other social bonding). So while these texts relish disorder, they ultimately bring the eccentric or maverick under the jurisdiction of the normal through socially warranted (albeit often distant) disapproval. The comic spirit grants license but also reins it in—thus proving entertainment's ideological worth.

Screen Culture

Watching TV or film is an activity shared by multiple classes and, further, the same content is enjoyed by multiple ranks, unlike the more highly differentiated tastes in literature, the visual arts, or music (Bennett et al., 2009, p. 132). However, professional media products are generally created by economically advantaged elites ultimately for other elites (those who own or advertise), and so it may be no surprise that the poor (whom advertisers don't target) are either invisible or often crudely or negatively portrayed. This is especially the case in the predominantly commercial American system. Britain has had a strong tradition of sustained and variegated working-class portraits in melodramas, soaps, and comedies from both commercial and public broadcasters, whereas if lower-class characters appear on US screens (outside the occasional documentary), they are often either criminal or comic or both: either threatening villains (news programs and police procedurals), or misguided bigots (Archie Bunker, Homer Simpson), or harmless fools (*Beverly Hillbillies, Family Guy*) (see Richard Butsch's chapter in this volume). It is notable, also, that some of the most important American working-class comedies were based on British series: *All in the Family* (CBS, 1971–1979) being inspired by *Till Death Us Do Part* (BBC1, 1965–1975) and *Sanford and Son* (NBC, 1972–1977) by *Steptoe and Son* (BBC1, 1962–1974). With few exceptions (e.g., the working-class Rosanne Barr), American producers do not reproduce a sympathetic lower-class perspective or view working-class individuals as complex and rounded human beings.

Reality TV and the Working Class

Reality TV offers distinct advantages for laughing at the poor and has indeed featured a number of working-class figures in recent years; not, I suggest, because producers feel obliged to give voice to the underrepresented but because it suits commercial and ultimately conservative goals (Deery 2012; Deery, 2015, p. 137).[3]

These portraits are no more complex than in past programming but there are more of them and, as we shall see, their presence illustrates some of the advantages of reality TV for class ridicule, given that it involves real people playing themselves whose behavior is nevertheless caricatured and even outrageous but seemingly self-determined and unscripted.

Some reality TV portraits are positive, many more are negative, and some go back to comedy to process class judgments. Among the most positive, non-comic images of the working class are depictions of masculine and manual activities that require bravery and stoicism (Palmer, 2014; Deery, 2015). These figures are more like self-reliant frontiersmen than factory workers: the latter, less romantic figures are rarely portrayed sympathetically, or even at all, on American TV except for a few sentimental, philanthropic formats like *Undercover Boss* (C4, 2009–; CBS, 2010–). A congratulatory rags-to-riches story enhances other reality formats, especially the talent show or makeover varieties, but even here the poverty of the person's origins is not dwelt upon. When cameras illustrate living in poverty in documentary-like formats it is often to mock or criticize individuals as criminal (*Cops*, Fox, 1989–), immoral (*Benefits Street*, C4, 2014–2015), mentally disturbed (*Hoarders*, A&E, 2009–), abusive (*Toddler and Tiaras*, TLC, 2009–2016), or just immature and irresponsible (*Teen Mom*, MTV, 2009–2012, 2015–). In these critical portraits, reality TV producers have learned how to spectacularize class, exploiting class positions for their exoticism and shock value, while offering weak legal or therapeutic rationales for the programming.

Their ontological situation is significant also. Since it is reality TV, there is (seemingly) some subject agency. Viewers needn't worry about writers being prejudiced and laughing at the lower class because these people are purportedly playing themselves (even if viewers suspect it is at least "lightly scripted"). And to the extent that they perform as part of a group identity viewers may feel more at liberty to criticize. However, this group identity does not appear to constitute a political form of class consciousness. Meanwhile, they are being exploited not only as characters but also as employees, for thanks to reality TV they have become a cheap labor force in a media economy that has benefitted from non-professional actors in non-unionized productions.

Comedy tends to be excessive in both form and content: it both exaggerates in its depiction and what it depicts is often its characters' own excess. As we shall see, a strong strain of reality TV relies on the comic excess and exhibitionism of overt lower-class positions. In these instances, class distinctions become something of a joke and the satiric edge is sanctioned because participants seem happy to perform their class identities as caricatures. Viewers may know these portraits are constructs and exaggerations of sorts but find them just realistic enough to grant the cathartic release of feeling superior to real-life others. Part of the catharsis could also be in the form of scapegoating, where the individual failings of these shameful subjects are offered up to carry off the viewers' possible feelings of guilt and blame for larger social flaws and injustices.

Red, White, and Blue

Classism, and in particular denigrating the lower classes, is countenanced in a way that is no longer the case with racism. Even when there are accusations of "poverty porn" or widespread disgust, these provoke not political protest but enhanced ratings, and for-profit companies have little incentive to stop. Nevertheless, if producers want to encourage mockery without appearing to be overly exploitative they can utilize those who caricature themselves, and for this they have discovered the comic utility of the American redneck.[4] These Colored Whites (Deery, 2015, p. 132) can be openly mocked without raising charges of racism (they are White) and class prejudices are made palatable by inflecting class with regional or ethnic "color." In American English, "blue-collar" is the positive term for working-class and "white trash" is negative,[5] but "redneck" is in transition—thanks in some measure to reappropriation within comic entertainment (Jeff Foxworthy and others). "Redneck" usually implies religious fundamentalists who are politically conservative, not well-educated, and maybe contrarian enough to not embrace modern ways. Self-professed rednecks are a great find for comedy producers because they identify themselves as at the lowest rank but are largely uncomplaining and so short-circuit pity. The redneck TV craze began as the economy was contracting in 2008 and, I have elsewhere suggested, this programming's pious pronouncements about the supreme importance of family and friends may be reassuring for viewers who themselves lack financial security (Deery, 2015, pp. 142–143). Not since the 1960s, with series such as *Green Acres*, *Petticoat Junction*, and *The Beverly Hillbillies*, have rural, working-class characters been so prominent on TV. As in the past, today's portraits gloss over poverty's restrictions by portraying people as folksy and funny and as guardians of a nostalgic rural, White lifestyle.

Comdocs

Reality TV's comdocs—reality shows that are structured like sitcoms (Deery, 2015)—are a rather boisterous form of the *comedy of manners*, less cold than open and biting satire. I will examine two varieties: the cartoon vulgarity of *Here Comes Honey Boo Boo* (TLC, 2012–2014) and the wittier *Duck Dynasty* (A&E, 2012–2017). These have been among the most watched and most talked about shows on American cable TV and part of a wave of shows from *Swamp People* (History, 2010–) to *Moonshiners* (Discovery, 2011–) that feature real-life characters who self-identify as rednecks. The *Honey Boo Boo* characters are hopeless, almost abject, and firmly entrenched in the lower class (it is not even clear if the family is working class), whereas *Duck Dynasty*'s selling point is that its cast are nouveau riche but still self-identify as rednecks. Both series amuse audiences by laughing at the culture of the poor through some similar displacement techniques.

For centuries, comedy has gone to the country to find inferior others to safely mock. In the contemporary redneck show, this *rustication* has a Southern inflection, which makes it doubly exotic in mainstream media. Today's comedies of manners enliven fundamental American tropes such as the division between North and South (associating the defeated South with stupidity and backwardness) and more global prejudices regarding rural versus urban living.[6] For the majority audience, these Southerners are Americans-with-subtitles, the foreign interior whose differences make them not threatening but amusing—and for producers a valuable commodity for market differentiation (Deery, 2015). They are the familiar-but-unfamiliar. They are how many might imagine poor people to be, but more exotic and colorful. Given the lack of serious attention to the lower classes in mass media, when they appear on our screens they are out of place immediately and more so as they break or offend more mainstream, middle-class conventions.

Reality TV gives these portraits the frisson of real-ness (they are "real people"), but they exaggerate, they ham it up, and viewing caricatures allows almost anyone else to feel superior and to point to missteps and incongruities. Like other sitcoms, the redneck series focuses on home life and leisure: it does not represent the grinding routine and physical endurance of more typical working-class labor. Instead, the atmosphere is often playful and carnivalesque, with carefree subjects who appear to have more liberties and childlike freedoms than the buttoned-down middle class. This emphasis may be driven by comic needs but it could reinforce some viewers' convictions that the poor are work-shy and so deserve their lower economic status. Also like fictional sitcoms, the focus is on isolated families with little sense of a wider community or systemic inequalities.

The characters often display rituals and attitudes that express pride in their lower-class culture—albeit self-consciously and defensively and no doubt as encouraged by producers. Fellow rednecks can therefore share the pride, or more privileged viewers shed the guilt. Even if real people are being mocked, both producers and viewers can claim special dispensation if the comic subjects appear to be laughing at themselves, or at least voluntarily appearing and reappearing in a show which they must know provokes laughter. Again, because it is reality TV, theirs is seen as a self-identification, not something patronizingly written by a more privileged media professional.

Here Comes Honey Boo Boo became notorious as an emblem of lower-class vulgarity. Viewers and journalists exuberantly blamed the family for their outrageous behavior, or the producers for exploiting it, or both, although over time some viewers also reported that they found the family sympathetic in their honesty and love for each other, so it was not universally read as a purely negative portrait. At least some of this sympathy may be due to the genre: as a television series broadcast over multiple seasons, the sympathy that comes with familiarity may lessen the affective displacement introduced by the comic mode. Nevertheless, as a situational comedy, any given episode of *Honey Boo Boo* consists mostly of surface and farce, with any graver issues (e.g., pedophilia) being kept off-camera.[7] There is no documentary voice-over or sociopolitical framing: instead the standard reality TV *hidden-producer-interview* technique seems to be letting us in and granting us intimacy but is in fact shaping the producer's comic narrative more than anything else. Shannon[8] family members appear to have limited powers of expression and so viewers don't enter far into their inner lives. We see them in action that we suspect is often staged and that ranges from the silly to the preposterous, but they are not so pathetic or reprobate as those in, say, gypsy series or *Cops*. The *Honey Boo Boo* family appear to be proud of their license and their ability to amuse and are complicit in a long tradition of containing the lower orders by making them into figures of fun. Instead of being portrayed as tragic or deserving of pity, poverty becomes entertaining because it is comic or bizarre and because the underclass is depicted as being happy with their lot. As proud rednecks, they are not even trying to be upwardly mobile and this begins to look like self-imposed class limits (Deery, 2015, p. 138). Even more chilling is the suggestion that they probably *prefer* being poor or that poverty is *a voluntary lifestyle*. Of course, by being on the show they are to some degree attempting upward mobility: like many others on reality TV, they can be considered immigrants from real-world anonymity to TV-granted celebrity. Although, on screen, they are discouraged from displaying their TV earnings or breaking their role as poor folk.

The particular kind of fun they exhibit and the comedy it produces can be summed up as gross. "Gross" encapsulates various forms of the repulsive, especially in American usage: it denotes overly large, vulgar, shameless—all features for a long time associated with the working class and reasons for moral censure. The most obvious sign of this grossness is the overweight body. As has long been recognized, bodies, as part of our habitus (Bourdieu, 1984 [1979]), signal class identity: the shape of, behavior of, and attitude toward. On *Honey Boo Boo*, the mother's body can be read as a monstrous symbol of excess, of things getting out of control. One in a long line of unruly women (Rowe, 1995) going back at least as far as Noah's wife in medieval drama, she is not only physically large but also dominates her mate and so is transgressive also in patriarchal terms.[9] In addition to being overweight, these characters openly display bodily functions and vocalize the scatological in a base and bawdy form of comedy that is traditionally marked as lower class. However, some of this translates as authentic as well as vulgar and so is validated and admired in the world of reality TV. Viewers may admire their being down-to-earth and grounded, which means that the ultimate validation of reality TV culture—being considered authentic—becomes politically conservative when it is accorded more worth than being wealthy or powerful (Deery, 2015, p. 143).

On *Duck Dynasty*, there is again a self-conscious performance of class identity but there are distinct ways in which this series allows viewers of higher rank to feel less guilty about the poor and those of lower rank to feel content with where they are. First, there is the rags-to-riches narrative. The Robertson family became wealthy before this TV series started, but being on TV means they have been able to self-brand with considerable enthusiasm, becoming an impressive neoliberal model of success. Second, because they are real people, their brand can be carried over into their real lives and their success may assuage viewer guilt about reality TV voyeurism since, by watching, the audience is adding to the family's celebrity capital. Then there is the fact that the Robertsons are not trying to imitate the more privileged and so can be admired for their authenticity. Being wealthy yet still maintaining the manners and rituals of a lower-class background makes the hegemonic pride in the lower rank even more pronounced. If the Shannons seemed to enjoy being redneck, this is reinforced by the Roberston clan, who clearly could live differently (although it is in their current economic interest to play redneck on TV and, indeed, growing beards is apparently in their contract). Viewers can admire their haute redneck lifestyle and economic success but also like them for upholding the values and rituals of a lower rank (a formula also seen in the series *Bayou Billionaires* [CMT, 2012]). The Robertsons are somewhat eccentric but are ultimately sanctioned in real life by their wealth and on the TV show by their control of the commentary ("eccentric" usually aligns with rich and "monstrous" or "stupid" with poor). Shannon family members make jokes about themselves but they are not so articulate or self-aware. The Robertsons' wry humor and their gentle self-mockery reduce viewer alienation and possible accusations of pretension. We laugh *with* them as much as *at* them.

Where *Here Comes Honey Boo Boo* is monstrous and stupid, *Duck Dynasty* invokes the wily and resourceful trickster.[10] The Robertsons circumvent rules and seem to possess their own forms of power. They reflect some ideological peculiarities of American culture that have historically slowed or blocked a more socialist distribution of wealth: the immigrant and frontier mentality of making your own way, of hard work leading to achievement, and the suspicion of authority and regulation. The Robertsons often display a comic ingenuity which suggests that "rednecks" can improvise within the strictures of poverty. They also reflect another Americana topos of the regular guy. These are "god-and-country" people, armed patriots whose narrative illustrates how nationalism distracts from class conflict. Indeed, one could argue that this family ultimately represents the legion of lower-class supporters of conservative ideologies that are instrumental in dampening consciousness of class competition.

The Robertsons differ from most entertainment casts in that they have a definite political awareness and affiliation, although this is generally excluded from the program lest it spoil the fun—or (just as important) alienate advertisers. Not surprisingly, producers tend to play up the humor and downplay more serious elements, such as the patriarch's apparent racism or religious bigotry. However, this family's real-life political views, their passionate support of Christian fundamentalism and right-wing politics, are known to many—since they are real people who exist between series and not fictional characters who only exist in a script. Several family members went on the campaign trail in 2016 to support Republican candidates, culminating in Willie Robertson's prime-time speech at the Republican National Convention in support of Trump. In addition, before entering the White House, one of Trump's chief advisors, Steve Bannon, presented the patriarch Phil Robertson as an apocalyptic prophet in a film entitled *The Torchbearer* (2016), which asserts that a godless society brings depravity and terrorism. The conservative message seems to be resonating, for it was discovered that there was a stronger correlation between Trump voters and *Duck Dynasty* viewers than those who voted previously for a Republican president (Katz, 2016). Clearly this show was tapping into something the pundits missed.

Nouveau Riche Docusoaps

Before moving on to portraits of the upper class, it is worth comparing the above examples to the noveaux riches in docusoaps like *The Real Housewives* (Bravo, 2006–), also a successful and long-running franchise. The Roberstons chose to ignore to some extent their elevated socioeconomic status, but the arrivistes of *The Real Housewives* ever strive to match their behavior and new class position. Channels like Bravo feature many such newly rich because, whereas fictional drama can create genuinely upper-class characters, it appears factual entertainment can only attract the striving and insecure (i.e., those who will sign a TV contract) (Deery, 2012). These are a fascinating hybrid whose behavior has brought to millions of viewers an explicit attention to class differentiation. These characters' class elevation is often so rapid that it becomes comically disruptive.[11] As parvenus, the "housewives" suffer what Bourdieu called a cleft habitus (*habitus clivé*) where their original class dispositions and current position don't quite align, leading to psychological dislocation. Bourdieu (who himself moved from humble to elite circles) uses the term hysteresis for those whose habitus has not yet adjusted to the new situation (1990 [1980], p.62) and who suffer the "double isolation" of one who doesn't fit in either within their original or new class group (1996 [1989], p. 107). Certainly, most of the "housewives" experience a pronounced lag between the acquisition of economic capital and of cultural capital and this incongruity produces an ironic form of comedy based on delusion, hypocrisy, and lack of self-awareness. Whereas the rednecks are somewhat self-conscious in their performances, these nouveaux riches are more anxious to pass and they repeatedly illustrate the insecurity and ambivalence many people feel about class positions, especially in American culture. Again, they are real people but their inconsistent and stagey performances underline that class is, indeed, a learned performance and that some are better at it than others.

Judging by online commentary, some viewers regard theirs as a cautionary tale about class ambitions and others as a shining example of class mobility. Cast members explicitly make claims about being upper class or "classy", but their behavior and values belie this (for viewers in socially superior positions) and, as with arrivistes throughout world drama, their more humble roots keep tripping them up. For centuries, comedy has been used to skewer pretension, putting the overly ambitious or self-aggrandizing back into their place (from the *miles gloriosus* to Malvolio), but it is worth pointing out that these are more docusoaps than comedies and that while there are many opportunities for viewers to feel superior and to regard inept performances as comic, there are also elements of intimacy and empathy as these women's trials and tribulations play out over several years. Their stories are capable of generating sympathy beyond the derision provoked by their class misrecognition.

Melodrama

Finally, we come to a more fully sentimental form where the affective displacement takes the form of a diffusion, of an ecumenical dispersion of sympathy for all ranks. Melodrama is a term used to describe a narrative that relies on exaggerated characters and improbable plots to create a sensational effect operating on a sub-tragic level—if, in drama, the author plays god, in melodrama god is easily bored. Serious critics tend to be bored too and generally demote melodrama to a second-rate status. (Perhaps controversially, where comedy is often seen as masculine, melodrama is seen as feminine). In recent years, one well-financed Anglo-American production attracted a huge global audience and enjoyed critical acclaim despite being described as a melodrama. *Downton Abbey* (ITV and PBS, 2010–2015) was broadcast in more than 200 countries to over 100 million viewers and was the highest rated drama in PBS history.[12] It got closer than most entertainment forms to looking at class from a structural perspective: we see broader patterns, collective identities, and larger mechanisms. But it still focuses on individual stories and intimate emotions and is safely contained within fiction and the past.

Downton Abbey faces class and wealth disparity head on but creates a safe space for exploring its personal ramifications. Though of course any given viewer can activate class content in various ways, this fiction comes from a Conservative politician who admires much about the English upper crust. His work dwells on class difference but softens its abrasions by peering at it through a deeply nostalgic and semi-opaque lens. *Downton Abbey* begins when the upper-class characters recognize that their way of life is changing and their privileges are slipping away. They accept this transition with more grace than bitterness and the audience is positioned to feel sympathy for their loss. Author Julian Fellowes, now Lord Kitchener-Fellowes, grew up in the outer circle of an aristocratic world that he clearly admires. When he married, he took his wife's illustrious name (Kitchener) and pushed legislation to allow her (like the fictional Lady Mary Crawley) to inherit a hereditary title (an unsuccessful bill dubbed the "*Downton Abbey* law"). He currently sits in the House of Lords.

Because of its ontology, fiction can inspire a strong but ephemeral emotional attachment, so the displacement happens over time: we can weep or cheer with enthusiasm as the drama occurs, but this reaction evaporates with the story. Knowing the characters do not exist in real life also encourages an ethical as well as affective displacement; for if we witness people suffer, they are not real people and we can enjoy feeling sympathy without guilt or responsibility. Fiction is also useful ideologically because it is not obliged to stick to facts, such as about actual class relations.

Another temporal form of affective displacement available to fiction is the historical. Fellowes' costume drama uses nostalgia, disarming historic aesthetic appeals, and the incongruous injection of modern sentiment, all to make class division palatable. Its costumes are, in fact, rightly admired but also function as an indicator of the often-superficial treatment of historical realities. It is generally agreed that this series presents a literally and metaphorically sanitized view of the life of the lower classes, with clean language and spotless uniforms. Those upstairs don't sneer at or punish those below them as might have happened in real life, and if the Dowager is particularly snobbish, then she is forgiven for delivering her prejudices in quick, Wildean one-liners. Whereas full-blown ridicule or satire can be ugly and miserly, here comic elements work to diffuse tension or allow the politically incorrect to survive.

A related distancing is geographic and cultural. For most viewers, the upper class is quite exotic, an exoticism that is reinforced when set in a different historical period. This allows audience members the pleasures of wealth voyeurism and escapism without political conscience. For the enthusiastic American audience there is, in fact, a double displacement, both temporal and geographic, which builds on the Anglophilia of the American middle classes who regard British culture as prestigious in-and-of-itself, despite their constitution's official disapproval of aristocratic societies (and without always recognizing the different class position of the characters/accents they revere).

As the title of the series indicates, people serve the institution represented by an imposing physical structure that requires those both upstairs and downstairs to fulfill their functions. This takes some of the heat off personal demands for service or individual privilege. Further, by aestheticizing the class hierarchy, Fellowes is also removing some of its sting. From the opening credits that dwell lovingly on simple artifacts and rituals, there is an almost fetishistic adoration of upper-class life. The narrative is heady also with signature music used to orchestrate emotion—harkening back to the roots of melodramatic manipulation (*melos* being the Greek for song). The physical beauty of the elegant settings distracts us from the harsher realities of the economic underbelly; pervasive in human societies is the belief that beauty is associated with rightness, with intelligence, and with virtue. Indeed, the attraction of sumptuous privilege and responsibilities may be one reason for a slew of upper-class or royal dramas on American TV in recent years: *The Tudors* (Showtime, 2007–10), *Reign* (CW, 2013–), *Wolf Hall* (PBS, 2015), *The Crown* (Netflix, 2016–), and *Victoria* (PBS, 2016–) (see Littler and Williamson in this volume).

In the many plotlines of *Downton Abbey* sentimental generosity tends to override competing interests. The script acknowledges numerous inequities and deprivations, but there is also plenty of noblesse oblige and benevolent paternalism. So while class differentiation is thematized, serious conflict is *not* and one class is rarely directly pitted against the other. The emphasis is on interdependence and people being measured by their worth as individuals: there are good and bad in all ranks, although mostly good. Class hierarchy is an important stage set, but the ultimate focus is interpersonal. Political consciousness is embodied in certain odd individuals (an Irish chauffer, an outspoken schoolteacher, a newly educated kitchen maid), but they tend to either come around or go away. Most notably, the former revolutionary chauffer is absorbed into the status quo and loses his structural awareness of class relations because, it seems, he feels the aristocratic family who now accepts him are just awfully nice. It is in his frequent repetition of this sentiment that the writing is often weakest. In another managed sociopolitical eruption, a radical schoolteacher's gauche interruption of genteel dinners is ultimately dismissed as bad form and she obligingly disappears.

Generally, middle-class figures are seduced by the upper-class life and values, which is presumably a cue to viewers about how to react. Indeed, an emotional ecumenism invites viewers to care about all ranks and illustrates how emotional intimacy can breed political neutrality. There is some pointed critique of upper-class privilege to be sure, and some real pathos for the lower class (at times maudlin), but in this long-running melodrama there is plenty of empathy and sympathy to go around. The overarching theme is an elegiac and sweeping view of the decline of the British aristocracy which is portrayed in many ways as a shared cultural loss (the British manor home).[13] Landowners, as the stewards of their estates, are sympathetically portrayed as having their own burdens, and the class hierarchy is just liberal enough to appeal to a modern audience. The author chose a time when class relations were going from almost feudal to modern-industrial and he blends nostalgia for an older regime with recognition of the necessity for a more progressive future (this includes optimistic scenarios of tolerance toward Jews, Catholics, and Blacks).

Class identity is always on display, but individualized. The author essentially dwells on one household, and because in this arrangement upper- and lower-class intimacies did historically occur, he is able to portray inter-class relationships as at once formal and very close. Successful cross-class romances and examples of social mobility rely on viewers embracing sentiments like "love conquers all" or "we're all in this together and the same underneath"—thereby evading a more rational perspective that would point to competing interests and agendas. This is not to say that Fellowes avoids class conflict altogether; for indeed some of this is essential for creating his energetic plots. We are reminded quite frequently that the servants have few liberties and are dependent on their employers' generosity for basic needs. Sometimes the aristocrats are unfair or harsh with their staff, and there is social division and unkindness below stairs too, with some servants being hostile toward any of their own who elevate their status. Fellowes acknowledges wider social injustices also, for example, people facing destitution if pregnant or in bad health. As in traditional melodrama, lower-class characters endure unfortunate circumstances which demand stoicism and sacrifice, but this leads to self-growth not political rebellion. Particularly in the final season, we see a highlighting of self-generated social mobility. Now (without benefit of aristocratic marriages) lower-class characters become more economically successful through hard work and modest savings, some even becoming bourgeois homeowners. This pattern reflects real changes in the 1920s and the move from service to other forms of employment, but it still conjures a rosy picture compared to the drudgery of factory work that was a more common path.

So what might be the effect or appeal of all of this for contemporary viewers? We can only speculate. Those who have observed that wealth disparity is once more extreme might be reassured by the suggestion that the way ahead will be more progressive, as it was in the early twentieth century. Or it may be that however benighted they feel about social inequality today, they can at least say their society is not as divided as Edwardian England—or not as openly divided. For if wealth disparity is again pronounced, then at least few are in the position of servant or obliged to display class deference in public settings. The counter response, of course, is that this is cold comfort if the underlying economic conditions are as extreme and not having to curtsey or touch the forelock is small compensation. Another appeal might be aspirational, especially among American viewers on whom the hegemonic "American Dream" still exerts a pull (Deery, 2012). Those watching may have the vicarious pleasure of empathetically enjoying an elevated lifestyle and feel that they, too, will someday achieve a modern equivalent. Others who *can* have imitated the lifestyle already, for it is thought that the popularity of this series has led to a surge in demand for British butlers around the world, particularly among the newly wealthy in China, Russia, and the Middle East (Galvin, 2013; Buckley & Kan, 2017). A less successful real-world imitation destroyed the career of US Congressman Aaron Schockin in 2015 after news emerged of his aspirational *Downton Abbey*–themed office. It is not clear if the main objections were to the lavish nature of the décor (and possible illegal gift from the interior designer) or to the apparent homage to a British class hierarchy in a publicly funded Congressional office.

Conclusion

We have seen comedy that short-circuits radical critique and melodrama that reduces its charge. With *Honey Boo Boo*, viewers can laugh off inequalities or, more seriously, conclude that the lower classes don't deserve better or wouldn't know how to behave if they were elevated. The exceptions, like the entrepreneurial *Duck Dynasty* family, imply that with initiative and self-sufficiency the poor can, in fact, make it big. *Downton Abbey* suggests that not everything is fair but that there is something seductive about the life and values of the upper class, whatever the price paid by other ranks. The series also suggests, in true melodramatic fashion, that sentiment overrides politics and love transcends all.

Notes

1. Although the programming is still seen from the perspective of the middle class—also my own class position.
2. The Pale was the colonized and "civilized" area around Dublin beyond which the less civilized native Irish lived.
3. Reality TV began with a portrait of the British working class in *The Family* (BBC1, 1974).
4. Since the late nineteenth century, "redneck" has been used to refer to poor Whites, i.e., those who get sunburned by laboring outdoors.
5. White trash is a term originally used by Black house slaves to denigrate poor Whites to whom even they felt superior.
6. Not all Southern shows are working-class or rural: *Southern Charm* (Bravo, 2014–) is a docusoap that features more wealthy city dwellers. They, too, are hardly paragons of good behavior.
7. However, charges of pedophilia against the mother's boyfriend eventually ended the show's run.
8. Family members are named Shannon and Thompson, but I will use the mother's and the majority's surname.
9. More recently, producers are selling bodily excess by focusing on its loss, in a spin-off weight-loss show called *Mama June: From Not to Hot* (WE tv, 2017).
10. A trickster is a character who is clever or has secret knowledge and uses it to upset normal rules and to mock or bypass authority.
11. Some "housewives" are better able than others to perform as elite; for instance, the New York cast is generally more sophisticated than the New Jersey or Atlanta casts.
12. A similar, long-running British series called *Upstairs Downstairs* (ITV, 1971–1975) also foregrounded class relations in the same historical period as *Downton*, i.e., 1910s–1920s. It was unusual for being created by working-class producers, in this instance Jean Marsh and Eileen Atkins.
13. British manor homes often survive today by turning themselves into commodified entertainment as tourist sites. Indeed, being televised has allowed the actual setting of Highclere Castle to prosper as a TV location and tourist destination.

Works Cited

Bakhtin, M. (2009 [1968]). *Rabelais and his world* (H. Iswolsky, Trans.). Bloomington, IN: Indiana University Press.

Bennett, T., Savage, M., Silva, E., Warde, A., Gayo-Cal, M., & Wright, D. (2009). *Culture, class, distinction*. London, UK: Routledge.

Bourdieu, P. (1984 [1979]). *Distinction: A social critique of the judgment of taste* (R. Nice, Trans.). London, UK: Routledge.

Bourdieu, P. (1990 [1980]). *The logic of practice* (R. Nice, Trans.). Stanford, CA: Stanford University Press.

Bourdieu, P. (1996 [1989]). *The state nobility: Elite schools in the field of power* (L. Clough, Trans.). Stanford, CA: Stanford University Press.

Buckley, C., & Kan, K. (2017, January 14). Rich Chinese, inspired by 'Downton,' fuel demand for butlers. *The New York Times*. Retrieved from: https://www.nytimes.com/2017/01/14/world/asia/rich-chinese-inspired-by-downton-fuel-demand-for-butlers.html?_r=0.

Deery, J. (2012). *Consuming reality: The commercialization of factual entertainment.* New York, NY: Palgrave Macmillan.
Deery, J. (2015). *Reality TV.* Cambridge, UK: Polity Press.
Galvin, L. (2013, July 11). Demand for British butlers doubles in one year from world's wealthiest families 'influenced by Downton Abbey.' *The Daily Mail.* Retrieved from http://www.dailymail.co.uk/news/article-2239672/Downton-Abbey-effect-Demand-British-butlers-DOUBLES-2-years-wealthiest-families.html.
Katz, J. (2016, December 27). 'Duck Dynasty' vs. 'Modern Family': 50 Maps of the U.S. cultural divide. *The New York Times.* Retrieved from: https://www.nytimes.com/interactive/2016/12/26/upshot/duck-dynasty-vs-modern-family-television-maps.html.
Palmer, G. (2014). The wild bunch: Men, labor, and reality television. In L. Ouellette (Ed.), *A companion to reality television* (pp. 247–263). Chichester, UK: Wiley Blackwell.
Rowe, K. (1995). *The unruly woman: Gender and the genres of laughter.* Austin, TX: University of Texas Press.
Shohat, E., & Stam, R. (1994). *Unthinking Eurocentrism.* London, UK: Routledge.
Stott, A. (2014). *Comedy* (2nd ed.). New York, NY: Routledge.

5

SEX, CLASS, AND TRASH: MONEY, STATUS, AND CLASSED "DREAMS" IN CLASSICAL HOLLYWOOD CINEMA

Andrea Press and Marjorie Rosen

When Laura Mulvey published her signature piece "Visual Pleasure in Narrative Cinema" in 1975, she singled out the Hitchcock films *Rear Window* (1954) and *Vertigo* (1958), as well as Depression-era *Blonde Venus* (1933), to illustrate her now well-known thesis that women were most often portrayed as the fetishized *object* of the gaze in classical Hollywood cinema. Mulvey's short article, though extremely influential and still cited today with some regularity, was immediately and widely challenged. Feminist film scholars, in particular, objected to its seeming portrayal of female passivity in mainstream movies. Three fundamental arenas of cinematic history were often invoked in this challenge: the highly sexual femme fatale of film noir (Kaplan, 2008); the typical heroine and ensemble cast of the woman's melodrama (Gledhill, 1987); and the specific persona of Marilyn Monroe, who in her films appealed as much to women as to men (Arbuthnot & Seneca, 1990; Banner, 2003).

Each gave challenge to Mulvey's argument in a different way. Film noir heroines seemed more powerful than the women Mulvey had discussed, though they often used their power for evil. Women's melodramas seemed to engage a collective audience and to feature an ensemble of distinctive and active female characters, rather than a central male protagonist. Finally, Marilyn Monroe was cast as a sex object, of course, but often within the context of the kind of ensemble cast that characterized the woman's film—as in *Gentlemen Prefer Blondes* and *How to Marry a Millionaire*, the two initial roles that cemented her star persona and ensured that she appealed to other women (perhaps sexually, perhaps otherwise), as well as to men.

What we argue here is that what has been overlooked in this literature is the strong social class dimension underlying each of these modes of representation. This has been ignored in much of academic film criticism and, especially, in feminist film literature. Though Hollywood, the American public, film critics, and film theorists rarely, if ever, articulated it as such, these iconic images of female sexuality are often "classed." That is, the category of social class is central to understanding the meaning of American popular film, yet it has rarely received attention comparable to that of gender or sexuality. However, in film criticism—and in our lives outside of film criticism—we have come to realize the importance of intersectionality in discussing issues of gender, even as the very category of gender itself is being interrogated in both academic and popular circles. But most scholarly attention to intersectionality in the gender literature has focused on racial and sexual differences, with class differences often ignored. Recent political developments like the 2016 election have made it obvious that we simply must pay more serious attention to those who feel disadvantaged vis-à-vis social class. Moreover, when we throw gender into the mix, the issues become even more complex, as intersectional theorists argue and as we hope to demonstrate in this chapter.

Social class is central to the filmic traditions often offered in feminist film literature as counterpoints to Mulvey's sweeping statements. Depictions of sexuality in the 1946–1962 period reflected more general cultural concerns regarding gender, social class, race, and ethnicity. With these interests in mind, we went back to the immediate post-war period of Hollywood film, which witnessed the flowering both of Hitchcock's stereotypical "cool blonde," the mainstay of Mulvey's thesis, and the three main currents contradicting this thesis. While the woman's film is, of course, an important development, because sexuality takes a backseat role in its portrayals of women, we turn our attention primarily to the other two developments: the vampy femme fatale of *film noir*, and the establishment of the Marilyn Monroe star persona, both very sexual in nature.

We argue in the following pages that these highly sexual images in post-war Hollywood were specifically "classed" in distinct ways that solidified earlier pre-war (and pre-Code) trends. During the late forties and early fifties, while much of the US was preoccupied with the upward mobility made possible by the GI Bill, which enabled veterans to get free educations and low-interest suburban home loans, American moviegoers developed a fascination with earthy, hyper-sexualized, hyper-physical images of lower-class men and women. Though Marlon Brando's characters are probably the most remarkable and powerful examples of this—his t-shirted Stanley Kowalski in Tennessee Williams' *A Streetcar Named Desire* (1951) and Terry Malloy in Elia Kazan's *On the Waterfront* (1955) arguably transformed our concept of film acting—here, we discuss the phenomenon as it played out in women's sexual images, starting in 1945 and continuing throughout the decade of the 1950s.

Moving to the areas of film noir and the star persona of Marilyn Monroe, we also find that classed identities are integral to the depiction of female allure. In contrast to the Hitchcock theory of allure, we focus here on a lower-class sexuality. With both Monroe and the film noir femme fatale, it is the quality of "trash" that excites. "Trash" means a lot of different things when considered as a component of female identity. It means, as Monroe sings along with Jane Russell in the opening lines of her most famous film *Gentlemen Prefer Blondes*, coming from the "wrong side of the tracks"—being poor. In the words of Jane Austen's Elizabeth Bennett, poor women "have nothing but our charms to recommend us." But poverty alone does not give rise to a powerful, trashy sexuality: there are other qualities that trash heroines display, and while most viewers know it when they see it, it remains relatively unarticulated in the literature about sexuality and film. In popular film, the representation of this quality falls into one of two broad categories, and we consider both of them here: the manipulative, powerful, and dangerous heroine of the film noir, and the peculiar, powerful but childlike innocence of the Marilyn Monroe persona.

With a few notable exceptions,[1] the femme fatale of film noir is a trashy, wrong-side-of-the-tracks type figure. Notable examples include Barbara Stanwyck, in the iconic film noir *Double Indemnity*, who plays an ambitious nurse who achieves middle-class prosperity by marrying her boss (after poisoning his first wife). Rita Hayworth in *Gilda* (1946) portrays a young woman of unknown background who weds the wealthy Nazi Ballin Mundson. And finally Jane Greer, in the similarly iconic film noir *Out of the Past*, displays her rough edges as the ruthless heroine who shoots her lover (Kirk Douglas) and then steals $40,000 from him.

With almost every role she plays, Marilyn Monroe portrays a sexy, lower-class, penniless woman, vulnerable and in need of male support, financial and otherwise. Some scholars have pointed also to the homosocial nature of Marilyn's lower-class heroines, who often bond strongly with other females (Doty, 2000). Feminists have noted her closeness to the other women in her films, often her buddies (Arbuthnot & Seneca, 1990). This was certainly true of the films *Gentlemen Prefer Blondes* and *How to Marry a Millionaire*, which, as we've said, cemented her star persona. What unites these images as well is the "down-and-out" penniless character of such essentially disadvantaged characters. They are lower class, lacking in education, money, and connections. Like Elizabeth Bennett, Monroe's women have only their charms to recommend them.

In sum, with some notable exceptions, both the femme fatale and Monroe's image in virtually all her movies were distinctly lower class. We consider each of these examples in turn, describing and articulating their class dimension. Ultimately, we argue, class is as central as sexuality to American film, but in ways which remain relatively untheorized by American film scholarship.

Film Noir and Its Vampy, Knowing, Sexualized Heroines

It is worth noting how men, returning home from the war in 1945, resented the women who were occupying the jobs they once had. With eight million soldiers coming home, welcoming them back into the workforce emerged as a patriotic duty. That meant that women had to be pushed out and, in whatever ways were possible, made obsolescent. These realities are reflected in the conditions for screen women of the era. We see in most *films noir* how narrow screen women's job opportunities were. Usually, the choice was between diner waitress (*Mildred Pierce* in 1945, *The Postman Always Rings Twice* and *Fallen Angel* in 1946) and nightclub chanteuse (*Gilda* in 1946). Occasionally, the woman had formerly worked as a nurse, and we are asked to believe that that had been the profession of Barbara Stanwyck's Phyllis Dietrichson in Billy Wilder's great noir *Double Indemnity*—even though the movie reveals no sign that Dietrichson had any humanistic impulses whatsoever. And, of course, there was always the (subtly) kept femme fatale such as Gloria Grahame in *The Big Heat*, and perhaps the most sublimely cold-blooded mistress of all, Jane Greer in *Out of the Past*. All these women were working-class gals, and all exuded a steamy, sexy aura that weakened male resolve.

Clearly, certain attributes of *film noir* contribute to what we identify as the hyper-sexualized image of women that appears repeatedly in Hollywood films of the immediate post-war era. While much has been written about the sexual nature of African-American and Latino women's film images, little appears in the literature identifying the interrelationship between being lower class or poor *and* sexy. However, Bogle (2001) and King (2015) have effectively pointed out a series of stereotypical portrayals that are often associated with the African-American women who do appear in Hollywood film. Though not all of these are highly sexual—Bogle mentions the "mammy" image, for example, which is more motherly than sexual—the "Jezebel" is explicitly sexual in nature, and a key component of African-American women's portrayals. Think of the character played by Dorothy Dandridge in her biggest hit, *Carmen Jones* (1954), and in several other of her more well-known roles including *Island in the Sun* (1957) and *Porgy and Bess* (1959). Or note Jennifer Jones' fire-breathing image in *Duel in the Sun* (1946). Here, in "woman-of-color" makeup and ironically named Pearl, she embodies one of the sexiest, trashiest, and most compromised images produced in post-war Hollywood. And what gives that image its special shock value is that she is a Mexican, and by the terms of the film and of society back then, she was non-white.

In fact, social class identities themselves are often highly sexualized identities in American cinema. Witness Linda Darnell in *Fallen Angel*, a 1946 Otto Preminger movie about an entire town that is fixated on her character, Stella, a working-class waitress at Pop's, a local dive; this is one working-class broad who distracts the area's male population, driving some to obsessive stalking, others to insanity, despair, and, in one instance, murder. Stella, a gal from nowhere with nothing but her body and her beauty to recommend her, illustrates our argument that these hyper-sexualized female figures are endowed with an almost mystical power to intoxicate and transfix all male onlookers. Her presence shatters the will of all these men; they, and, in turn, their penises—clearly the driving force in their actions and emotions—surrender all rationality in the face of her overwhelming sexual force. They must possess her, or they cannot go on.

True, in the small town of Walton, 150 miles from San Francisco, where the action of *Fallen Angel* takes place, the male population seems to be both waning and wanting. To be blunt, the pickings are slim. Maybe the decided lack of young and eligible men is because the action takes place in 1945, at the end of World War II; whatever, all suitors seems to be a gaggle of bottom-of-the-barrel types—Pop, an ancient, shriveled fellow, who owns the diner; Atkins, a traveling jukebox repairman (great profession!); Judd, a graying former New York City copper; and Eric Stanton (Dana Andrews), a scheming drifter who has just been thrown off a bus heading to San Francisco because he does not have the fare to continue on and, as a stop-gap, must seek his (interim) fortune here in Walton. Tough guy that Stanton is—a con man who can con even the creepiest of traveling psychics, one Dr. Madley (John Considine)—he cannot, however, persuade Stella to completely capitulate to his charms.

Part of this is because Stella defines herself differently from other femmes-noir leading ladies and more like the virtuous good girls in any town. She has no vendettas to fulfill, and no real passionate hatred; her primary goal is to marry a guy with a few dollars in his pocket and to become respectable. When we first meet her, she has been missing for three days, and her worried cache of boyfriends at Pop's, the diner where she is a waitress, are filling out a police report. Could she have committed suicide, one wonders? No way, says Judd, "Stella's not the type." Moments later, she enters the dive, disheveled and exhausted, but exquisite in a large picture hat, ruffled blouse, tight skirt, and heels that have made her feet ache; all her beaux seem to be on their way in or out, and all worry because she had disappeared for a few days. Now she explains, she had run off with yet another guy who had had his way with her but did not have a nickel in his pocket. The men here are all babbling with concern. "One look at him, and I knew he was no good," says Pop. "You make me sick," she retorts, totally inoculated against fawning sympathy.

The manly drifter, Stanton, however, persuades her to take a ticket to hear the visiting psychic, Professor Madley. Later, Stanton takes her dancing and to the beach, where they kiss passionately. When he tries to go further, she pulls away and says pointedly, "No, that's okay for kids, but not for me. *Not anymore*." She sums up her history here in three little words.

Stanton tries to woo her by telling her that he is a one-time publicist who ran a "publicity mill" and hobnobbed with movie stars. "The Stork Club, that's where you belong, smothered in mink. I see you there," he coos.

"And do you see me with a ring on my finger, somebody to give me a home?" she responds pointedly. Nothing coy about her.

"Sure, sure." But his voice contains not a shred of conviction,

"Now look," she says, pushing him away again, "last night I made up my mind, that's the way I want it. . . . Well, you've got the wrong girl." She struggles out from his grip and says, "Tomorrow you're going (to skip town). Where does that leave me? You got into town with one dollar in your pocket. You're a *fake*."

That roils him. "Oh, now, you little gyp," he responds, reminding her that he saw her steal a dollar from the cash register earlier in the evening. She responds by slapping him.

As they part, he flings one last insult at her: "Go on back to your one-armed joint and wait for someone to come and marry you."

But, of course, he wants her so much that he begins scheming how to make enough money to be worthy of her. His plot? To bilk the movie's really good girl, its blonde angel, its whiff of summer—June, played by Fox's top musical star, Alice Faye, in her first dramatic role.

At this point let us stop to consider Stella and June, their differences and similarities. For here the director Otto Preminger, with the help of his screenwriter Harry Kleiner and the original novelist Mary Holland (billed on screen as "Marty Holland," perhaps because a male author sounds tougher and more film-noirish), develops some interesting good girl/not-so-good-girl contrasts: Stella, of course, means "star," lighting the dark noir night; June means the first month of summer, which we can interpret as all lightness and warmth. In the course of *Fallen Angel*, Preminger plays up the exotic dark beauty of Stella/Darnell in traditional noir style by situating her almost entirely either indoors at night, in moody evening shadows, or under a brooding night sky. At the same time, he bathes June/Faye in light. Indoors and out, this church organ player (!) wears pale, schoolmarm-ish clothes, primarily business suits (although she does not go to an office job) and picture hats, and she braids her golden hair in a prim, Germanic way, very much like Heidi, the Alpine goatherdess. Let's not forget that the town of Walton seems almost as isolated as the Alps. However, poor June has fewer companions than Heidi, who had a wealthy playmate, Clara, and could always count on her animals as well. Still, June must deal with her sister, also named Clara (played with terrifying severity by Anne Revere), who looks and acts more like a punishing mother. Nobody, not even Eric Stanton, is going to pull the wool over Clara's eyes, even though her sister is desperate to be fooled. That desperation may well have its roots in Walton's striking dearth of eligible men.

Preminger even provides contrast regarding the way the two women, Stella and June, live. He shows us Stella's cramped, gloomy rented room—the room of a transient—with its cheap floral chintz accents and yet also stuffed animals to let us know that while she may have a trampy record with men, Stella is basically childlike and good-hearted; then he takes us to the bright, spacious, but not too ostentatious middle-class home that June and Clara share—the kind of all-American, sun-flooded home that is worth fighting a world war for.

Stella's trashy back story in *Fallen Angel* is also prototypical of that of other desirable and sexually potent femme fatales in post-war film noir. You could practically smell the cheap perfume on Lana Turner in *The Postman Always Rings Twice*, Barbara Stanwyck in *Double Indemnity*, Jan Sterling in the sun-drenched desert noir *Ace in the Hole*, Joan Bennett in *Scarlett Street*, Jane Greer in *Out of the Past*, Rita Hayworth in *Gilda* and *The Lady from Shanghai*, and Marilyn Monroe in the Technicolor-noir *Niagara*. On the other hand, the upper-class bad girls of film noir either stalked the men in their lives, just as the unhinged heiress, Jean Simmons, stalked Robert Mitchum in *Angel Face*. And as for the victimized, moneyed good girls, Joan Fontaine in *Suspicion* and Ingrid Bergman in the period melodrama *Gaslight*, they suspected correctly that their mates did not sufficiently desire them and perhaps had other motives.

It's worth noting that in *Fallen Angel*, as June and Stanton become closer and more committed to each other, she begins to morph into a fair-haired version of Stella. Her dresses become more provocative; her hair, looser, flowing more sensually around her face; her manner, tougher and more knowing; her behavior, riskier.

By the way, Darnell re-enacted the sexually potent lower-class babe to perfection in Joseph Mankiewicz's *A Letter to Three Wives* in 1949, playing Laura Mae Finney, who captivates and snaps up her wealthy boss, Porter Hollingsway (Paul Douglas), the refrigerator mogul. He arrives at her home—one that is clearly located on the wrong side of the tracks—for the very first time and might have been taken aback but for the fact that he spots one of his company's new iceboxes in her mother's kitchen and is duly impressed and distracted by its presence.

Iconic films noir *Double Indemnity* and *Out of the Past* both feature this slutty, trashy female predator as their center; her power is underscored by the presence, as well, of a good girl, a virtuous alternative. In *Double Indemnity*, Lola, Phyllis's stepdaughter, represents youth and innocence; she also has a conscience and real feelings of love for her dead father as well as solid suspicions about her stepmother. It is an irony of sorts that the insurance salesman, Walter Neff, who has become involved with Phyllis, in part because she is a cool bitch—"I never knew that murder could smell like honeysuckle," he says in voice-over—actually develops a real affection for and attraction to Lola because she is so pure and upstanding.

Similarly, in *Out of the Past*, the beautiful but deadly Kathie's opposite is Ann (Virginia Huston), a wholesome and pretty blonde, who is always pictured in nature, whereas Kathie lives in darkness and shadows. Sweet Ann makes her home with her parents in a modest rural cabin, and we always see her in daylight, where she and Jeff Bailey (Robert Mitchum) talk about a modest post-war future: buying a little house together and living happily ever after.

They wish. As it turns out, both Phyllis and Kathie betray the men they ostensibly love, trying to use them to break away from their lives of crime. Kathie double-crosses everybody; she tries to steal the money from Whit and uses Jeff to get away.

Phyllis seduces Walter in order to get her hands on her husband's insurance money; he may be planning to run off with her and their stash, but she has clearly planned a future without either him or Lola.

However, in the end both Phyllis and Kathie get caught in the webs that they themselves have spun. And both die as a result. So do the men they had once seemed to adore.

An interesting note about the sexuality of these women: they both understand that men find them attractive and so play up their sexuality for their notorious ends—financial freedom. Neither seems to have any genuine sexual feelings of their own. For them, sex is a bargaining tool, a way to get men to comply with their wishes and plans. There is no such thing for them—or for most screen heroines of that era—as joyous sex or sexuality for its own sake.

But a few exceptions did exist, namely, Rita Hayworth and Gloria Grahame.

Being so sexual, they also used their powers, and in movies like *The Big Heat* (1953) and *The Lady from Shanghai* (1947), they emerged as sociopathic characters. By contrast, the sexy Marilyn Monroe was, for the most part, an innocent, a naïve little girl. And a total opposite from these film noir characters who are sexy, know it, and know how to use it. (Ironically, Monroe, in *all* her films, and Linda Darnell in *Fallen Angel*, both want the same thing: marriage.)

Marilyn Monroe: Sex, Class, Trash, and the Otherwordly Qualities of an Innocent Screen Goddess

> "Primarily, she was a victim of her fit, a biological victim of life itself. I think Marilyn Monroe was a tragedy of civilization."
>
> —Diana Trilling, writing in 1962

> "Marilyn Monroe is like nothing human you have ever seen or dreamed. She is astonishingly white, so radically pale that in her presence you can look at others as easily as you can explore the darkness around the moon. Disdaining all lingerie and dressed in tight white silk emblazoned with countless red cherries, she becomes at once a symbol of impartial and eternal availability. And her smile, when she directs it clearly at you, is exquisitely, heartbreakingly sweet."
>
> —Alice McIntyre, writing for *Esquire*, from the set of *The Misfits*

While some may argue that Marilyn Monroe is the most salient sex object of post–World War II American cinema, an analysis of her cinematic image supports and confirms our thesis that female sexuality in the post-war film is inherently classed. Repeatedly, Monroe portrays what film analysts have called "the Marilyn Monroe persona" in her important movie roles (Banner, 2012; Spoto, 2014). Think of her steamy Rose Loomis, the one-time waitress who is two-timing her mentally ill husband (Joseph Cotton) in *Niagara* and also planning his death-by-waterfall. (Unfortunately, he beats her to it, chasing her up a winding staircase and then throwing her off it in a scene that clearly inspired Hitchcock to send Kim Novak up that bell tower in *Vertigo*).

The truth is that whether Monroe appeared in noir suspense movies, in comedies, or musicals, she never veered from that hyper-sexuality or from those working-class roots: her characters, including the gold-digger Lorelei Lee in *Gentlemen Prefer Blondes*, the naïve dance hall gal Cherie in *Bus Stop*, the penniless Pola Debevoise in *How to Marry a Millionaire*, nightclub dancer Elsie in *The Prince and the Showgirl* (1957), and the ukelele-strumming band singer Sugar Kane Kowalsiczyk in *Some Like It Hot* (1959), all identify as lower class all the way, girls who are often saddled with distinctly ethnic names and super-sexy personae that are almost always the focus of these films. This persona motivated even her bit part as Miss Caswell, the voluptuous starlet in *All About Eve* (1950), one of her arresting early performances. In this role, Monroe plays a wide-eyed, aspiring actress trying to figure out how to charm powerful producers and so further her career. George Sanders, as her mentor Addison DeWitt, urges her to use her sexuality to make the producers happy. Her youth, powerlessness, and overflowing sexuality combine to create the incipient Marilyn Monroe persona of a poor, aspiring, friendly, and overwhelming sexual young woman, which she develops more fully in later roles.

Some would point out that Monroe's sexuality became a major focus of American popular culture in the 1950s, and remains so to this day. And in part because once the Monroe persona was developed, Monroe became such a big box-office attraction for Fox and even saved the studio from bankruptcy, even in her own time Hollywood spawned a series of second-rate imitations—big-breasted blonde starlets such as Jayne Mansfield, Diana Dors, Stella Stevens, Barbara Nichols, Anita Ekberg, Mamie Van Doren, and Monique Von Voren, to name a few.

But no one was quite like Monroe herself. And no one did as well at the box office. In particular, her portrayals of Lorelei Lee in *Gentlemen Prefer Blondes* and Pola in *How to Marry a Millionaire*, arguably the roles that made her a big star, are worth dissecting because these are where she fully develops her "classed" persona that both celebrates her sexuality and defines her as a working-class woman looking for a guy with a big, thick wallet. As we learn from "Two Little Girls From Little Rock," the opening song in *Blondes*, Lorelei Lee and her brunette counterpart, Dorothy (Jane Russell), immediately identify themselves this way:

> "We're just two little girls from Little Rock,
> and we lived on the wrong side of the tracks."

Yet from the beginning it is clear that Jane Russell's Dorothy has very different motives from those of her musical partner, Lorelei. In a song-and-dance number set at the ship's swimming pool, Dorothy sings in a sexually suggestive manner to the entire men's Olympic relay team: "Ain't there anyone here for love?" At this point she lets everyone know what she is looking for:

> "I need a shoulder to lean upon
> and a couple of arms to hold me.
> I'm not in condition to wrestle."

As the camera closes in on her face, Dorothy, who on the surface seems like a no-nonsense, business-like gal, in fact becomes even more specific—and more physical:

> "Show me a man who can wrestle,
> and I'll pin a medal on him.

Doesn't anyone want to play?
I like big muscles and red corpuscles,
I like a beautiful hunk of man.
But I'm no physical specimen.
Ain't there anyone here for love?"

On the other hand, Lorelei, the bombshell who looks like walking desire, is not on a sexual quest at all; she is much more interested in upward mobility. In other words, she wants to marry a rich man, period. And she uses her outsized sexual power to do so, deliberately luring into her web every wealthy man she meets. No one is too old or too portly. The irony is that although trampy-seeming Lorelei *uses* her sexuality, she herself is neither sexual nor interested in a sexual liaison in and of itself. She wants love, diamond tiaras, and respect.

But she is nothing, if not aware of, her own gifts. When Dorothy tells Lorelei that she will need to get hold of $20,000 to repay the cost of Piggy's stolen diamond tiara, Lorelei cold-bloodedly calculates the time it will take her to charm a particular suitor out of that money. It is a computer-like commodification, and Lorelei, with quick mathematical instincts that belie her "dumb blonde" image, says instantly: "One hour and 45 minutes."

Here we see how smart she is as she puts her sexual power to work. Later, she lets us know *why* she poses as the breathy dumb blonde all the men think she is. First, she gives Gus's wealthy and disapproving father a sweet, guileless, and well-thought-out *raison d'etre* for being a gold-digger. "Don't you know that a man being rich is like a girl being pretty," she tells him. "You might not marry a girl just *because* she is pretty, but my goodness, doesn't it help? And if you had a daughter, wouldn't you rather that she didn't marry a poor man? You want her to have the most wonderful things in the world, and to be very happy. Well, why is it wrong for me to want those things?"

She persuades Gus's dad with her simple logic. "Say, they told me you were stupid," he responds. "You don't sound stupid to me."

And Lorelei answers, again with her disarming honesty, "I can be smart when it's important, but most men don't like it."

Let us underscore here that Lorelei's persona almost precisely mirrors Monroe's. The Monroe "star" persona is not just working class but also, primarily, naive and childlike. This was true in almost every one of her movies, certainly all the comedies.

As with Monroe in real life, Lorelei accepted her sexual power and used it to her advantage. Though we never see Lorelei "becoming" the bombshell, Monroe, in real life, took several hours to apply her hair and makeup to emerge as her character, "Marilyn"; many friends report that, with her face scrubbed and her clothing nondescript, she could walk New York's streets without attracting any notice whatsoever. Yet when she "became" Marilyn, she could seduce any and everyone—and did. Frank Sinatra, Joe DiMaggio, John F. Kennedy, Robert Kennedy, Elia Kazan, Arthur Miller—presidents, politicians, sports and movie stars, Hollywood agents, and clothing designers alike all found themselves susceptible to her charms—for a while, at least.

And Monroe, in real life, seemed to be a creature of nature—a bountiful goddess with no sexual hang-ups, no sexual boundaries. Some say she had exchanged sexual favors with numerous studio executives for roles in various movies. In her "autobiography," co-written with Ben Hecht, she claimed that she hardly ever felt sexual pleasure (Monroe & Hecht, 2006). And, indeed, it is a sad irony that she took on the role of a sexed-up flower child perhaps a decade too early. If sex was easy and natural for her, it is also true that in Hollywood she was judged poorly for it. Her penchant for relating to men sexually, her nude calendar, her foster-home background, and her image as a working-class bimbo all contributed to her Hollywood devaluation. In the highly "classed" and moralistic fifties, studio executives like Darryl F. Zanuck, the head of 20th Century Fox until 1956, when he left for Europe to produce movies starring a succession of his mistresses, seemed unable to appreciate Monroe.

And although the strong profits from her movies almost singlehandedly kept Fox afloat, it was a difficult decade at best. Not only were the studios competing with television for viewers, but in 1948, in *U.S. v. Paramount Pictures, et al.*, the courts dealt another blow to Hollywood by upholding anti-monopoly laws which decreed that all studios must divest themselves of their movie houses over the next few years. The result? The studios deliberately created movies that starred he-men lording it over large-breasted sexpots in dresses with plunging necklines. The blatant idea: to bring those ex-GIs back to the movie-going tradition.

Hitchcock Blondes: Mulvey Missed the Class Act

Hitchcock's development of the definitive "Hitchcock blonde" involves a growing focus in many of his works, culminating in his peak period from the 1950s to 1964, on blondes with an upper-class flair. Think of actresses such as Grace Kelly, Kim Novak, Eva Marie Saint, and Tippi Hedren, each of whom brought an upper-class quality even to the lower-class women they portrayed.

In fact, Grace Kelly was perhaps the most perfect embodiment of Hitchcock's icy blonde. She represented a respectable and elegant woman, a creature of restraint and beauty on the outside, but one who smoldered with sexuality on the inside—a phenomenon that illustrates our point about the classed nature of sexuality in post-war Hollywood. While, for Hitchcock, a refined, cultivated, sophisticated, and understated sexuality was the sexiest—and he often articulated this quite specifically—much of the film-viewing audience preferred figures who were more overtly sexy, figures who were earthy and sometimes vulgar, and who often took the form of lower-class film noir heroines or were embodied by Marilyn Monroe's unique persona, that of the smart dumb blonde. By contrast,

Hitchcock's perfect blonde kept her passion buttoned up within a veneer of upper-class refinement and manners.

Nowhere is the social class dimension of the Hitchcock blonde more obvious than in his crowning achievement, *Vertigo*, a film which the British Film Institute's *Sight and Sound* magazine voted in 2012 to be the greatest film of all time. In *Vertigo*, Hitchcock contrasts his idealized and fundamentally unattainable blonde heroine with a more earthy, working-class double who is, poignantly, also more real; yet, in part because of her reality, this woman is *not* the object of male desire. Though both women are played by Kim Novak, the contrast is stark, thanks to Hitchcock himself, who famously oversaw every detail of fashion, makeup, and hairstyle used in the construction of each woman, each a specific image that reflects back on her opposite.

Though young Grace Kelly (along with Elizabeth Taylor and Audrey Hepburn, who often played a similar role in non-Hitchcock films) was emphatically beautiful, she was, however, *not* the sexual animal who had men salivating in every scene. She often, as with Kim Novak's Madeleine in *Vertigo*, embodied a wealthy, glamorous image, which channeled the golden era of Hollywood glamour. Even in *Fallen Angel* this image's counterpart—the blonde "angel," Alice Faye, is not simply buttoned-up and virginal, she is moneyed, virtuous, and belongs to one of the town's best and most respected families. And when her character falls for Dana Andrews, who has worked very hard to get into her good graces, he never goes weak in the knees, he goes weak in the wallet—and begins calculating how he can bilk her out of at least part of her fortune.

Hitchcock was intimately acquainted with these two contrasting visions of female sexuality, as described first in Mulvey (1976), with its antithesis articulated by her critics. He played with these conflicting visions in his masterpiece, *Vertigo* (1958), when he cast Kim Novak to play the contrasting roles of Madeleine and Judy. Madeleine was a heroine of the classical Hollywood cinema. The genius of *Vertigo* was to construct the image of Madeleine as inherently unattainable; she was object, rather than subject, of James Stewart, who stood in for the Hollywood male audience with his overwhelming, crippling desire. Yet Madeleine remained just out of reach in the film because she was only an act put on by Judy as part of a murder plot; but more broadly, in the classical Hollywood cinema she represented Stewart's desire. He had created in his imagination an unattainable perfection, inciting unquenchable desire that dooms its subject to eternal, unfulfilled longing.

For Hitchcock, the working-class Judy had an "out-there" sexuality which did not entice. He dressed her in distinct contrast to the Madeleine character, even including different foundation garments, makeup, and hairstyles. In a famous example of her working-class difference, Judy is spied walking down a San Francisco street in a tight sweater with no bra underneath, a style that the refined Madeleine would never adopt (the big-breasted Novak later remarked she was "proud" she could pull off the no-bra look, large as she was). Judy was "out there," in Marilyn Monroe style—in fact, Hitchcock often expressed disdain for Monroe's sexual image, stating that he and his male audience would never find such an overt sexuality appealing. Truffaut quotes Hitchcock on this issue:

> [Alfred Hitchcock speaking]: Sex on the screen should be suspenseful, I feel. If sex is too blatant or obvious, there's no suspense. You know why I favor sophisticated blondes in my films? We're after the drawing-room type, the real ladies, who become whores once they're in the bedroom. Poor Marilyn Monroe had sex written all over her face . . .
>
> (quoted in Truffaut, 2015, p. 224)

Box office receipts, however, continually high for Monroe throughout the 1950s, proved him wrong, at least in his prediction that audiences would reject a Monroe-like, obvious sexuality.[2]

For Hitchcock, what was most appealing was the idea that the "volcano" of sexual desire lay underneath a refined and reserved exterior. He constructed his signature blondes with almost no window into their own sexual desire or activity. They were the ultimate "ladies" of the cinema, but unfortunately this meant they lacked a certain depth of character. Beyond their ostensible desire for Hitchcock's too-old leading men (who overwhelmed no one with their sexuality, except perhaps the ageless Cary Grant), we know nothing of what they really wanted in life, or what their characters were really about. It is no accident that the penultimate Hitchcock "blonde" was, as many have noted, Grace Kelly, who was in real life to become an actual princess, and in this role she had to permanently subordinate her own desires (among them, the desire to return to acting, which tragically she was just beginning to do when she was killed, too soon, in an automobile accident).

It's interesting to note that Ingrid Bergman never really conformed to the strictures of the Hitchcock blonde. She was an actress of such depth that even Hitchcock could not contain her image. Of course, she starred in Hitchcock films of the 1940s, and we would argue this was before he perfected his ultimate "icy blonde" image in such 1950s productions as *Rear Window, Vertigo, To Catch a Thief, North by Northwest,* and on into the 1960s with Tippi Hedren's two iconic roles in *The Birds* and *Marnie.* Bergman in her best 1940s roles with Hitchcock, in which she portrayed a spy in 1945's *Notorious* and a psychiatrist in 1946's *Spellbound,* seemed to create characters with more depth than the cool blondes that populated his later works.

Conclusion

The legacy of the 1950s remains compelling and surprisingly relevant. Even today, Marilyn Monroe's image retains its power as one of the most widely recognized in the world, even if young people have never seen a film of hers. What's more, *noir* style, particularly the "look" of the typical femme fatale—which involves elegant dresses, crisp trench coats, peekaboo pageboy hairstyles a la Veronica Lake, fervent puffs on a cigarette, and, most important, cool, knowing glances—remains an important influence on a variety of current filmmakers like Quentin Tarantino and his muse, Uma Thurman. Or like Roman Polanski, who in *Chinatown* (1974) created Evelyn Mulwray (Faye Dunaway), an elegant woman of mystery. Denzel Washington in *Devil in a Blue Dress* (1995) and Russell Crowe in *LA Confidential* (1997), playing opposite high-class prostitute Kim Basinger, who, coincidentally, impersonates Veronica Lake in hairstyle and looks, all attest to the currency of noir archetypes. More fundamentally, however, the legacy of the 1950s has been to inextricably connect our sexual imaginations to the landscape of social class. Articulated most profoundly by Carolyn Steedman in her 1987 tract on social class and gender identity, *Landscape for a Good Woman*, class is the unarticulated foundation of a plethora of wants and desires that our culture simply doesn't have the means to represent. Steedman describes the aching desires of her lower-class mother: "Mam ... wanted things," she writes, and her goal in the book is "to admit her [mother's] desire for the things of the earth to political reality and psychological validity," given that "politics and cultural criticism can only find trivial the content of her desires, and the world certainly took no notice of them" (Steedman, 1987, p. 109).

But when you put aside style, the "classing" of sexuality has changed dramatically. Perhaps most saliently, women now have the opportunity to earn their own livings. Recent statistics on marriage indicate that men and women are more likely to marry when each has similar earning power. This has led to a drastic shift in the romantic and sexual imagination, particularly as represented in Hollywood film. Gold-diggers are out; today's film students react with some horror to their frequent portrayals in classical film history, seeing the gold-digger persona as simply immoral. These early movies convey more successful images of working women, but they are not necessarily sexualized. More troublingly, hyper-successful, powerful, wealthy women are often portrayed as undesirable, untrustworthy, and downright evil (cite counting).

Much has changed since the heyday of the original films noir and Marilyn Monroe's brief period of stardom. The National Organization for Women was formed in 1966. During the decade that followed, we survived Watergate and the defeat of *Roe v. Wade* and made notable advancements in the workplace. More women than ever before were graduating from colleges and universities, and from law schools and medical schools, which once had strict quotas. What's more, women were pushing their way into the workforce, onto magazine staffs, and also, with some difficulty, onto Wall Street.

Why were the hyper-sexualized working-class heroines discussed above so popular and so iconic, and what do they reveal about Hollywood's—and the American viewing public's—notions of female sexuality and social class? Clearly, the proliferation of provocative, lower-class sexual images created box office profits during a particularly difficult financial period for the studios; but it was also indicative of the *particular* flux around class identity and consumption patterns characterizing

American society in the post-war period. These images foreshadowed the upcoming social upheavals of the sixties, including the sexual revolution, which we may still be experiencing. The ferment during this post-war decade led to the transition from "old Hollywood" studio pictures to a more modern, independent, and innovative type of cinema, one featuring directors like Stephen Spielberg, Martin Scorsese, and Brian de Palma that is young, vibrant, and as we write is still grappling with the nature of sex, class, and the nature of women's onscreen image.

We have established in this chapter that social class identities are integral to some of the most highly sexualized images produced in post-war Hollywood film. Here, we can use the tools of intersectionality to analyze the juxtaposition of social class and gender identities that are integral to the construction of many sexual images. We urge that scholars pay more attention to the social class narratives underlying popular film, and popular media in general. This could facilitate more effective communication across class boundaries, which, recent political events indicate, is a pressing need in our culture. We hope that this work, through discussing what has long been implicit in these representations, is a first step in that direction.

Note

1. One notable exception here is the chilling upper-class femme fatale played by Jean Simmons in the noir thriller *Angel Face* (1953), starring Robert Mitchum.

Works Cited

Arbuthnot, L., & Seneca, G. (1990). Pre-text and text in *gentlemen prefer blondes*. In P. Erens (Ed.), *Issues in feminist film criticism* (pp. 101–125). Bloomington, IN: Indiana University Press.

Banner, L. (2012). *Marilyn: The passion and the paradox*. London, UK: Bloomsbury.

Bogle, D. (2001). *Toms, coons, mulattoes, mammies, and bucks: An interpretive history of blacks in American films* (4th ed.). London, UK: Bloomsbury Academic.

Doty, A. (2000). *Flaming classics: Queering the film canon*. New York, NY: Routledge.

Gledhill, C. (1987). *Home is where the heart is: Studies in melodrama and the woman's film*. London, UK: British Film Institute.

Kaplan, E.A. (2008). *Women in film noir*. London, UK: British Film Institute.

King, K. (2015). Do African American stereotypes still exist in television? A descriptive character analysis of Olivia Pope. *Inquiries*, *6*(2), 1/1.

Monroe, M., & Hecht, B. (2006). *My story*. New York, NY: Taylor Trade.

Smith, S.L., Choueiti, M., & Stern, J. (2013). Occupational Aspirations: What are G-rated Films Teaching Children About the World of Work? The Geena Davis Institute on Gender in Media. Retrieved from: https://seejane.org/wp-content/uploads/key-findings-occupational-aspirations-2013.pdf

Spoto, D. (2014). *Marilyn Monroe, the biography*. New York, NY: Dansker Press.

Steedman, C. (1987). *Landscape for a good woman: A story of two lives*. New Brunswick, NJ: Rutgers University Press.

Truffaut, F. (2015). *Hitchcock: A definitive study of Alfred Hitchcock* (rev. ed.). New York, NY: Simon and Schuster.

PART II

Documenting Class

6

PERFORMING CLASS AND TASTE THROUGH THE DOCUMENTARY LENS

John Corner

Representations of social class are an inevitable, recurrent presence in British documentary, sometimes explicitly engaged with but much more often indicated obliquely in relation to occupation, accent, dress, and the social settings in which a documentary account develops. As documentary production, across its wide range of aesthetic-journalistic-diversionary options, attempts to connect with varied aspects of social reality through its recorded images and sounds, class routinely "comes through," often unintentionally and often unrecognised by the producers themselves. This is particularly true within the British media system given the depth, complexity, and multiple, sometimes subtle, indicators which social class takes on in a society still in slow transformation from its traditional structures of difference and deference.[1]

In the 1930s British Documentary Film Movement, which regularly examined the world of industrial work and the profile of the (usually male) "worker," aspects of class were often consciously present, an unavoidable if understated thematic ingredient. Classic films of the 1930s—*Coalface* (GPO Films, 1935), *Housing Problems* (British Commercial Gas Association, 1935), and *Spare Time* (GPO Films, 1939), for instance—variously make contact with class as, among other things, an economic variable as well as a matter of clothes and appearance. The exploration of social class, often nervous of too much "politicisation," continued as a theme through the development of British television documentary from the 1950s, as it explored the changing social landscape of Britain, quite frequently by looking at varieties of occupation and at aspects of the "ordinary" (categories which, of course, can displace "class" rather than give it sharp focus). In a social report series like *Special Inquiry* (BBC, 1952–1957), strong connections back to the classic expositions of 1930s documentary cinema were evident but they were tempered by the need for the "domestic" intimacy of address of television and recognition of the changing political and economic order in which social differentiations now operated.[2] However, although television documentaries often began from occupational, regional, or thematic categories (e.g., health, education, housing) rather than directly engaging with class (allowing for the considerable overlap between these terms), their focus on the routines and self-accounts of "working lives" began to position their participants less narrowly than earlier modes of "top down" investigation. Instead, they allowed, both in visual design and in forms of speech, an expanded, richer sense of ordinary living to be articulated, including its hopes and hardships. The arrival of commercial television (ITV) in 1955 accelerated this stronger, more affirmative, connection "downward" which can be seen in a number of programmes.[3]

The positioning and treatment of class-sensitive themes showed variations as documentary programmes expanded across a range of stylistic approaches beyond the expositional/reportorial. For instance, Denis Mitchell's strikingly original *Morning in the Streets* (BBC, 1959) explored it indirectly as part of its impressionistic urban ethnography, mixing various voices over montage sequences of Manchester and Liverpool. Much later, Mike Grigsby's *Living on the Edge* (Central/ITV, 1987) located it more firmly within a political frame by selecting different working-class families and communities for detailed observation as they lived through the hardships of the Conservative government's economic policies. Occasionally, television documentary has taken a more head-on approach not just to depiction but to analysis, an example being Melvyn Bragg's *Class and Culture* (BBC2, 2012) which attempted to place it in the context of national social history.[4]

The broad, changing relationship between matters of class and documentary depiction was modified significantly with the initially slow and then increasingly rapid development of reality television strands from the late 1980s onwards.[5] Undoubtedly, an important early precursor here was Paul Watson's series *The Family* (BBC, 1974), which followed the weekly life of a working-class family, including its conversations and arguments. This was an observational documentary offered more as popular sociology than as entertainment, but its "living soap" appeal made it a ratings success and helped establish a precedent and a template for later work.

Experiments with different "reality" formats took very different routes in tone and theme but generated programmes in which the economic and lifestyle dimensions of class were often foregrounded with a new frankness.[6] The portrayal, for instance, of economic inequality in recent programmes like *Benefits Street* (Channel 4, 2014–) took implicit class framings to stronger levels. In the process it generated accusations of "poverty porn" and the charge that those on social welfare depicted in it were being set up as targets within a national polity which viewed "benefit culture" as a drain on national resources by specific kinds of people (seen as an "underclass" but also as a lower rung of the contemporary working class).

Class from Within and Without

Within the broad context sketched out above, this chapter places its focus on the quite distinctive approach to mediating questions of class in two programmes from the three-part British television series *All in the Best Possible Taste* (Channel 4/Simply Media, 2012, DVD available). The series was presented by a well-known figure in the British cultural scene, the artist Grayson Perry, whose flamboyant transvestism has combined with the qualities of his creative work to give him high public visibility.

The programmes' exploration of taste is strongly organised through the categories of social class. Their development is structured around different class groupings and activities to the extent that, for most of the time, class rather than taste is the dominant point of focus. What gives the programmes a unique character in the context of the previous documentary approaches noted above, however, is the way in which Grayson not only operates as a reporter, through visits and interviews, but also as a performer/impersonator, inserting himself within the different class milieu as "one of them" (including in both male and female dress). I shall argue that this approach generates a richly provocative viewing engagement with the class/taste relationship, one which opens out into territory well beyond conventional modes of documentary portrayal, including those of "reality" formats, at the same time as it displaces certain kinds of possible answer to the questions about class difference which it poses.

In what follows, I want first of all to look at the expositional scheme and discursive design within which Grayson constructs his particular form of documentary account and "performs" class. I then want to focus on the accounts he offers of the working class and the middle class, since these are the most sociologically ambitious and the issues they engage are familiar outside of Britain, whereas the third programme's consideration of the British upper class is more restricted both in focus and in its terms of exploration.[7] I shall conclude with some observations about how the project works both as tele-mediation of class/taste relations and differences and, in part, an attempted explanation of them. My approach requires quite close attention to the speech and images since what I am doing is attempting to follow the various (and sometimes contradictory) ways in which class appears within the textual fabric of the programmes, both intentionally and otherwise.

However, despite my concern with form, my analysis is concerned as much with what is outside the textual structures as inside them. It is their wider resonance that counts. At almost every point both the programmes and my inquiry open out onto much broader issues not only about the sometimes conflicting testimony concerning class experience but about the visual, aural, and spatial profile of social class in Britain. I make connection with these issues regularly in the course of my comments and then return to them at the end.

The "Documentary Eye" and Performative Ethnography

The opening sequence of the first programme, and therefore of the series, gives some of the key terms organising its design, assembled as a "hook" for the viewer:

> *VO For the past year this man has been watching what you do. He's been travelling around Britain to the events and social rituals where you reveal the most about yourselves.*
>
> *Perry meeting home owner: "Tell me about your loo. Show me your loo. I'm quite interested in your loo."*
>
> *VO He's been looking around your houses, inspecting your possessions, your décor and your cars. He's been watching what you wear and even dressing up like you do because he believes that gives him an insight into who you think you are.*
>
> *His name is Grayson Perry, he's one of Britain's leading artists, a winner of the Turner Prize. . . .*
>
> *In this series, Grayson Perry goes on safari through the taste tribes of Britain. Not just to observe your taste but to tell you in his biggest artwork yet what he thinks it means. He's making 6 huge panoramic tapestries—his personal interpretation of the taste of 21st century Britain.*
> *Perry: In this [first] program, I want to get to grips with working-class taste.*

Clearly, the promise of the series is offered as being partly about the pleasures of "snooping," although "we" as much as "they" are notionally positioned as the target. The line about "loos" (toilets) suggests that very little will be considered off limits. The metaphors are those of sightseeing in the wild and visiting communities whose members are tightly connected by their rituals and beliefs. The art of tapestry will be put to the service of something very different from its former role and the engagement with taste will be a vigorous one ("get to grips"). The speech is run over visuals of various types of class-indicative events and places (e.g., polo matches and football crowds), showing people in class-related dress, including Perry himself.

However, the opening emphasis on the "ethnographic" eye is vigorously complemented in the programme itself by Perry's strongly performative role, in which the "experience of class" is briefly sampled in order to inform the external assessment. Such a play-off is further complicated by another, third, set of articulations at work—the autobiographical connections Perry makes as a result of his own working-class origins. The nature of the interplay across these points can best be approached by selectively examining sequences from the first programme, the one on working-class taste, which is set in Sunderland.

The First Programme. Going Local 1: Sunderland

For the series, social class is explored in terms of localities with which it is perceived as being closely identified. Perry starts the first programme's investigation with the following commentary, one in which the autobiographical element is signalled clearly.

> *I've come to Sunderland. Because this is a town built on traditional old industries of shipbuilding and coal and has a proud working-class tradition and I want to see what the contemporary manifestation of working-class taste is. For somebody who's from a working-class background myself but since spent most of my life in the very middle-class world of contemporary art, I've learned that people can get uncomfortable when I talk about taste in class terms.*

Men

Perry begins his exploration of the class profile of the town by looking at the men, at for instance their cult of "hot cars," in which performance goes well beyond requirement. This example he sees as one of "male display" with "primal, primitive" aspects. However, the way in which the men talk about their cars almost as if they were sculptures, bringing out their aesthetic qualities, he sees as "quite heartening." Other examples of masculine working-class taste given visual attention with encounters and inquiries are tattoos (where again a comparison with painting and sculpture is made), cage-fighting, and then gym culture, where a tough body is developed for display rather than being an occupational consequence and requirement of the heavy industrial work, which was once the dominant mode of male employment.

The strong local interest in soccer gives him the opportunity to dress up in supporter's kit and go along with a group of men to an important league game. He sees the event in terms of "banners" and "heraldry" and talks about this as a key moment of "belonging to the tribe." A slow montage of scenes related to the match (game) gives the programme a brief passage free of speech, one richer in visual associations. The match sequence leads through to an evening at a club, where much beer is drunk and a male singer moves an audience of both sexes powerfully with his sad ballads, including Perry himself (provoking a class comparison in his comment, "Could the tears at Glyndebourne be any more vintage?").[8]

Throughout these scenes, Perry's warmly positive relations with those he is with and his approval of what they are doing comes through strongly and sometimes seems awkwardly related to the anthropological language through which he offers his main insights ("tribe," "primitive," "ritual," etc.). Glancing parallels with middle-class culture (painting, art, and opera) are used to provide not so much a sense of difference as of *equivalence and validation* even if, for instance, using the idea of "painting" to appreciate "tattoos" risks a level of suppressed condescension in the terms of approval.

Women

Perry then turns his attention to working-class female taste, particularly in respect of clothing, wondering whether he "can pull off the look himself" when preparing for a night out dressed as a woman with a suitable hairdo and fake tan. In the context of the choices of "artifice" he is making, he wonders if "tasteful" people might not be missing out. As the night out proceeds, he asks a number of males about what his "look" (inflected towards the "classy") scores and what might have been done better.

This sequence clearly gives Perry his strongest performative opportunity—to go out on the town dressed as a working-class woman. What is significant about it, however, is the way in which throughout, as with male companions earlier and now with female ones, Perry behaves as a man cheerily operating within the working-class milieu. The "matey" element of his behaviour and speech, the same as in the soccer match sequence despite the cross-dressing, complicates the performance, giving it something of the comic character of theatrical drag, in which the obvious and strongly projected *contrast* between person and role is central. Any sense of getting "inside" the gendered experience of class is clearly compromised as a result.

"Roots"

Perry's third area of exploration concerns the older generation and their relationship both with the past and with contemporary culture. In the house of one of the older residents he examines the pottery figures she has collected. Here, he further develops a positive valorization of working-class taste, as part of a strong "folk culture," against those who would "look down" upon it (what he calls the "sneer factor").

In conversation about a graduation photograph of the resident's daughter, he reflects on the movement from one class to another ("At what point do you become middle class?"). The mother suggests that going to university did allow her daughter, if not to become middle class, then to "go a little further up the rungs of the ladder."

Here, it seems that the programme begins to have a serious problem with the play-off between the idea of "class travel" and the idea of "class stability." Perry is drawn to the former for strong autobiographical reasons but for most of the people he has met there has been no significant "travel." The question of whether the chief focus is on the enabling, if disconcerting, experience of class mobility or the problem that there is not enough of this becomes an awkward one. This is particularly true when it is suggested that "looking down" on working-class taste may largely be a problem of "distancing ourselves" from "who we used to be." This draws on the autobiographical strand to imply that the real problem of "sneering" issues from those who were born into the working class and then moved out of it rather than being an attitude shown by established members of the middle class. Given that the programme itself points to the limited amount of class mobility, this position complicates if not completely undercuts some of the main assumptions being traded on elsewhere. The localised dynamics of interaction, the spaces into which Perry's sociable explorations and performances have taken him, create a degree of incoherence at the level of "findings." This comes through again as he talks to a hairdresser about his own "necessary" move to the middle-class art world because "there is no working-class art world." In part, this seems to be offered as a regrettable reason for his leaving the working class. His big theme, he says, is prejudices and tastes and how these "reflect our own class journey in life." Here, as I indicated earlier, autobiography has become confused with sociology. The question of how many people have a class journey in their lives and what this proportion says about the economic and social system has been exchanged for the suggestion that we all do.

Presenting the Results

The programme ends with Perry presenting the tapestries he has made, influenced in their design by a range of artists including Hogarth and the people to whom he has talked in his explorations. A model of the "Rake's Progress" is at work here, displaced uncertainly from 18th-century matters of changing status in relation to personal behaviour to a 21st-century class frame. The images are discussed with delight and approval by those attending, who are often seeing themselves, their places, and their activities portrayed. Perry's own cultural status (validated as a "celebrity artist" in another world from that of the working class) is never in doubt and the respect shown to his work veers at times into the embarrassingly deferent for a programme with class relations as its topic (e.g., "I am honored to be portrayed like that"). Perry picks up on his inclusion of an image of the graduate photograph, noting that it is a "story of class mobility" that "is not as common as it should be." He thereby obliquely indicates an interpretation in some conflict both with the earlier implication that all of us undergo a class journey and his choice of this theme as a focus.[9]

The quite specific terms of television's capacity for the intimate, the personally revealing, and the sociable clearly frame the project with strong performative-dramatic as well as documentary qualities. However, by narrowing down his focus to specific aspects of taste and by operating with congenial taste-pairings (e.g., hot cars–sculpture; tattoos–painting) Perry is able quite easily to divert any engagement with the economic and social inequalities underpinning cultural options into a matter of noting and *affirming* "differences." There is no exploration of the wider sphere of literature and music and only a passing connection with education, one which raises more questions than it addresses. The programme is finally as much about evaluation (of something initially placed as "other") as it is about explanation and this becomes quite an easy evaluation to make, projected positively against the potential for a "sneer." It is made even easier by the way in which his account is grounded in autobiographical comments and stances which, as I noted, work to undercut the initial, anthropological terms of his inquiry but are never properly recognised as doing so.

The Second Programme. Going Local 2: Tunbridge Wells

The second programme sets out to explore "modern middle-class taste" and does so through a two-part exploration. First of all, the new estate of Kings Hill near Tunbridge Wells is visited to examine the taste of Britain's "new, upwardly mobile" middle class. Then, Tunbridge Wells itself provides an opportunity to assess what is going on within the more established middle class. The opening sequence shows images which include organic aubergines on a market stall, people drinking wine, and a farmers' market.

Perry begins the programme with a provocative proposition concerning class affiliation: "In a recent survey more than two thirds of Britons identified themselves as middle class when only 25 years ago two thirds of us said we were working class."[10] So something has happened to a sense of class belonging which appears to have expanded the middle class. Perry goes on to note the "important story" for him—*the relationship between our taste and our class journey in life.* The idea of the "class journey" thus reappears early on here, raising once more the questions I noted earlier.

The New Middle Class

As in the Sunderland programme, but more directly, Perry positions himself as inside the middle class despite his origins (*I suppose I'm middle class myself. . .*). However, this does not stop him from noticing how Kings Hill area is different from the middle-class spaces he is familiar with (it is "cleaner, no litter"). This allows him to repeat a theme from the earlier programme's trip to working-class spaces—*I feel like an anthropologist who has wandered into a different tribal territory.*

His first social occasion is a party, for which he is properly attired by a local outfitters (designer clothes with good detailing). At the party, he notes the décor and the way in which a "village feel" is part of the attraction of those who have moved here. He discusses class definitions and is told by one man that being "middle class is all about aspiration." When asked "aspiration to what" he is told "to live a better life." Another man raises the question of whether there is a single middle class or whether there is upper middle class and lower middle class. He says he is "moving towards" upper middle class (a class journey *within* a class?) because of his income and in answer to Perry's questioning says he thinks income is the decisive factor in class mobility.

Across the range of his subsequent encounters and his explorations of choices in cars, home interior design, and kitchenware, Perry observes that people liked "the clarity of meaning that a known brand could convey" and, once again, he contrasts the behavior with that of his own "Islington tribe" in London. He wonders whether middle-class taste is a function of a filtering down or whether, by contrast, it is a reaction to working-class taste. The women he is speaking to strongly indicate the latter. On a kitchen table they identify a tagine as the item that most clearly represents middle-class taste and its "difference." When asked "difference from what," one of them replies to general laughter "difference from working-class taste." Perry, who generally backs off from negative comments of any sort, is provoked by the case of a woman who bought a show home with everything inside it, including the furniture, as a way of avoiding the anxiety of choices. He comments to her that it seems to him "an amazing symptom of modern capitalist hyper-consumption," before going on to say, a little unconvincingly, he doesn't mean that is bad.

The Old Middle Class

The second part of the programme moves to Tunbridge Wells itself, where a more established middle class in older housing have established the "tone" of the place. He is told by an anthropologist he interviews that neither income nor occupation defines the middle class but matters of "speech, manner, and taste, lifestyle choices, what you eat, what you wear." Not for the first time in the series, a very questionable claim, one out of line with other comments made, is allowed through without challenge. The possibility that "speech, manner, and taste" themselves might have economic determinants, in a variety of combinations with family background, education, and occupation, is not considered.

In the cultural context of the first couple he meets in Tunbridge Wells, who speak confidently of their taste in a house full of high-quality fine art, with William Morris wallpaper and many books, Perry is pushed towards a series of more general reflections. First of all, on the nature of this kind of taste:

> *What Sue and Norman's taste spoke of to me was not money but a different kind of capital—cultural capital—the sum of all the knowledge, education, and culture they had worked so hard to accumulate.*

The formulation itself risks a degree of circularity. Once again, and in strong contrast to Bourdieu's use of "cultural capital,"[11] money is being displaced from the picture. But it is then not clear how the sum of "knowledge, education, and culture" works as an *independent* differentiating factor. Instead, it is a way of pointing to the advantages of education (references to Cambridge are made as the couple talk about their possessions) while ignoring the advantages of the privileged family background which, to judge from their accents alone, the couple clearly had. That Perry does not want to make the direct, economic links is made clear by his emphasis on "worked so hard to accumulate," as if the taste displayed were chiefly a matter of individual, effortful acquisition rather than socially structured opportunity.

But Perry moves into a further, broader generalization here. One that has implications not just for the whole program but the whole series:

> *I was learning something crucial from Sue and Norman. The important taste divide in British life wasn't between working-class and middle-class taste it was within the different tribes of the middle class itself. Between Kings Hill on one side and old Tunbridge Wells on the other stood the Berlin wall of British taste.*

Here, the premise of the original "tribal" framework is radically revised, introducing a division *within* the middle class which appears to exceed in its importance that division between the classes previously placed as central.

However, even here, as in Kings Hill, "anxiety" is a key theme of Perry's analysis and he notes that Sue and Norman "worry away" at their taste when, in fact, little or no evidence of this has emerged from his encounter with them. This theme is continued through a meeting with a local National Childbirth Trust group, where anxieties about children's food—its constituents and its sourcing—are aired, allowing Perry to judge that the middle class (not internally divided on this it seems) see "taste in moral terms."

The visit to Tunbridge Wells ends with a dinner party ("the central ritual of the middle classes," although the implication might be that the lower middle classes of Kings Hill are not included in this claim). Dressed elegantly as a woman, Perry drinks his wine and enjoys his food (including courgettes from his host's allotment). He observes that "taste for the middle classes is about the vanity of small differences" and that the class is the one "most self-conscious" about the meaning of their possessions. The theme of strategic taste, exercised for the primary purpose of impressing others, is thus continued.

As in the Sunderland programme, the ending is a reception at which the tapestries he has made are revealed to those whom he has visited and talked to. The images allegorically indicate the spaces, the clothing, the objects, the people, and the experiences which Perry has encountered in his trip to what are in effect the "two tribes" to be found in the Tunbridge Wells area. Interestingly, in introducing the event to the television camera, Perry notes, "I think it's telling when we've invited people to come and see these tapestries by far the greatest response was from Tunbridge Wells, the middle classes." There can be no surprise either for him or for us in the fact that the mode in which he has chosen to give his "feedback" is most popular with the group already aligned towards forms of "high" cultural practice. As in the earlier programme, there is appreciation by those attending of his imaginative depiction of what he has seen and heard during his visit, including where a level of satiric intent is perceived.

I have noted how this programme starts out by being about what seems to be a relatively identifiable class grouping which can be contrasted with the working class of Sunderland but then moves, if unevenly and awkwardly, to being about two groupings with the relationship between them and the possibility of mobility between them uncertain. Subsequently, the single and the dual idea both inform the account, depending on the particular trait being emphasised. The displacement of income and occupation as factors in middle classness, a displacement explicitly made by the professional anthropologist, is not borne out by what the programme itself finds, either in Kings Hill or in Tunbridge Wells, where in different ways, brazen or discreet, income is a major factor as also, implicitly, is occupation. Throughout, a wish to stress "anxiety" as a key aspect of middle-class taste risks overstatement against the available evidence and the kinds of social confidence, if not complacency, on display. This is so even though many of his respondents are happy to play into a self-deprecating humour in which "angst" is seen as pervasive. I have observed at several points how the idea of the autobiographically driven theme of "class journey" is present, as in the Sunderland programme, although here it is more implicit and less about movement from the working class to the middle class than mobility within the layers of the middle class itself.

Tribes, Journeys, and Values

Through a detailed examination of its organisation and examples of its local textual detail, I have wanted to suggest that *All in the Best Possible Taste* develops an account of social class with an immersive and performative character quite original in British television. Here, we are certainly a long way both from the indirect and often distanced "sociological" expositions of 1930s documentary cinema and the potentially exploitative, voyeuristic "surveillance" of the reality mode. The particular deployment of "televisuality" connects with class space—looks, experience, testimony—in ways which have the broadest significance. However, the primary linkage with "taste," productive though it is at certain points, works finally to constrain and even at times to undercut the propositions that it can make. The aesthetic-evaluative emphasis is allowed to lead to the relative banality of "difference" being proclaimed the key and sufficient finding. This is a relativism which, while it positions itself against evaluative prejudice, has the effect of implying against much of the evidence collected that social class itself is *primarily a matter of differences* rather than of inequalities. The way in which questions of wealth are often marginalized in the programmes gives support to this implication. I have also noted how the autobiographical element, however welcome in its honesty, further complicates the account, sustaining a "class journey" idea which is never squared with the programmes' local "findings."

Despite these limitations, and perhaps at times because of them (since they are the product of engaging with dimensions of class unrecognised or actively avoided in many media treatments), the programmes remain a richly provocative and illuminating venture. The alertness to pleasures as well as to fears generates an expansive experiential dimension going beyond the terms of analysis. Perry's project, structured for *reflective* engagement by an audience coming from different class positions, constitutes an imaginative landmark in British documentary approaches to its conflicted themes.

Notes

1. A comparison of documentary with drama is instructive here. In the latter, "class" is constructed imitatively through scripting, casting, acting, and the full range of directorial choices. Whereas in documentary class inflections emerge from production discourses interacting variously and sometimes awkwardly with existing people, spaces, and actions.
2. A discussion of this series in relation to changing ideas of British society, including interviews with those who worked on it, can be found in Corner (1991).
3. In Corner (1996), I look at one example of a documentary series, *Look in on London* (Associated Rediffusion, May–August, 1956), in which matters both of social class and class culture are given extended attention within a discourse which starts out as a "report" on occupations but quickly turns into something more informal and sociable in relation both to participants and viewers.
4. Among the range of books to attend to class in British documentary, Brian Winston (1995) is a major text, while Corner (1996) examines selected films from the 1930s to the 1980s with a strong emphasis on social representation.
5. Deery (2015) gives a concise, critical account of reality television, including a valuable discussion of the terms of its shift to ever more direct treatments of class. She observes how often, within it, "class identities are consciously performed" (p. 230) and notes the important relationship with matters of taste—both points central to the concerns of this chapter. Among the range of texts, a good, earlier account of the complex history of the "reality" form in Britain is Biressi and Nunn (2005).
6. On this, as well as Deery (2015) (above) see Bignall (2015) for a recent overview, while Morley (2009) offers an excellently theorized account of tendencies both in documentary and drama and Woods and Skeggs (2011) brings together a range of perspectives on the class relations of "reality" productions.
7. The emphasis here on the inherited wealth of the "aristocracy" and its relative continuity of taste is often illuminating but it lacks that sense of nervous inter-class relations which characterise the first two programmes, and Perry's approach here inclines towards the respectful rather than either the investigative or the autobiographical.
8. Glyndebourne is an opera house in south east England. Its annual opera festival is seen as a key event in the social and cultural calendar of the established middle class and sections of the upper class. Of course, Perry's use of "vintage" here connects with ideas of champagne (the signature drink of the Glyndbourne festival).
9. This compares interestingly with other autobiographical versions of "class travel," the most recent in Britain being Hanley (2016), which, in its impressive account of the mix of aspirations, anxieties, and hurts of prejudice involved, draws parallels with the classic account by Hoggart (1957). In both cases, and in many others, it is the rareness rather than the frequency of class travel that gives the narrative its significance.
10. A fine and detailed indication of the complexities and shifts of British class categories is Savage (2015), which includes data from a national survey.
11. Among the many references, see Bourdieu (1984).

Works Cited

Bignall, J. (2015). Authenticity and performance of class in British factual TV series. In N. Cloarec, D. Haigron, & D. Letort. (Eds.). *Social class on British and American screens: Essays on cinema and television* (pp. 58–73). Jefferson, NC: McFarland.

Biressi, A., & Nunn, H. (2005). *Reality TV: Realism and revelation*. London, UK: Wallflower Press.

Bourdieu, P. (1984 [1979]). *Distinction: A social critique of the judgment of taste* (R. Nice, Trans.). London, UK: Routledge.

Corner, J. (1991). *Popular television in Britain: Studies in cultural history*. London, UK: British Film Institute.

Corner, J. (1996). *The art of record*. Manchester, UK: Manchester University Press.

Deery, J. (2015). *Reality TV*. Cambridge, UK: Polity.

Hanley, L. (2016). *Respectable: The experience of class*. London, UK: Allan Lane.

Hoggart, R. (1957). *The uses of literacy*. London, UK: Chatto and Windus.

Morley, D. (2009). Mediated classifications: Representations of class and culture in contemporary British television. *European Journal of Communication, 12*, 487–508.

Savage, M. (2015). *Social class in the 21st century*. Harmondsworth, UK: Penguin (Pelican).

Winston, B. (1995). *Claiming the real*. London, UK: British Film Institute.

Woods, H., & Skeggs, B. (Eds.) (2011). *Reality television and class*. Basingstoke, UK: Palgrave.

7

HOW THE OTHER HALF LIVES: THE WILL TO DOCUMENT FROM POVERTY TO PRECARITY

Laurie Ouellette

In 2015, the US reality series *The Briefcase* cast a spotlight on cash-strapped Americans. On each episode, TV producers offered families steeped in debt, job insecurity, and chronic financial difficulties a briefcase filled with $100,000—along with instructions to keep the cash or share it with another struggling household. Before deciding, the participants must surreptitiously tour the homes of the potential beneficiaries, rifle through photographs, personal belongings, and stacks of unpaid bills, and examine other evidence of neediness (overcrowding, broken-down vehicles and appliances, medical conditions) while cameras roll. Unbeknownst to them, the subjects of their investigation have also been gifted a briefcase, and in a parallel plotline are carefully observing their own arduous circumstances, vulnerabilities, and hardships. At the end of the episode, the two families meet face-to-face for the cathartic reveal, and TV viewers learn whether they will share the money—or keep it all for themselves.

While billed as an edifying experiment, critics lambasted *The Briefcase* for exploiting the poor for dramatic entertainment purposes. Some noted that voyeurism and moral judgment were built into the formula; others said the economically disenfranchised were humiliated and put on display for middle-class audiences. Critics protested the merger of authenticity and showbiz, insisting that the realities of poverty were too harsh for slick commercial packaging. One commentator said it would be more ethical to shut down the TV production and give the contents of the briefcase directly to social service agencies. While *The Briefcase* was blamed on reality television's recent brand of sensationalism and ethical insouciance, similar tendencies operate across a genealogy of "serious" documentary and factual media. Since the late-1800s, "the poor" have been documented, surveilled, commodified, displayed, and judged in the name of ameliorating their suffering. While often rooted in humanitarian intentions, the history of poverty documentary is laden with uneven power dynamics, voyeurism, and sentimental appeals to middle-class benevolence (Rosler, 1989; Rabinowitz, 1994; Price, 1997).

Overlooked in the debate over *The Briefcase* is the increasingly precarious context in which it operates. From slum photography to television exposés, the impetus to make the poor visible peaked during the welfare stage of liberal capitalism, spanning the Progressive reforms of the 1890s to the New Deal and Great Society programs of the 1930s and 1960s. The American Dream of class mobility also flourished during this epoch, as the state progressively tempered the harshest consequences of capitalism and supported the well-being and productivity of the population. In recent decades, the state has retreated from this role, and individuals are expected to manage their own "fates and fortunes" with only the barest public safety net (Rose, 1996). In tandem with the shift from Fordism to a post-industrial, de-unionized, and "flexible" economy, the neoliberal approach to "governing through insecurity" (Lorey, 2015) that now prevails perpetuates precarity as a way of life for most people. Whereas the "old rule" of domination demanded "obedience in exchange for protection," the post-welfare state offers only "minimal assurance" of collective security and instead encourages individuals to compete against each other, says political theorist Isabel Lorey (2015, p. 2). Lorey uses the term precarious to describe the subjectivities and uncertainties perpetuated by "governing through insecurity." In the broadest sense, she argues, we are all *precarious* due to our contingent status as social beings. Under capitalism, however, political, economic, and legal processes have always made some populations (people of color, immigrants, refugees, the disabled, gender-nonconforming individuals, economically disenfranchised people) more vulnerable to systemic precariousness than others. Structural *precarity* refers to the "striation and distribution of precariousness in relations of inequality." In recent decades, says Lorey, a generalized precaritization of social life has also taken hold, blurring the boundaries between the "precarious and the immune." What Lorey calls the "destabilization" of life, bodies and "modes of subjectivation" is a dominant power dynamic in post-welfare capitalist societies where precaritization is "democratized" (Lorey, 2015, p. 13). As many have argued, the financial crisis of 2008, and the recession that followed, intensified a dispersion of precarity "from the margins" to a sense of insecurity that manifests "everywhere," in parcel with the "political and economic developments of the last decades" (Kunst, 2015, p. 6). Not only has the gap between haves and have-nots grown wider, the fantasy of the stable, middle-class "good life" (Berlant, 2011) has become more difficult for most people to imagine and sustain.

The Briefcase draws from a long-standing tradition of documenting the poor as "others" clustered on the outer edges of mainstream society. However, the reality series also registers the neoliberal rationalities and widespread insecurities of the current political conjuncture. The series catalogues everyday socioeconomic precarity as an increasingly common way of life for "real-life" families across intersecting differences of race, ethnicity, education, gender identity, sexual orientation, religion, and place. In the process, it registers the ubiquitous, "governmentalized" form of precaritization that now dominates neoliberal societies according to Lorey, and potentially unsettles the distance between needy "others" and middle-class audiences. This chapter explores the tension between poverty and precaritization in recent reality-based media culture through an analysis of *The Briefcase* and *American Winter*, a 2013 documentary about multiple families similarly grappling with housing eviction, food insecurity, health care costs, unemployment, indebtedness, and financial distress. While *The Briefcase* was created by the showrunner of the popular makeover series *The Biggest Loser* and serialized over six episodes on commercial broadcast network television (ABC), *American Winter* was directed by independent filmmakers, screened at prestigious film festivals, and released on a "quality" premium cable channel (HBO). Rather than taking these cultural pedigrees as a sign that *American Winter* must be more perceptive and politically engaged, I situate *both* productions within a genealogy of poverty documentation and consider how each navigates the shift from liberal welfare capitalism to neoliberal precarity. By situating these case studies historically, we can think more complexly about how the "will to document" poverty operates in the 21st century, and identify possible fissures and points of resistance to the contemporary "state of insecurity" (Lorey, 2015).

Liberal Reform and the Poverty of Sympathy

Genealogy, as Michel Foucault (1977) reminds us, is a method of mining the past to make critical sense of the present. Toward that end, it is helpful to revisit the aims, contexts, and representational techniques that have governed the "will to document" the poor historically. According to Gareth Palmer, "twin histories" haunt the origins of documentary in the late 19th century. On one hand, photography was used to surveil the Victorian slums and develop a new "science" of policing. Here, the will to document targeted the poor and the working class as potential threats to socioeconomic order and buttressed the "repressive, classifying and ordering powers of the State." On the other hand, humanitarian reformers embraced the camera as a technology for observing and recording the lives of the poor, with the "aim of raising awareness" and improving their conditions. Here, documentary was "woven into a discourse on improvement for the less well-off led by charitable middle-class campaigners" (Palmer, 2014, p. 248–249). Techniques of documentation developed through these parallel histories overlapped and informed each other. Hardly a neutral recording device, photography was stitched into the management of the social, intertwined with "ways of thinking about," representing, and acting on problems such as criminality and poverty (Tagg, 1993, p. 5). While police departments and other modern disciplinary institutions developed "instrumental" uses of documentary behind the scenes

(Tagg, 1993), reformers generated documentary evidence for other purposes. Photographers (and later filmmakers) made substandard housing, sanitation, indigence, child labor, and other problems visible to government agencies and the middle-class public; in so doing they participated in the production of knowledge and the problematization of social life (Palmer, 2014).

As advocates for social reform, documentarians helped constitute what political theorist Nikolas Rose calls the "the state of welfare." The liberal state, he explains, was called upon to become more directly involved in the care of citizens in the late 19th and early 20th centuries. As relations between capitalist owners and workers became increasingly antagonistic, rulers were "urged to accept the obligation to tame and govern the undesirable consequences of industrial life, wage labor and urban existence in the name of society" (Rose, 1996, pp. 39–40). In making these problems visible, liberal documentary was vital to the formation of a "new social contract" between the State and the population that exchanged allegiance and cooperation for "social protection" in the form of increased government regulations, social insurance programs, and universal services, including public education (Rose, 1996, p. 49). In the United States, relief programs for the unemployed and the impoverished also appeared in the turbulent 1930s and 1960s. It is easy to celebrate the liberal documentary project at a juncture when the social contract discussed by Rose has given way to neoliberal ethics of privatization, self-enterprise, and personal responsibility. Rising indifference to the poor—as evidenced when conservatives claim that people who can't afford healthcare and other needs are making the "wrong choices" and/or spending too much money on iPhones, cable TV, and other "luxuries" (Sheffield & Rector, 2011; Miller, 2017)—only accentuates the humanitarianism of earlier eras. However, it is also important to understand how the impetus to make the poor visible in the name of societal reforms coincided with practices of surveillance, othering, and social regulation. Understanding the role of media in the "state of insecurity" requires unraveling these contradictions.

According to art historian Derek Price, the earliest "actuality photographs" took on a class inflection that would shape the documentary project for years to come, as "photography established itself as part of a tradition of enquiry into the health, housing, education, economic condition and moral state of the poor" (Price, 1997, pp. 66–67). Jacob Riis, a former police reporter, is the most famous example of documentary as a type of social work (Rosler, 1989). Riis took his camera into the slums of late 19th-century New York, using the earliest flash equipment to record scenes of overcrowding and abject poverty (Yochelson & Czitrom, 2007). His photographs of tenement dwellers, many of them immigrants, were presented as "evidence" to the New York Board of Health, and circulated in newspapers and magazines. In 1890, his book of photographs and commentary, *How the Other Half Lives: Studies among the Tenements of New York*, became a bestseller (Riis, 1890). Riis's photojournalism provoked awareness and reform, but it also exposed its subjects to the gaze of authorities (philanthropists, social workers, police) and middle-class consumers. Riis is reported to have barged into tenement buildings unannounced and bullied the occupants into submissively posing for his photographs—tactics he undoubtedly learned in the police force (Price, 1997, p. 71). In so doing he cast the poor as "victims deserving pity and charity," as opposed to the subjects of political struggle or even their own lives (Yochelson & Czitrom, 2007, p. 119).

As cultural theorist Martha Rosler points out, documentarians like Riis appealed to the self-interest of the privileged classes as much as their sympathy, to the extent that they stoked the fear that the "ravages of poverty, crime, immorality, prostitution, disease and radicalism would threaten the health and security of polite society" (1989, p. 306). They also moralized the politics of poverty by classifying and dividing the "deserving" and the "undeserving" poor. According to historian Michael Katz, the deserving poor (often women and children) were sympathetically viewed as victims of circumstances beyond their control; the undeserving poor were said to have brought on their own poverty through their own insolence, laziness, or drunkenness. Masking the structural exploitation inherent to industrial capitalism, this framework provided a "powerful incentive to work," facilitating the need for "cheap labor," Katz contends (2013, p. 6). The impetus to classify the poor also rationalized the ongoing production of knowledge about them of which documentary was a part.

According to historian Daniel Czitrom, Riis pioneered a co-mingling of factuality and entertainment, reason and sentimentality that many attribute to reality TV and related spectacles. His quasi-social scientific method of "careful observation and deployment of statistics and photographs" would become a hallmark of the Progressive era (Yochelson & Czitrom, 2007, p. xviii). At the same time, he tapped into the class voyeurism that made "slum tours" fashionable during the Gilded Age. Riis's lantern slide-show performances had a pre-vaudeville sensibility to them, says Czitrom, with Riis giving "improvisational talks" laced with ethnic jokes and humorous stories from the police beat against the backdrop of his projected photographs, interspersed with bursts of song and lively organ music (Yochelson & Czitrom, 2007, p. 87). Middle-class audiences were invited to "learn to what depths of social and physical degradation human beings can descend" from a safe distance that reinforced their power over the nameless poor depicted in the images and flattered their sense of genteel benevolence. The "beauty of looking into these places without actually being present there . . . is that the excursionist is spared the vulgar sounds and odious scents and repulsive exhibitions attendant upon such personal examination" (Riis, quoted in Yochelson & Czitrom, 2007, p. 50, p. 9). Besides disrupting any easy bifurcation of "serious" documentation and popular entertainment, early slum photography constituted power differentials that continue to vex poverty documentary.

The impetus to reveal "How the Other Half Lives" continued during the Progressive Era, most notably in the documentary photographs of Lewis Hine, a sociologist-turned-reformer whose images of poor children were instrumental in the passage of child labor laws. The 1930s were especially receptive to liberal documentary due to the economic turbulence of the era and the public funding for documentary that materialized during this time. In the US, the federal government employed skilled photographers to surveil the social landscape of the Great Depression, collecting "visual facts" for state agencies and public dissemination (Price, 1997, p. 82). In the context of mounting economic hardship and political unrest, these images were intended to harness support for New Deal programs. The Farm Security Administration (FSA) documented the need for public works and welfare programs, focusing on the rural poor and migrant workers. Their iconographic images of breadlines, minimalist rural shacks, and ragged children have become synonymous with the "deserving" poverty of the Depression era, even as they now command space in art museums and coffee table books.

Unlike slum photography, FSA photographers aestheticized their subjects, blending factuality and artistry and thus encouraging the consumption of the poor in new ways. Their "densely constructed works" were nonetheless designed to produce a similar response in the spectator (Price, 1997, pp. 82–83). As William Stott shows in his study of the 1930s, there are no "tramps" or "aimless dregs" in the FSA archive, nobody who is "poor as a result of laziness or moral dereliction." Without exception, the deserving victims of these photographs possess a "decency" achieved through carefully selected settings and "sentimental poses." Stott's research reveals the strategy involved in producing the mournful, plaintive "look" so prevalent within the FSA's documentary oeuvre (Stott, 1986, pp. 59–60). Like slum photography, FSA photographs invited viewers to witness the intimate realities of poverty from a distance. As film scholar Paula Rabinowitz points out, this constituted a social hierarchy between the surveyors and the surveilled: "The scene of class domination is the same as the scene of voyeurism," she explains, with both depending on the desire to possess difference (1994, p. 36). This "difference" was interchangeable and anonymous across the ritualistic images, as the subjects of FSA photographers were rarely named (and never consulted in the manner of their representation). While New Deal-era documentation legitimated the expansion of the welfare state, few of its subjects benefited directly from their images, financially or otherwise. Critics like Rosler claim they were exploited—as exemplified by the impoverished farm woman featured in Dorthea Lange's infamous photograph "Migrant Mother." In her field notes, Lange recalls the exhausted-looking woman with a baby at her breast: "She thought that my pictures might help her, and so she helped me" (Rosler, 1989, p. 315). But when Florence Owens Thompson was tracked down to a trailer park in California in the late 1970s and found to be still living in poverty, she expressed her disappointment with the outcome. Thompson told the Associated Press that she had tried unsuccessfully to get the photograph suppressed for many years, because she "never made a penny out of it, and that it had done her no good" (Rosler, 1989, p. 315; Price, 1997, p. 83).

In the moving image culture of the 1930s, the "victims" of poverty were allowed to speak for the first time, potentially disrupting the power dynamics of their documentation. British filmmaker John Grierson coined the term "documentary" in 1932, defining it as the "creative treatment of actuality." Taking real life as the raw material for storytelling, Grierson expanded on the instrumental uses of recording technology operational since the late 1800s, setting the stage for documentary film and television for decades to come. Like Riis, Hines, and the FSA photographers, Grierson approached documentary as a cultural tool for social education and reform. Harnessing the narrative possibilities opened up by film, he cast its subjects within a "social problem framework" (Price, 1997, p. 77) that aligned the documentary project with the civic ambitions (and paternalistic impulses) of public service broadcasting. Grierson worked comfortably within the bureaucracies of the welfare state, but also welcomed sponsorship from gas companies and other corporate benefactors. *Housing Problems* (1935), one of his most famous productions, presents impoverished slum dwellers who describe the wretched living conditions inside decrepit city tenements—a scenario reminiscent of *How the Other Half Lives*. However, in this case the working class was interviewed on film (Winston, 1991, p. 39). As film scholar Barbara Halpern Martineau notes, *Housing Problems* offered an early experiment in direct cinema when a "slum dweller tells her story of an encounter with a rat, not so much to the camera, as in front of it." While the scene was visually framed to highlight her poverty and interpreted by "strong-upper-class male commentary . . . so that she tends to become a piece of local color," the "spirit of this working-class woman telling her story" still comes across very strongly, Martineau contends (1989, p. 256).

Sponsored by the Gas, Light and Coke Company, *Housing Problems* was created to promote housing reform in Britain; by the end of the film, scenes of urban poverty had given way to shiny new housing developments where some of the people appearing in the film had been moved. With its reformist (but not radical) impetus to improve the housing conditions of the working classes, *Housing Problems* set in motion what Brian Winston calls "tradition of the victim" in moving image documentary (1991). In a provocative essay, Winston questions the assumption that documenting the hardships of the poor can ameliorate their problems. On the contrary, he contends that by constructing the disadvantaged as "poor suffering victims" in need of saving by middle-class filmmakers, documentary perpetuates a type of symbolic violence (Bourdieu, 1984) that rarely leads to substantial change in the real world. To support this argument, Winston points out that despite many decades of reform-minded documentary cinema and television, poverty is still very much a problem. At its worst, he claims, the social-problem approach to documentary pioneered by Grierson exploited disadvantaged "others" to justify the purpose (and funding) of documentary and attract middle-class audiences: "Documentary found its subject in the first decade of sound, and by the late 1930s the now familiar parade of those of the disadvantaged whose deviance was sufficiently interesting to attract and hold our attention had been established"

(Winston, 1991, p. 34). The arrival of factual television as a staple of primetime programming in the 1950s, he contends, "cemented the tradition into place" as the "problem of the week" promoted empathy over radical analysis and structural change. Even direct cinema, which "dispensed of narration" and claimed to observe reality without mediation, latched onto the tradition of the victim: The "more fruitful strand turned out to be not the powerful but the powerless . . . direct cinema gave the victim tradition the technology that allowed a degree of intrusion into ordinary people's lives which was not previously possible," Winston contends (1991, p. 41). While Winston's treatise may oversimplify the place of documentary in social change, it raises crucial questions about the uneven power dynamics between documentary producers and subjects already disadvantaged by structural inequalities.

The 1960s stand out as the most recent era during which liberal reformist documentary developed and flourished in the United States—this time on television. Edward R. Murrow's television documentary *Harvest of Shame* (1960), famously broadcast on CBS the day after Thanksgiving, revitalized the will to document poverty, setting the stage for a slew of similar programs. As media scholar Michael Curtin (1995) points out, the documentary powerfully critiqued the exploitation of migrant farm labor—but it ultimately cast migrant laborers as unfortunate victims who had "slipped through the cracks in an otherwise rational system" (1995, p. 168). For Rosler, this lack of agency was magnified by the program's address to civic-minded TV viewers at home, who were called upon by Murrow to "write their Congressmen to help the migrant farm workers, whose pathetic, helpless, dispirited victimhood has been amply demonstrated for an hour" (1989, p. 307). The "discovery" of domestic poverty in the United States animated documentary production of the 1960s, from network television programs to educational films produced by the Office of Economic Opportunity (Charbonneau, 2016, p. 101). The impetus for establishing agencies like the OED was Michael Harrington's bestselling 1962 book *The Other America: Poverty in the United States*, which claimed pockets of poverty persisted in midst of rising consumer affluence, and that the hidden poor were "increasingly isolated from contact with, or sight of, anybody else" (Harrington, 1962, pp. 3–4; Charbonneau, 2016, p. 100). The US government declared a War on Poverty and new social welfare programs, from Head Start to Pell grants for college, were authorized to ensure "equality of opportunity" for all Americans. While these were monumental achievements, the rationales behind them generalized and infantilized people living in chronic poverty without addressing the causes of socioeconomic inequality. The poor were cast as "others"—backward rural whites and urban people of color—whose self-perpetuating "culture of poverty" (Ehrenreich, 1990, pp. 49–51) prevented them from realizing the achievements of the white, educated, suburban middle class. According to media historian Chad Raphael, the documentaries that came out of this era advocated reform but not radical critique: the poor were "portrayed as sympathetic victims who deserved assistance in breaking out of this cycle," but liberal reformist discourse "did not identify the interests at stake in redistributing wealth and economic opportunity." This made it possible to present their problems as "maladies" and "social ills" that could be "cured" by experts and professionals (Raphael, 2005, pp. 50–51).

> "Even in what we now think of as the liberal sixties, the notion that the poor were alien members of a 'culture of poverty' had a profound effect on how middle-class people . . . plotted solutions to their distress,"

writes historian Barbara Ehrenreich. Even the more activist and community-based approaches of the time, she notes, ascribed to a middle-class view that felt the poor deserved "services and programs" but could not be trusted with money (1990, p. 55).

Raphael traces the crucial role of television documentary in problematizing poverty—and its solution. His analysis of the typical 1968 CBS documentary *Hunger in America* details how an abundance of professionals (including social workers and medical doctors) perpetuated the "culture of poverty" thesis. The poor were limited to "the familiar role that they most often play in sympathetic treatments of poverty: as victims who testify about personal experiences to illustrate or dramatize a larger point made by experts or journalists" (2005, p. 52). As with slum photography, abject poverty is put on display to stimulate audience interest and middle-class sympathy. The program opened with images of emaciated children, while a narrator told TV viewers, "Hunger is hard to recognize in America. We know it in other places like Asia and Africa. But these children, all of them, are Americans. And all of them are hungry" (quoted in Raphael, 2005, p. 43). Then the camera fades to a doctor, who is trying without success to resuscitate a newborn baby who is dying of starvation. Scenes of malnourished families on Navajo reservations, an African American woman with ten hungry young children in Alabama, and poor Mexican children in San Antonio, Texas evoke the aesthetic of New Deal photography, says Raphael. While the poor are allowed to speak of their circumstances, their voices are framed by expert analysis and the interviews take place "against the iconographic and stereotypical backgrounds of rural poverty (interiors of shacks, the fields, amidst large families)" rather than government hearings or political organizing activities like the Poor People's Campaign of the era (Raphael, 2005, p. 59). While *Hunger in America* advocates expanding food aid and federal hunger programs, it reproduces the conventions of documentation traced so far by presenting the poor as helpless victims to a more powerful and privileged audience expected to be sympathetic to their cause.

Precarity and the State of Insecurity

Since the 1970s, the "state of welfare" has been under assault. Critics across the political spectrum have contested the welfare programs created during the 1930s and the 1960s, and advocated the unregulated free market as the best way to manage social life. During the 1980s, this discourse took on a racialized dimension as conservatives demonized the poor as "undeserving" people of color, inventing the stereotype of the welfare queen to undermine white middle-class support for welfare programs (Raphael, 2005, p. 56). In the 1990s, the push to "de-statize" welfare was distanced to some extent from overt racism (Duggan, 2004) and linked to neoliberal ethics of personal empowerment and "freedom" from government dependency. Everyone of all genders, races, and social circumstances was called upon to "maximize" their freedom and "optimize" their futures. Within this shifting context, the will to document the passive victims of poverty lost currency.

On television, reality-based entertainment (the makeover, the competition show) proliferated, proving itself more synchronic with the market rationales and self-enterprising expectations of the neoliberal era. Reality shows transformed the victims of documentary into enterprising subjects by inviting "real-life" families coded as poor and working class to perform stereotypical versions of themselves—and achieve a (temporary) career and even minor celebrity status in the process. These programs work in tandem with "governing through insecurity" (Lorey, 2015) by ritualistically narrating, and helping to inculcate, the self-enterprise, competitive ethos, and perpetual "hustle" expected of neoliberal personhood.

While documentary exposés of poverty have appeared from time to time, there's been no equivalent to the surge of reformist documentary evidenced during the Progressive Era, the 1930s, and the 1960s—until now. In recent years, a cluster of television documentaries have taken TV viewers inside the lives of families residing in rundown residential motels (*Poor Kids*, PBS, 2012), supporting themselves on minimum wage (*Paycheck to Paycheck*, HBO, 2015), and coping with generational rural poverty (*Rich Hill*, PBS, 2014). These productions recognize the persistence of poverty in the neoliberal era, but offer few solutions. Indeed, reflecting the divestment of state responsibility for the poor and the self-enterprising ethic of the current conjuncture, some documentary producers have taken to setting up crowdsourced GoFundMe sites for the impoverished subjects of their films. Addressed to TV viewers imagined to be securely middle class, this wave of documentary attempts to humanize and elicit empathy for the poor—a gesture that makes a certain amount of sense at a time when right-wing politicians (especially since the election of Trump) feel entitled to blame the economically disenfranchised for their circumstances. However, these reformist projects also reproduce the class voyeurism, passive victim motif, uneven power dynamics, stereotypes, and impetus to classify the deserving and undeserving poor of earlier eras.

Since the financial crisis, another strand of documentary has taken viewers inside the financial circumstances and affective experiences of downwardly mobile families who once identified as middle class. Some productions document first-time experiences of unemployment, financial troubles and social dislocation (*Downsized*, WEtv, 2010; *Hard Times: Lost on Long Island*, HBO, 2012), while others document the precarious socioeconomic circumstances of people referred to as the "shrinking middle class" (*My Reality: A Hidden America*, ABC, 2017). Documenting eight ambiguously classed families, *American Winter* (HBO, 2013) promises an intimate look at human costs of the recession long after the economy was said to have bounced back. Filmed in Portland, Oregon during the deep chill of winter, the documentary begins with an audio compilation of dozens of calls to 211, a nonprofit telephone referral service for people who need food, shelter, utilities, and other necessities. This cacophony of voices establishes the needy as an amorphous "multitude" (Negri & Hardt, 2004) that far exceeds the marginalized "others" and pockets of poverty familiar from previous documentaries. Weaving together interviews with families selected from the 211 exchange, observational footage of the participants in their daily lives, and interviews with experts (social workers, politicians, local business people), *American Winter* attributes the mounting financial insecurities of a broad swathe of city residents on diminished social services. One takeaway is that the downsized safety net is too frayed to be very helpful to 211 callers—and by extension the "shrinking middle class" writ large. Another is that people at risk are not "others," but potentially all of us. At a time when "46 million Americans are living in poverty, or near poverty—the highest number of poor since we began keeping records, *American Winter* seeks to bring a human face to these statistics," claim the directors. According to the program's website, the goal is to expose how "In the Richest Country on Earth, Millions of People have been Left Out in the Cold."

American Winter simultaneously reproduces and unsettles the conventions of poverty documentary. According to the directors, the program aims to challenge "myths and stereotypes" about who needs help by revealing the commonalities of different "families who have lost their jobs and can't find work, or who are working full time and overtime, yet don't make enough to pull their families out of poverty" (Ganz, 2013). Despite the use of the term poverty, the families are ambiguously classed: some graduated college and have recent memories of financial security, others live with remnants of the middle-class "good life" acquired during better times. Their direct testimony to the camera, along with observational footage of their daily lives and expert commentary on the "decline" of the middle class, position *American Winter* as a precarity document, a catalogue of the generalized precaritization discussed by Lorey (2015). Here, social experience is marked not only by acute economic hardship in the present but by an anxious structure of feeling about the future (Berlant, Butler, Cvejic, Lorey, & Vujanovic, 2012; Lorey, 2015). The audience is offered multiple points of entry into the intersecting insecurities and vulnerabilities that compose this structure of feeling. Many of the participants describe feelings of worry and shame; in one scene, a white woman who imagines herself to be middle class becomes nervous and cries when she visits a food bank for the first time. Children situated amidst the accoutrements of the consumerist "good life" (ranch house, large screen TV) describe the embarrassment of having their electricity shut off or having to eat meals at friends' houses because there is no food. A middle-aged white man who has lost his accounting job and is facing the foreclosure of his home says he feels inadequate when forced to borrow money from his parents to care for his son, who has Down syndrome. While the subjects of the documentary do not critique the infrastructures of neoliberal capitalism, they are invited to have a "voice" in narrating its experiential consequences (Couldry, 2010)—a rare opportunity in contemporary media culture. This potentially disrupts the distance between the objectified poor and audiences who may share these anxieties and fears.

However, by highlighting the experience of people who have lost secure middle-class status, *American Winter* downplays the structural dimensions and continued unevenness of precarity. As Lorey reminds us, "precarity in capitalism is nothing new." Insecurity in working and living has been the "norm for many people under industrial capitalism," with the state of welfare as the exception. It has long been distributed according to relations of inequality that depend on "processes of Othering" (Lorey in Berlant et al., 2012, p. 165). *American Winter* perpetuates this hierarchy by downplaying racial, gender, and class inequalities and positioning the precarious as victims of unfortunate events (such as job loss). Sympathy is engendered by positioning the featured families against historical constructions of the "undeserving" (lazy, entitled, dishonest) poor and classed and racialized populations trapped in a dysfunctional "cycle of poverty." The documentary takes great pains to cast its precarious characters as moral, industrious citizens who have "never needed help" before and, in the case of the accountant, would "clean toilets" to provide for his family and avoid dependency on social services. The only African American to be featured, a single mother with a useless for-profit college degree struggling to raise a family on minimum wage, speaks of selling her plasma and is shown "scrapping" at junkyards during her off hours to make ends meet—activities that affirm her status as deserving, and distance her from the stereotype of the welfare queen. While raising the possibility that we are *all* precarious now, *American Winter* perpetuates a moral hierarchy of neediness.

American Winter presents its human subjects as evidence to support an understanding that social services are crucial and worthy of continued support. Throughout the documentary, experts from the nonprofit, public, and private sectors argue that it is in the interest of US society to assist the needy and help lift families out of poverty. The shrinking safety net is called into question by many of these experts, including a local entrepreneur who explains that it is cheaper to assist poor families than not, given the productivity needs of the capitalist economy. While *American Winter* advocates a progressive challenge to neoliberal policies, it also reproduces the uneven power dynamics of earlier approaches to poverty documentation. The precarious subjects of the film bear the burden of the flexible economy, but they are not treated as experts. While they are invited to share their experiences and emotions, they are not invited to assess and critique their circumstances in broader sociopolitical terms. By focusing on individuals who never meet, the documentary also downplays solidarity and activism among the disenfranchised and dispossessed. While the individualized stories combine to suggest a shared experience of economic struggle at odds with the fantasy of the "good life," connections among the participants aren't explored. Still, repetitive scenes of anxious and displaced everyday life, framed by the recurring chorus of overlapping voices calling into the 211 hotline, suggest a common experience that exceeds the boundaries of liberal ideology and neoliberal exceptionalism.

Unlike *American Winter*, the reality television series *The Briefcase* does not attempt to situate precarity within a "social problem" framework. The opening sequence reminds TV viewers that "Across America, hard-working families are feeling the impact of rising debts and shrinking paychecks," but there are no experts on hand to explain why, or offer solutions. The formula hinges on a different enigma—whether struggling Americans who have lost sight of the "good life," or have always lived on its outer edges, will act selfishly or with collective interests in mind in the aftermath of a financial windfall. Families who have been told they are participating in a documentary about money problems are enlisted in a multilayered form of close observation within this experimental framework. On the one hand, participants and by extension TV viewers at home are asked to peer inside the intimate lives of another family and gather "facts" about their daily circumstances and needs. At the same time, the audience is called upon to observe the participants as they grapple with whether or not to share the $100,000 with their peers. The voyeurism is complicated by the "ordinariness" of the subjects, who are not presented as poor others, but rather as representatives of a downward shift in economic security that impacts "millions" of Americans. As with *American Winter*, the everyday hardships on display (massive debt, unemployment, minimum wages, lack of affordable health insurance) are repetitive across the families and are cued as problems the TV audience may face as well.

Reinforcing the moral classification of the poor, the inspection consistently reveals that the families on *The Briefcase* are "deserving." In the opening episode, one family lives in a middle-class suburban house, but is actually deeply in debt and virtually without income. The father was laid off and has been unable to find work; he and his wife started a neighborhood ice cream business, but their truck is broken down and they can't afford to fix it. Inside the house, appliances are broken, the refrigerator is nearly empty, and bills are everywhere. When they investigate their compatriots—a pregnant nurse, her husband, who lost a leg in the Iraq war, and their small child—they discover a cramped apartment that is not equipped for disability, overwhelming debt, and a breadwinner (the wife) forced to work long hours of overtime. There is no ambiguity here about whether or not help is needed; indeed, after examining the tiny apartment, the female ice cream truck entrepreneur becomes so upset she vomits on camera. On one hand, this reinforces the legacy of the victim tradition, with its "worthy" poor who must do everything right to earn the empathy of reformers and audiences. At the same time, it constitutes empathy as reciprocal, rather than top down. While critics lambasted *The Briefcase* for its voyeurism and judgmental framework, the similar socioeconomic status of the show's participants actually complicates the class voyeurism and uneven power dynamics so common to liberal reformist documentary. The upset woman, for example, tells her husband that she identifies with the needy family they have spied on, explaining "they remind me of us when we were younger." When both families decide to split the contents of the briefcase, they refuse to adopt the selfish self-protectionism theorized by Lorey as a tactic of neoliberal "governing through insecurity." In this sense, a type of collectivity registers (filtered through commercial television's conventions) as an alternative to competition and market values.

The Briefcase emphasizes differences within neoliberal precarity—even if structural inequalities are ignored. The struggling families are often partnered with "opposite" types—as is typical on reality television. Everyone is living with the material and affective dimensions of acute financial distress—but within this shared condition diversity is emphasized. Families with racial, ethnic, religious, political, and physical differences are encouraged through the formula to identify their precarious commonalities, but must also negotiate their receptiveness to social experiences and values that may not be their own. On one episode, a family featuring a Latino trans man, his wife, and their child is partnered with a conservative Christian white family. The pairing is done to enhance drama in the vein of "cross cultural" reality programs like *Wife Swap* (ABC, 2004–2013). However, it also constitutes generalized precaritization as a condition—and a point of commonality—that cuts across many social and cultural differences. This in turn raises the possibility of collective action.

The Briefcase does not promote this type of activism. As with *American Winter*, precarious subjects "voice" their feelings and experiences but do not critique neoliberal conditions (including the dismantled safety net). Still, it is significant that the families always agree to split the money, in some combination or another. However stage-managed by producers, this solution to widespread precarity feels authentic in the context of the reciprocal empathy the program narrates and encourages. At a conjuncture when we are all called upon to think and act in self-interested market terms, this small gesture toward a communal ethic of care and responsibility partly ruptures the all-encompassing ideology of capitalist realism (Fisher, 2009). *The Briefcase* does not incite political critique, but it does allow us to see and feel the dispersion of precarity outside the liberal reformist reformist paradigm. In so doing it moves the will to document to a potentially different register.

Works Cited

Berlant, L. (2011). *Cruel optimism*. Durham, NC: Duke University Press.

Berlant, L., Butler, J., Cvejic, B., Lorey, I., & Vujanovic, A. (2012). Precarity talk: A virtual roundtable. *The Drama Review, 56*(4), 163–177.

Bourdieu, P. (1984 [1979]). *Distinction: A social critique of the judgment of taste* (R. Nice, Trans.). London, UK: Routledge.

Charbonneau, S. (2016). *Projecting race: Postwar America, civil rights and documentary film*. London, UK: Wallflower Press.

Couldry, N. (2010). *Why voice matters: Culture and politics after neoliberalism*. London, UK: Sage.
Curtin, M. (1995). *Redeeming the wasteland: Television documentary and Cold War politics*. New Brunswick, NJ: Rutgers University Press.
Duggan, L. (2004). *The twilight of inequality: Neoliberalism, cultural politics and the attack on democracy*. Boston, MA: Beacon Press.
Ehrenreich, B. (1990). *Fear of falling: The inner life of the middle class*. New York, NY: Harper Perrenial.
Fisher, M. (2009). *Capitalist realism: Is there no alternative?* Winchester, UK: Zero Books.
Foucault, M. (1977). Nietzsche, genealogy, history. In D. Bouchard (Ed.), *Language, counter-memory, practice: Selected essays and interviews* (pp. 139–164). Ithaca, NY: Cornell University Press.
Ganz, J. (2013, April 5). American Winter: It's a cold reality for millions of struggling families. *Huffington Post*. Retrieved from http://www.huffingtonpost.com/joe-gantz/american-winter-its-a_b_3021514.html
Harrington, M. (1962). *The other America: Poverty in the United States*. New York, NY: Penguin.
Katz, M. (2013). *The undeserving poor: America's enduring confrontation with poverty*. New York, NY: Oxford University Press.
Kunst, B. (2015). The institution between precarization and participation. *Performance Research*, *20*(4), 6–13.
Lorey, I. (2015). *State of insecurity: Government of the precarious*. London, UK: Verso.
Martineau, B.H. (1989). Talking about our lives and experiences: Some thoughts about feminism, documentary and talking heads. In T. Waugh (Ed.), *Show us life: Toward a history and aesthetics of the committed film*. Lanham, MD: Scarecrow Press.
Miller, H. (2017, March 7). Jason Chaffetz: Poor people shouldn't buy iPhones if they need money for health care. *Huffington Post*. Retrieved from http://www.huffingtonpost.com/entry/jason-chaffetz-iphone-health-care_us_58bea6aae4b09ab537d6a395
Negri, A., & Hardt, M. (2004). *Multitude: War and democracy in the age of empire*. New York, NY: Penguin.
Palmer, G. (2014). The wild bunch: Men, labor, and reality television. In L. Ouellette (Ed.), *A companion to reality television* (pp. 247–263). Malden, MA: Wiley-Blackwell.
Price, D. (1997). Surveyors and surveyed. In L. Wells (Ed.), *Photography: A critical introduction* (pp. 33–102). London, UK: Routledge.
Rabinowitz, P. (1994) *They must be represented: The politics of documentary*. London, UK: Verso.
Raphael, C. (2005). *Investigated reporting: Muckrakers, regulators, and the struggle over television documentary*. Urbana and Chicago, IL: University of Illinois Press.
Riis, J. (1971 [1890]). *How the other half lives*. New York, NY: Dover.
Rose, N. (1996). Governing 'advanced' liberal democracies. In A. Berry, T. Osbourne, & N. Rose (Eds.), *Foucault and political reason: Liberalism, neoliberalism and rationalities of government* (pp. 37–46). Chicago, IL: University of Chicago Press.
Rosler, M. (1989). In, around, and afterthoughts (on documentary photography). In R. Bolton (Ed.), *The contest of meaning: Critical histories of photography* (pp. 303–342). Cambridge, MA: MIT Press.
Sheffield, R., & Rector, R. (2011). *Air conditioning, cable TV., Xbox: What is poverty in the United States today?* Washington, DC: Heritage Foundation.
Stott, W. (1986). *Documentary expression and thirties America*. Chicago, IL: University of Chicago Press.

Tagg, J. (1993). *The burden of representation: Essays on photographies and histories*. Minneapolis, MN: University of Minnesota Press.

Winston, B. (1991). The tradition of the victim in Grierson documentary. In L. Gross, J.S. Katz, & J. Ruby (Eds.), *Image ethics: The moral rights of subjects in photographs, film and television*. Cambridge, UK: Oxford University Press.

Yochelson, B., & Czitrom, D. (2007). *Rediscovering Jacob Riis: Exposure journalism and photography in turn-of-the-century New York*. Chicago, IL: University of Chicago Press.

PART III

Media Leisure/Labor

8

THE WORKING CLASS, ORDINARY CELEBRITY, AND "ILLEGITIMATE" CULTURAL WORK

Helen Wood, Jilly Boyce Kay, and Mark Banks

Introduction

In the last decade or so, there has been an increased academic interest in the rise of "ordinary celebrity" (Turner, 2014; Williamson, 2016). Chris Rojek (2001) has coined the term the "celetoid" to refer to an individual who gains notoriety without any discernible cultural talent, often via the visibilities afforded by reality television. Much of the literature surrounding this figure focuses on it as part of the celebrity economy, which invites new forms of self-commodification and performance "labour"—and yet there is curiously very little interrogation of this form of celebrity work *as work*. This chapter argues for attending closely to the labour of ordinary celebrity, its relation to broader inequalities within work and employment, its denigration as a form of "illegitimate" labour, and its relationship to the structural formations of class.

As we go on to show, some critics, particularly in journalistic discourse, have settled on a moralising view of ordinary celebrity as exemplifying the worst excesses of "workshy" working-class narcissism and vulgarity, whilst other commentators (and many academics) have tended to view such celebrities as victims of an advanced capitalist media industry that exploits and degrades in equal measure. Yet each perspective contains very little consideration of the actual *work* that is involved in becoming or being an ordinary celebrity; our knowledge of workers' *time* and *toil*—how their labour is empirically embodied, lived, and exploited—remains obscure. Furthermore, we know little about participants' motivations to partake in such work, or the pleasures and rewards they might gain from it, beyond simplistic understandings of them as being narcissistic, naïve or "fame hungry." Could such work actually provide other goods or benefits—akin to that of conventional work perhaps?

In this chapter, we want to interrogate the ways in which the terms of labour are deployed in the literature around "reality" celebrity. It begins by outlining the structural changes within the media industries that have facilitated the rise of ordinary celebrity, and how reality television and social media in particular have generated new labour models and forms of exploitation. It then considers how, in broader cultural narratives, reality celebrity is seen as both responsible for and emblematic of the moral decline of the working classes, and in particular as having destroyed a traditional ethic of what in British English is known as "graft" (or "honest labour" in the US).[1] It moves to review the academic literature, where reality celebrity labour has most often been analysed via the reality television text; we argue that in order to adequately theorise its labour relations we must also pay attention to the time and investments of workers as well as the organisational structures that pre-exist and circulate beyond the text. We then consider examples of reality celebrity work in order to suggest that this allegedly superficial and contentless activity is both a form of "immaterial" labour *and* involves forms of mental and corporeal toil that connect it with older, more conventional forms of industrial labour, both through the time investments of its workers and the tolls it takes on the working-class body. We conclude with a general plea for more sustained and situated investigation into the labour politics, practices, and organisation of ordinary celebrity.

The Structural Changes That Enable Reality Celebrity

In recent decades, the definition of celebrity has been expanded to incorporate "ordinary celebrity" (Williamson, 2016), the "real celebrity" (Turner, 2014), "reality celebrity" (Curnutt, 2009; Grindstaff & Murray, 2015), "DIY celebrity" (Turner, 2014), or "celetoids" (Rojek, 2001). Many of these terms imply the much more visible presence of the working class within celebrity culture—for instance, through the intensified visibility of so-called "celebrity chavs" (Tyler & Bennett, 2010). The category of "celebrity" has been fundamentally reconfigured by its apparent new openness to people whose fame is not generated through traditional notions of talent, but rather through a performance of spectacularised ordinariness, or the subjection of one's body and "life force" to intimate, public scrutiny (Kokoli & Winter, 2015).

While in popular discourse ordinary celebrity is seen to have emerged either from the individualised psychological deficits of young people, or through the rise of a more advanced and pathological cultural narcissism, such explanations serve to efface the profound changes in the structural conditions of the media industries. For instance, the rise of reality television has clearly been a driver of these new models of fame (Williamson, 2016). Television has always mobilised forms of celebrity based on "personality" rather than the more distant "star" figure, but reality television has more intensively exploited the medium's affinity with the ordinary (Holmes, 2004). This desire to engage with the ordinary is also a commercial strategy necessitated by increases in competition and technological change. Whether competing for public funding or commercial income, broadcasters and producers must seek to extract maximum value from minimum inputs. Reality productions offer significant advantages in this respect: lucrative returns are enabled by low setup and production costs and the genre's foundational reliance on a pool of non-unionised, low-paid or unpaid labour, both front- and backstage (Andrejevic, 2004, 2011; Jost, 2011; Mayer, 2011; Williamson, 2016). Indeed, reality television has pioneered the use of dubious employment contracts, payments through "perks," and bars to accessing unions, all of which are recognisable in other forms of capitalist exploitation. Andrew Ross (2014, p. 32) notes how reality television gained the status of a "scab genre" within the US television industry for taking commercial advantage of writers' strikes and undercutting unionised labour. Ross also points to reality television's central role in restructuring the creative industries into "doughnut economies" with a high-wage core and a large periphery of precarious workers (ibid.).

Reality television has also pioneered the use of mobile, flexible production technologies and more "authentic" (cheaper, less polished, and less "professional") filmic styles. Simultaneously, reality television now operates in a co-constitutive relationship with less regulated digital and social media platforms, which provide an important context for the growth of what Graeme Turner (2014, p.70) calls "DIY celebrity." As a result of these changes, the possibility of becoming a "micro-celebrity" (Senft, 2013; Marwick, 2013) is extended to allow the individual to exploit the capacities of "broadcasting yourself" (to cite YouTube), and user-generated content is deployed extensively to extend the personality "brand." Reality celebrities themselves must make use of many alternative spaces to preserve their visibility, often in order to maintain their ongoing relevance to the more "legitimate" channels of the mainstream media industries (Curnutt, 2011). So there is a significant blurring here between "accessible" forms of celebrity (self) production and the organisational practices of exploitation by the television industry. The term "labour" is often now used to describe all such mediated practices; however, as Milly Williamson (2016) suggests, we must maintain a distinction between forms of consumer labour performed via social media which are *commodified* and labour which is directly *exploited*. It is true that "micro-celebrity" is significantly constituted by new forms of "self-work" and "performance labour" which exist outside the employment relation. However, as we argue, we must not neglect the labour of ordinary celebrity that operates *within* this relation; that is to say, labour that is exploited because it generates surplus value for capital, and labour undertaken in direct exchange for income within a relationship of economic dependency. We must not lose sight of the fact that this is a form of work under capitalism and that it is at once distinctive and pioneering, but also continuous with, and comparable to, "conventional" work in the broader economy.

Fools, Shirkers, and the Decline of the Working Class

The very intense resistance towards considering reality celebrity as "work" tells us something of the current climate in which certain kinds of work are valued and legitimated. Writing in 2001, for Chris Rojek, "celetoids" were lottery winners and one-hit wonders whose stories were ultimately disposable. More recently, Rojek has identified the cultural figure of the "fool," whose celebrity is not necessarily temporary and yet is ultimately devoid of agency or hope:

> They become life-long celetoids, but their careers are fatefully constrained by the label that they wear around their neck. The essence of the natural fool is not to develop but to remain the permanent, misshapen naif. They are not "anybodies," they are fools. They are ritually defined and culturally confined. This is the immoveable straitjacket of their celebrity existence. (Rojek, 2012, p. 172)

Such "fools" are also often implicitly positioned as belonging to the working class. Particularly in the UK, within the broader context of austerity and intensifying disgust for the unemployed (Tyler, 2008), reality celebrity has come to symbolise the antithesis of commitment to a career—rather, it signifies a particular kind of narcissistic worklessness, being "workshy," or even pursuing unemployment as a "lifestyle choice." Here reality celebrity appears as an affront to the ideals of meritocracy, the fair reward of talent, and of an honest wage for an honest day's work. These ideas have also gained popular currency around the fears over young people's aspirations. For example, a 2014 article from the Labour-supporting tabloid the *Daily Mirror* lamented reality celebrities' status as "role models" for children:

> [They are] people who are famous for absolutely no reason whatsoever. They just turn up at nightclubs or the launch of a fake tan brand, have their picture taken, pocket some cash and go home again. Now I really do wonder what job satisfaction Joey Essex, Sam Faiers[2] and their like get from their so-called careers? What have they contributed to society? What difference have they made to the world? Can they go home at night and look back at their day and think that it really was worthwhile? (Killelea, 2014)

This discourse of ordinary celebrities accruing undeserved rewards is also evident in the conservative press; for example, an article from 2015 in the broadsheet *The Daily Telegraph* lamented the lack of role models for working-class white children, specifically pointing to "ghastly" reality television as the problem: "Not only are poor white children shown a standard of behaviour based on drunkenness and stupidity (and mocked for it by the country as a whole), they're told such behaviour is rewarded with fame and fortune" (Kirkup, 2015). Similarly, a 2012 GirlGuiding report discussed a "role model deficit" for young girls within celebrity culture, pointing to the pervasive and unfortunate influence of shows like *The Only Way Is Essex* on young women (see BBC, 2012). Here the burden of "value"—of being a "role model" for the working classes, and of "making a difference to the world"—is placed at the feet of the reality celebrity. It does so in a way which perhaps harks back to and laments the decline of an industrial society, where value could be more visibly seen in the end product of labour—when working-class "graft" or hard labour was "productive," masculinised, and perhaps more humbly undertaken in service to the needs of an industrial economy.

However, while "celebrity" is often invoked to narrate a history of moral decline in the labour force, it is important to note that there are classed and gendered distinctions in the way that it is (de)valued and (de)legitimised. For example, Kim Allen and Heather Mendick (2013) analysed young people's talk about celebrity for the ways it structured their ideas about their own educational and work futures (see also Mendick et al., forthcoming). While for many of their interviewees, reality celebrity was seen as lacking worth, for others—and particularly working-class young women—it was seen as an "opportunity structure" (2013, p. 87, drawing on Skeggs & Wood, 2008). For example, while Jade Goody (the now deceased British celebrity whose media career originated in the British *Big Brother*) was widely positioned in the broader culture as illegitimate and undeserving of her wealth because of her poor education and "low" intelligence, for many working-class young women, her "graft" was acknowledged and valued. For example, Anusha, a working-class arts student, said of Goody: "She's clever and she's worked hard for what she's got and she ain't changed for no one either, [...] so I've got a lot of respect for her" (Allen & Mendick, 2013, p. 88).

Dominant narratives which frame young people's "choice" to pursue media visibility in pathological terms also chime with fears over the decline of a more "authentic" and morally valuable working class. For instance, Andrew O'Hagan laments "a working class [who] were no longer a working class [....they were now] people who craved not values but designer labels and satellite dishes" (cited in Todd, 2014, p.5). An ideology of lack of achievement and catastrophically misdirected aspiration is therefore part of a broader culture of blame in which the working class are made individually responsible for the conditions in which they find themselves (Skeggs & Wood, 2012). According to Tyler and Bennett (2010) celebrity "chavs"—and most especially women—are figured as embodying this moral collapse of the working class. By fusing welfare dependency with excessive consumption, these celebrities stand accused of promoting a "something for nothing" culture to which the young and poor are especially in thrall.

Lifestyle and reality television has in the last two decades drawn on the economically fruitful "spectacularization of the working class" as figures of failure in need of improvement in the neoliberal landscape (Wood & Skeggs, 2008). But in more recent years this trope has intensified precisely around the terms of work and *lack* of labour, seeking out spectacles of "worklessness." In the UK, the moniker "poverty porn" has come to describe a particular version of reality television which focuses on "benefits cheats," "shirkers," and "scroungers"—for example *Benefits Street* (Love Productions/Channel 4, 2014); *The Great Big Benefits Handout* (Dragonfly/Channel 5, 2016); and *Gypsies on Benefits and Proud* (Channel 5, 2014). There seems to be an increasing symbolic entanglement between media visibility on the one hand, and "dependency" on state welfare payments on the other, whilst the proliferation of this television genre and its affinities with tabloid newspaper coverage means that participants coded as belonging to an "underclass" are courting some of the perks afforded by media attention. In other programmes like MTV's *Geordie Shore* (2011–) in which working-class youth party, drink, and have sex, participants seemingly stage a nightmarish possible future in which the workless—liberated from the responsibilising qualities of wage labour, and intoxicated by the spoils of consumer capitalism—spend their time shamelessly indulging in the unproductive pursuits of hyper-glamour, hyper-sex, and hyper-emotion (Wood, 2017). They are the "revolting subjects" of contemporary neoliberal culture (Tyler, 2013) and some are seemingly shamelessly basking in the opportunities afforded by media visibility.

Reality Television: "The Work of Being Watched"

In the core literature, various commentators have of course evaluated reality TV participation as the "work of being watched." Mark Andrejevic (2004) adroitly outlines how reality television participation can be conceived as related to Fordist models of monitoring the health and well-being of the workforce. Regimes of surveillance are highly attuned to capitalist modes of enhanced production, and he describes how forms of reality television then help to acculturate audiences into the normalisation of "being watched" in the service of the capitalist economy. Bev Skeggs and Helen Wood (2012) situate the imperatives of reality television in a longer history of the measurement "the self"; many others see the genre as giving ideological force to particular neoliberal cultures of work through its representational practices. For example, scholars like Laurie Ouellette and James Hay (2008), utilising ideas of governmentality, see this move as part of the pedagogic function of reality television, which "teaches" audiences how to position themselves flexibly in relation to the shifting demands of the contemporary labour market.

This emphasis upon reality television's role in the teaching of self-branding techniques—as part of a broader culture of surveillance—seems to assume that it works rather straightforwardly on the naïve audience. Skeggs and Wood's (2012) research, on the other hand, understands the more ambiguous function of texts, as audiences must locate themselves within circulating ideas of person value. The notion that audiences straightforwardly accept the commodification of subjectivity and its reification of consumer capital also tends to support ideas about the role of ordinary celebrity in eroding civic culture and collectivity, which is what renders it so disturbing to many social critics. This scholarship can therefore function to frame many of the popular arguments that see reality television participants as victims of the powerful regimes of neoliberal governance who naïvely collude in their own exploitation. Much of this particular critique sees reality television's idea of "work" as brokered through an ideological attachment to neoliberal ideas of "self-branding." For instance, Hearn (2008, p. 213) argues that:

> The phenomenon of self-branding can be understood as labour in its simplest sense as "the process by which people transform nature into objects of their imagination" (Burawoy, 1979, p. 15). Indeed, the production of self must always involve some form of labour in order to create a public persona that might be of practical or relational use.

"Self-branding" becomes labour because of its returns to the industry, suggesting the ultimate absorption of "the self" into the service of capital. As such, it is understood here that all aspects of life in post-industrial societies are absorbed into models of capitalist production where affective and immaterial labour are constitutive of the production of value (see Hardt & Negri, 2005; Lazzarato, 1996). In this context, reality television and its diffuse incorporation of individuals into various practices of branding "stands out as at the forefront of new models of capitalist value generation" (Hearn, 2017, p. 12).

We do not necessarily reject that position, but we want to point to some crucial parts of the process that we see as sometimes missing from this critique. Firstly, we suggest the need for a more precise understanding of the economically valuable *time* of celebrity labour as it is actually spent to add value to the assets (here the TV programme or the celebrity commodity). What is the socially necessary labour-time, in Marxist terms, that is expended in these new sets of relations? Or what is the "real" work involved, on and off camera? The way that value is created, and transferred through time from inputs into outputs, cannot (only) be captured by a critique of the end product or text. In fact, we argue that some critiques which concentrate only on the television text might themselves contribute to the fetishisation of the celebrity commodity—by reading off the patterns of "affective labour" without attention to the actual time, effort, and investment in production which pre-exist and circulate beyond the text. Secondly, we propose a more complex focus on the celebrity worker-subject. We know little about the meanings and uses of ordinary celebrity work for those who choose to undertake it—in terms of the ethical or normative values, as well as the different kinds of benefits and rewards it might afford. How is the worker understandable as a conscious, motivated (and labouring) agent, *as well as* a subject of exploitation?

There has of course been some valuable empirical academic research into the motivations and practices of those people who appear on reality television and attempt to forge careers as "ordinary celebrities." For instance, Laura Grindstaff's (2009) interviews with character-participants on MTV's *Sorority Life* illuminate the affective pull of reality celebrity in its implicit promise to give recognition and value to lives, bodies, and identities that are otherwise not legitimated within dominant social and political orders. As Grindstaff has noted, the desire for celebrity is too often easily conflated with the personal, psychological desire for exposure or fame; she suggests that such explanations have dominated due to the paucity of more situated analyses of "the activities, practices and talk of those who produce these texts, from both behind and in front of the camera" (2009, p. 84). We take our cue from Grindstaff to argue that more empirical research is required to understand comprehensively the range of reasons why people—and most especially working-class people—might wish to take up such work, which might include (say) the need to make a material living, to achieve a social standing, have a voice within the public sphere, or secure some sense of control by escaping an inherited social fate.

Revaluing the Work of Ordinary Celebrity

Devalued celebrities must operate intensively *across* different and multiple media in order to sustain themselves commercially, and yet, despite the efforts, energies, and *time* that this requires, their practices are conceptualised as a rejection rather than an embrace of work. The effect of reality celebrity's association with "non-work" domains of intimate life and leisure time has been to occlude the managed and intense forms of biopolitical labour that are, in fact, intrinsic to it. For example, Kokoli and Winter (2015, p. 166) discuss how Jade Goody had to work to a schedule of weight loss and gain that was strategically planned for up to six months in advance to capitalise on the post-Christmas workout DVD market. For them, such labor fully involves and consumes the human body and its capacities as a living organism. Weight gain and weight loss, pregnancy, physical transformation through plastic surgery, physical symptoms of emotional distress, and even illness and death are all photographically documented and supplemented by extended textual commentary, usually with direct input from the celebrity (Kokoli & Winter, 2015, p. 157).

Occasionally this strategic manipulation of celebrities' bodies is discussed in popular discourse—for example, a former British celebrity magazine writer writing in the *i* newspaper (Barrett, 2016) describes "the tell-tale signs that a [fitness] DVD is on its way": firstly, there will be a series of pap shots from the celebrity's holiday. Their weight gain is immediately made obvious in several ways: the subject will be grabbing their belly, tucking into a huge portion of fish and chips, drinking a pint of beer, or walking down the beach with no makeup or a fake tan on.

Unflattering workout photos are then taken by a paparazzi photographer who "just happens" to be passing. And finally, there is the "unveiling" of the new body which coincides with the official announcement of the DVD, and which usually involves the celebrity standing next to a cardboard cutout of the overweight "before" image of themselves. This writer draws a distinction between "bona fide celebrity DVD workouts" and those made by reality TV stars, who are only in it for "an easy paycheck" and are "often promoting themselves rather than inspiring a desire for good health." As such, their motivations for participating in such work are denigrated as simple "self-promotion." It is "easy" money, with its implications of undeservingness and an absence of any legitimate labour; and their desire for a "paycheck" is not associated with any reasonable need to make a material living, but only with greed, narcissism, and acquisitiveness. We would insist here that these practices must be understood as labour that takes place within an agreed contractual or employment relationship; and that, furthermore, it is not an "easy" way of making money, but rather involves embodied labour, intensive corporeal toil, and the significant and calculated investment of time and effort akin to other kinds of embodied work.

Such work can be understood as typical of the array of portfolio activities and bodywork now intrinsic to the labour of ordinary celebrity. In similar terms, Helen Wood (2017) has detailed how the participants on MTV's *Geordie Shore* (2011–) generate income by exploiting their recognisability as they sell their labour at promotional appearances in nightclubs, among other forms of precarious paid work. Celebrities must work intensively to sustain their media visibility while simultaneously defending themselves from criticisms that they are "fame whores." And yet celebrity work may simply offer a better or more attractive option than other forms of work, given that many such celebrities tend to come from working-class backgrounds where low pay, low status, and insecure forms of employment are now more systemically entrenched.

The denigration of reality celebrities as "fame whores" is clearly deeply gendered, and it is women in particular who stand accused of narcissism, attention-seeking, and sexualised self-objectification as they use their bodies and intimate lives to make a living. Hearn (2017) suggests that some of the invisible labour practices of reality television are similar to what Maria Mies (2007) refers to as the "housewifization" of contemporary labour more broadly. That is to say, the gendered, invisible, and unregulated labour models of domestic work have spread outwards to the precarious work of the informal economy. While reality celebrity labour is increasingly "housewifized" for all its workers, it is important to attend to the gendered distinctions in the labour models within this category. For example, reality celebrities' nightclub appearances, Christmas light switch-ons, and supermarket openings predictably require different aesthetics and behaviours from men and women. These celebrities' social media accounts often read as constant streams of product placements for muscle-building protein shakes, gym-wear and their own nightclub businesses (men), and for weight-loss supplements, fake tans, hair extensions, and their own fitness DVDs (women). For women, the patterns of weight gain and loss, binge drinking, hangovers and detox, depression, and emotional renewal become highly exaggerated and the cycles carefully managed via their media appearances and engagements. Brenda Weber and Jennifer Lyn Jones (2014) introduce the term "transmediated grotesque" to capture the ways in which abject, female reality celebrities deploy their talents to keep themselves visible across a variety of mediated platforms, including reality television, social media, pornography, tabloids, and magazines. They are routinely reviled for doing so, but their financial rewards stem from the self-same practices for which they are condemned. Yet, again, while devalued and hidden as a form of labour, we should note that such work not only requires both sustained effort and involvement of its exponents, but that it is planned for, constructed, and managed in the context of a set of work relations that are somewhat more traditional in their organisation and techniques of value extraction than is commonly recognised.

More generally, we are interested in the reasons why the flexible (even entrepreneurial) orientations to the economy exhibited by ordinary celebrities are so intensively devalued whilst other forms of "portfolio" work in the media and creative industries are highly prized. Such forms of celebrity work are not so completely removed from what Andy Pratt (2000) has called the intensive and "bulimic" patterns of work in other media and creative industry careers—yet their misrecognition as "workless" renders them illegitimate. How do we explain such aggressive accounts of these celebrities as *NOT* workers—whilst others, including the mobile elites of finance capital, more easily evade censure for a lack of obvious "hard graft"? Who is preserving such a distinction and to what end? Partly, we surmise, it is because the value of the ordinary celebrity is realised only through their manufactured distancing from conventional notions of work—it is the *appearance* or *performance* of a disdain for work that is the best guarantee of a commercial prospect. These performances of worklessness range from the playful—for example, a male participant in *Geordie Shore* whose tagline on the programme is "the hardest graft I've ever done is doing me hair"—to those deliberately formulated to provoke public disgust, such as celebrified "benefits cheats" who appear in tabloid newspapers to "brag" about their "lavish," "taxpayer-funded" expenditures (and receive a fee for doing so). In both cases, the performance of eschewing "hard graft" is purposefully constructed in order to generate value—and yet the labour investments, the strategic organisation, and the processes of value extraction of this performance are all deliberately hidden. To publicly value and recognise the flexible, precarious labour involved in creating workless celebrity would be to undercut the conditions that allow for its exploitation. That ordinary celebrities "do nothing" (but do so recurrently, intensively, and across multiple sites and platforms) is fundamental to the successful generation of value.

There is clearly an ambivalent but constitutive relation between the economic rewards of reality celebrity (such as they may exist) and its cultural devaluation. We must ask how is this paradox constructed by capital—but also experienced and lived? For the subjects of this degraded and contradictory "portfolio" labour, what are the effects of their immersion in such work? How do such celebrities understand their own work, negotiate this paradox, and claim value for themselves? On the one hand, celebrity offers an "opportunity structure" amidst the fast-retreating possibility of working-class people obtaining any kind of secure or high-status careers in media, creative, and cultural work (Banks, 2017). On the other hand, for the working class to consciously and publicly avoid "graft" is seen as a "moral" crime; moreover, the fact that the apparent evasion of work is knowingly played upon in the limelight, as a spectacle of worklessness, cuts to the heart of that for which the working class were traditionally most valued—being "authentic."

Conclusion: Ordinary Celebrity as Ordinary Work?

While we want to make a case for researching the labour of ordinary celebrity, others have already begun to take up this challenge, with some of the more valuable preliminary insights coming from ethnographic work within reality television production. Vicki Mayer (2011) has explored how below-the-line casters use various forms of "immaterial" labour as they engage with and court potential reality stars. Laura Grindstaff's (2009) aforementioned research into the *Sorority Life* show permits important insights into the production of "ordinariness" and new, "self-serve" forms of celebrity. The valuable text *Fame Games: The Production of Celebrity in Australia* (Turner, Bonner & Marshall, 2000) analysed the workings of managers, advertising agents, and PR companies required for making celebrities and soap stars, mapping a previously underexplored sphere of work. Yet, seventeen years on from this important research, with profound cultural, political, and technological transformations in the interim, we wish to argue that much more needs to be done to capture the specific kinds of work and employment afforded by reality celebrity.

We argue for a more systematic analysis of the actual *operations* of this work whilst recognising the difficulties in gaining access and negotiating the non-disclosure agreements that help to preserve its opacity. The specific *experience* of the work of ordinary celebrities —its planning and management, its temporal and spatial dimensions, its moral economies, its exploitations and rewards, its subjective and objective possibilities, and its creative affordances and constraints—all require interrogation. Some of the debates around this devalued form of media visibility have proceeded without an informed or evidenced understanding of the labour that constitutes it. We do not know what the business models precisely are, nor what the "time and motion" of a working day look and feel like: We do not know what work, effort, and application are invested in the various tasks and processes that generate value, nor what the nuts and bolts—as well as pains and pleasures—of the labour one actually has to perform as a reality celebrity might be. Such labour exists—not only as a visibly mediated and publicly performed kind of "non-work" but also as a measured, calculated, embodied, and lived form of "real" labour around the screen.

The polarised accounts of blaming the workshy or wanting to protect the exploited have failed to consider the full complex of motivations and values that pertain to the lived *undertaking* of ordinary celebrity. Consequently, they appear to deny the possibility of ordinary celebrities possessing *any* kind of labouring subjectivity or antagonistic agency, so rendering their voices as workers largely silent and undifferentiated. Andrew Ross has argued that this new workforce need to be considered "arbiters of their own exploitation"—and that to suggest otherwise would risk falling back into old charges of "false consciousness" (Ross, 2014, p. 36). To recognise the legitimacy of ordinary celebrity—undertaken by people with complex motivations and intentions—is not to diminish or underestimate a critique of exploitation, nor to overlook the precariousness and harms that might be occasioned by what we might think of as an "illegitimate" form of cultural work; it is rather to try and better understand the complex class relations and economies of value that circulate in this somewhat opaque and degraded terrain of the cultural industries.

Notes

1. While in US English "graft" refers to a form of political corruption, in this chapter we are concerned with the British English use of the word, whereby it can be broadly understood as "hard work"—and most specifically the willingness to take on "dirty" or unglamorous manual labour. It is important to note that "graft" has gendered and racialised as well as classed connotations: "grafter culture," as Gunter and Watt (2010) note, is dominated by white men in the UK context, and implies a continuity with traditional, masculine, working-class labour cultures and practices.
2. These are character-participants from the British "real life soap" *The Only Way Is Essex* (Lime Pictures/ITV, 2010–).

Works Cited

Allen, K., & Mendick, H. (2013). Young people's uses of celebrity: Class, gender and 'improper' celebrity. *Discourse: Studies in the Cultural Politics of Education, 34*(1), 77–93.

Andrejevic, M. (2004). *Reality TV: The work of being watched*. London, UK: Rowman and Littlefield.

Andrejevic, M. (2011). Realizing exploitation. In M. Kraidy & K. Sender (Eds.), *The politics of reality television: Global perspectives* (pp. 18–30). London, UK/New York, NY: Routledge.

Banks, M. (2017). *Creative justice: Cultural industries, work and inequality*. London, UK: Rowman and Littlefield.

Barrett, J. (2016, October 25). The unfair secrets behind celebrity fitness DVDs. *i newspaper*. Retrieved from https://inews.co.uk/essentials/lifestyle/unfair-secrets-behind-celebrity-fitness-dvds/

BBC. (2012, May 11). Guides claim lack of female role models 'could be damaging'. Retrieved from www.bbc.co.uk/news/uk-18033198

Burawoy, M. (1979). *Manufacturing consent: Changes in the labor process under monopoly capitalism*. Chicago, IL: University of Chicago Press.

Curnutt, H. (2009). "A fan crashing the party": Exploring reality-celebrity in MTV's real world franchise. *TV and New Media, 10*(3), 251–266.

Curnutt, H. (2011). Durable participants: A generational approach to reality TV's 'ordinary' labor pool. *Media Culture Society, 33*(7), 1061–1076.

Grindstaff, L. (2009). Self-serve celebrity: The production of ordinariness and the ordinariness of production in reality television. In V. Mayer, M.J. Banks, & J.T. Caldwell (Eds.), *Production studies: Cultural studies of media industries* (pp. 71–86). London, UK/ New York, NY: Routledge.

Grindstaff, L., & Murray, S. (2015). Reality celebrity: Branded affect and the emotion economy. *Public Culture, 27*(1), 109–135.

Gunter, A., & Watt, P. (2010). Grafting, going to college and working on road: Youth transitions and cultures in an East London neighbourhood. In R. MacDonald, T. Shildrick, & S. Blackman (Eds.), *Young people, class and place* (pp. 58–72). London, UK/New York, NY: Routledge.

Hardt, M., & Negri, A. (2005). *Multitude: War and democracy in the age of empire*. London, UK/New York, NY: Penguin.

Hearn, A. (2008). "Meat, mask, burden": Probing the contours of the branded "self". *Journal of Consumer Culture, 8*(2), 197–217.

Hearn, A. (2017). Witches and bitches: Reality television, housewifization and the new hidden abode of production. *European Journal of Cultural Studies, 20*(1), 10–24.

Holmes, S. (2004). "Reality goes pop!": Reality TV, popular music, and narratives of stardom in pop idol. *TV and New Media, 5*(2), 147–172.

Jost, F. (2011). When reality TV is a job. In M.M. Kraidy & K. Sender (Eds.), *The politics of reality television: Global perspectives* (pp. 31–43). Abingdon, UK/New York, NY: Routledge.

Killelea, A. (2014, November 18). Simon Cowell and reality TV aren't solely to blame for the shift in kids' job aspirations. *Daily Mirror*. Retrieved from www.mirror.co.uk/news/ uk-news/simon-cowell-reality-tv-arent-4647338

Kirkup, J. (2015, November 11). I'm a celebrity 2015 and the curse of the white working class. *The Daily Telegraph*. Retrieved from www.telegraph.co.uk/news/society/ 11989263/Im-a-Celebrity-2015-and-the-curse-of-the-white-working-class.html

Kokoli, A.M., & Winter, A. (2015). What a girl's gotta do: The labor of the biopolitical celebrity in austerity Britain. *Women & Performance: A Journal of Feminist Theory, 25*(2), 157–174.

Lazzarato, M. (1996). Immaterial labor. In M. Hardt & P. Virno (Eds.), *Radical thought in Italy: A potential politics* (pp. 133–147) (P. Colilli and E. Emery, Trans.). Minneapolis, MN/London, UK: University of Minnesota Press.

Marwick, A.E. (2013). *Status update: Celebrity, publicity and branding in the social media age*. New Haven, CT: Yale University Press.

Mayer, V. (2011). *Below the line: Producers and production studies in the new television economy*. Durham, NC: Duke University Press.

Mendick, H., Allen, K., Harvey, L., & Ahmad, A. (Forthcoming). *Celebrity, aspiration and contemporary youth: Education and inequality in an era of austerity*. London, UK: Bloomsbury.

Mies, M. (2007). Patriarchy and accumulation on a world scale – Revisited (Keynote lecture at the Green Economics Institute, Reading, UK, 29 October 2005). *International Journal of Green Economics, 1*(3–4), 268–275.

Ouellette, L., & Hay, J. (2008). *Better living through reality TV: Television and post-welfare citizenship*. Oxford, UK: Blackwell.

Pratt, A. (2000). New media, the new economy and new spaces. *Geoforum, 31*, 425–436.

Rojek, C. (2001). *Celebrity*. London, UK: Reaktion.

Rojek, C. (2012). *Fame attack: The inflation of celebrity and its consequences*. London, UK/ New York, NY: Bloomsbury Academic.

Ross, A. (2014). Reality television and the political economy of amateurism. In L. Ouellette (Ed.), *Companion to reality television* (pp. 29–39). Malden, MA/Oxford and Chichester, UK: Wiley-Blackwell.

Senft, T. M. (2013). Microcelebrity and the branded self. In J. Hartley, J. Burgess, & A. Bruns (Eds.), *A companion to new media dynamics* (pp. 346–354). Chichester, UK: Wiley-Blackwell.

Skeggs, B., & Wood, H. (2008). The labour of transformation and circuits of value 'around' reality television. *Continuum: Journal of Media and Cultural Studies, 22*(4), 559–572.

Skeggs, B., & Wood, H. (2012). *Reacting to reality television: Performance, audience and value.* Abingdon, UK/New York, NY: Routledge.

Todd, S. (2014). *The people: The rise and fall of the working class.* London, UK: John Murray/ Hodder and Stoughton.

Turner, G. (2014). *Understanding celebrity* (2nd ed.). London, UK/Thousand Oaks, CA: Sage.

Turner, G., Bonner, F., & Marshall, P.D. (2000). *Fame games: The production of celebrity in Australia.* Port Melbourne, AU: Cambridge University Press.

Tyler, I. (2008). "Chav mum, chav scum": Class disgust in contemporary Britain. *Feminist Media Studies, 8*(1), 17–34.

Tyler, I. (2013). *Revolting subjects: Social abjection and resistance in neoliberal Britain.* London, UK: Zed Books.

Tyler, I., & Bennett, B. (2010). "Celebrity chav": Fame, femininity and social class. *European Journal of Cultural Studies, 13*(3), 375–393.

Weber, B., & Jones, J.L. (2014). Sperm receptacles, money-hungry monsters and fame whores: Reality celebrity motherhood and the transmediated grotesque. In M. Alvarado, M. Buonanno, H. Gray, & T. Miller (Eds.), *The Sage handbook of television studies* (pp. 325–335). London, UK/Thousand Oaks, CA: Sage.

Williamson, M. (2016). *Celebrity: Capitalism and the making of fame.* Cambridge, UK/ Malden, MA: Polity.

Wood, H. (2017). The politics of hyperbole on Geordie Shore: Class, gender, youth and excess. *European Journal of Cultural Studies, 20*(1), 39–55.

Wood, H., & Skeggs, B. (2008). Spectacular morality: Reality television, individualisation and the re-making of the working class. In D. Hesmondhalgh & J. Toynbee (Eds.), *The media and social theory* (pp. 177–193). London, UK: Routledge.

9

IDOLS OF SELF-PRODUCTION: SELFIES, CAREER SUCCESS, AND SOCIAL CLASS

Anita Biressi

Selfies: The Calling Cards of Neoliberalism

Much has been written in recent years about the rise of meritocratic culture and the triumph of neoliberalism as a philosophy, as a political practice, as governmental regime, and as a way of life (Harvey, 2005; Gilbert, 2013). It has been argued that the traditional class categories and the political party affiliations with which these classes were once associated have broken down, having been superseded by a neoliberal focus on the individual as the driver of personal success, social responsibility, and economic growth (Giddens, 1991; Beck & Beck-Gernsheim, 2002). Indeed, the resilience of neoliberalism when faced with macro-challenges to stability such as economic turbulence, recession, refugee flight, and nationalism seems to confirm that we are living in post-class times. But others have argued that these challenges, so many of which represent a struggle over resources (housing, medical care, jobs), have in fact reignited and refreshed class politics at a micro level, in communities and on the streets, as evidenced by anti-capitalist, communitarian, and other kinds of cross-affiliated agitation based on shared sympathies and perceived inequality (Gilbert, 2008; Tyler, 2013; Price & Sanz Sabido, 2015). Widening inequality, material deprivation, segregation by income and ethnicity, the peculiar insulation of capital cities from wider economic forces, and the social isolation of the very wealthy in gated residences—all point to the importance of maintaining an understanding of the dynamics of social class in the current moment of austerity.

Social media can testify to the mobilisation of class politics as a resource to challenge austerity's impact on various constituencies including women, the disabled, young people, migrants, and those subsisting on exploitation job contracts. Digital media platforms such as Twitter have usefully furnished activists with the tools to articulate dissent against neoliberal policies, to coordinate and to plan protest, and to insist on the relevance of class politics in the 21st century. The "distributed citizenship" of the digital public sphere is noisy with the voices of subjects who have become politicised through class injury and felt injustices brought about by the changing dynamics of capital and labour (Meikle, 2016, p. 177). But these voices are counterbalanced, and perhaps even overwhelmed, by the other messages conveyed in mainstream media culture, including in social media, which implicitly represent working-class politics especially, and class identification in general, as outmoded obstacles to social reform and economic growth (Biressi & Nunn, 2013). Broadly speaking, these countervailing messages are conveyed in two closely related ways—through negative, often shaming portrayals of "bad" citizens and through the relentless instruction of "good" citizens in self-improvement and properly directed ambition. The first we see in the plethora of television programmes and tabloid journalism which avidly attends to (and often stigmatises) the dispossessed, the apparently dissolute, the social failures, and those struggling in the communities that economic change has left behind (Nunn & Biressi, 2010; Biressi 2011). The second set of messages found in media culture work to recharge, refashion, and reinstruct the more energetic citizens in how to avoid falling into failure, how to weather stormy economic conditions, and, in short, in how to make a success of oneself. The vehicles for these include reality TV formats (Ouellette & Hay, 2008; Biressi & Nunn, 2014), makeover shows (Palmer, 2008), life coaching books, vlogs, and blogs (McRobbie, 2009), all of which demonstrate and celebrate the individual's potential to live a successful, satisfying life. In both scenarios, meritocratic "parables of progress" (Littler, 2017) direct us towards the proper conduct of the self and the strategies required to survive and to thrive in the current moment. As Negra and Tasker (2014, pp. 1–2) have observed, "any account of the economic conditions of the global recession will be incomplete without taking into consideration the cultural storytelling associated with the mass media."

In this chapter I am going to focus on one development of media culture which, I argue, connects to this second set of messages about the manufacture of the successful self—that is the production of the selfie as a personal project and especially in relation to the worlds of paid work, careers, and economic security.[1] As will be seen, work-related selfies are deployed across the social spectrum. Both working-class and middle-class subjects are invited to present their best selves via selfie culture. These are used to demonstrate their "passion" for work. Selfies bind together our personal biographies and social media profiles in the pursuit of advancement and financial security. I argue that worker subjects have become figured as the heroes of their own lives and self-portraiture is one important component of this self-fashioning. Bearing this in mind, I make the case for developing a new category of social role model, one which is fitting and theoretically useful for the current moment, namely the idol of self-production. I adapt the term from Leo Lowenthal's work. He charted the ways in which traditional social influencers (such as business leaders, politicians, engineers—idols of production) were being usurped in media culture by celebrity influencers. Now, in neoliberal times, we are emerging as our own idols, charged with both the ideals of entrepreneurialism and the ideals of celebrity self-fashioning. This new idol is expected to be self-made in the realm of work but also self-made in the media sphere, and the two collide in selfie culture. As Deborah Lupton (2015, p. 177) explains, "Taking and posting selfies is both an intensely personal practice as a means of representing the body/self . . . and a communal practice that demonstrates cultural norms about who should engage in this practice and how they should present themselves." Or in the words of Baym and Senft (2015, p. 1589), "Selfies function both as a practice of everyday life and as the object of politicizing discourses about how people ought to represent, document, and share their behaviors." From this perspective I wish to consider selfie culture as yet another popular discourse and practice of self-improvement, individualization, and personal choice whose "regulative dimension" helps to draw the lines "between those subjects who are judged responsive to the regime of personal responsibility, and those who fail miserably" (McRobbie, 2009, p. 19). Selfies are indeed the *personification* of neoliberalism because neoliberalism is both a narrative and a regime which places the individual centre stage. I make this argument because selfies not only demonstrate cultural norms (as noted above) but they also *produce* normative subjects through the action of the (self) regulatory practices.

There are as many selfies in circulation as there are people taking them, in fact, far more since so many of us take and circulate multiple shots. Google reported that we posted 24 billion selfies in one year alone.[2] Looked at cumulatively we have evidence that these are posted significantly more often by women than by men and that on some platforms the median age of posters is young, at 23 years old.[3] In many ways selfies are fairly generic; they are self-portraits usually taken on smartphones or other handheld devices. They are recognisable by the angle taken with outstretched arm or selfie stick, their (often composed or post-edited) spontaneity, their emphasis on the face, and their (sometimes faux) intimacy even when taken in public or group settings. As texts read in close-up, as the faces of individuals, these seem to offer few lessons or indications of how we might situate them in the landscape of post-class politics and society. But if we, in fact, choose to study selfies *across the piece*, from the imperative to produce them through to their content, distribution, address, use value, and the discourses that surround them, we will see that these are the perfect calling cards of neoliberalism and a testament to the enduring power of media culture to mask class relations.

Selfie production and exhibition functions as an affirming exercise which promotes one's visibility, which invites recognition and approval, and which courts popularity through self-branding (Lupton, 2015). To date, selfie regulatory practices have been discussed by scholars most extensively in relation to the policing of gender, femininity, and the body and largely in the context of debates about postfeminism and neoliberalism (Stover, 2014; Elias & Gill, 2016). For example,

Burns (2015) has argued, drawing on Foucauldian theory, that the critical public discourses around selfie production and the association of selfies with narcissism have worked to discipline young women to comply with patriarchal expectations. Young women are especially targeted because selfies have been disparaged as a feminine cultural practice (Burns, 2015). But these are not the only disciplinary directives being rolled out here. In addition to those described by Burns and others there are associated mechanisms of governmentality working through selfie production through compliance with directives around social mobility, social aspiration, and social class. In this chapter, then, I begin the work of exploring the argument that selfie culture may be understood as an innovation in the modelling and performance of competitive self-advancement and social aspiration in a supposedly post-class society (Pakulski & Waters, 1996).

Selfies: Your Confidence Calling Card

On November 12, 2014, a job recruitment agency claiming to operate across several continents Facebooked the findings of its own research which revealed that employees who took more selfies tended to be awarded higher pay rises.[4] The agency, called The Job Factory, announced in a press release:

> The survey of 287 employees in Australia, Singapore, the USA and UK who had received a pay rise in the past 12 months found that those who posted more than 20 selfies a month received pay rises averaging 3.7 per cent. Those who did not have a social media presence or who posted less than 20 selfies a month received pay rises averaging 2.4%.

The Job Factory's Director Craig Binnie was quoted as saying:

> Meek employees who sit in the corner with their eyes glued to their computer screens might be great workers, but they do not always stand out when bosses are thinking about who to reward during pay reviews. . . . The confident "look at me, let me take a selfie" employees are always going to be first in the boss's thoughts.

The story was picked up and circulated by various online media outlets including the South Carolina newspaper *The State*, which led with the question: "Can a selfie a workday keep poverty away?" A question that it did not go on to answer. It summarised: "Folks who take a lot of selfies naturally have a lot of self-confidence. . . . And behind ability, that's the No. 2 driver of a person's career."[5]

What interests me here is not the research itself (the sample is small and it is not open to scholarly scrutiny) but the way in which it ideologically yokes together the selfie, an economy of visibility, and the rhetoric of self-confidence in the pursuit of workplace success. The report indicated that there was a correlation between selfie output, financial reward, and personal recognition. Its overall message was circular—that effective workplace conduct is measured not only through work but through the performance of work; and that visibility itself was a marker of confidence and confidence a marker of effectiveness. It is notable that confidence as a personality trait is historically embedded in the politics of class relations and "self-confidence turns out to be a channel through which education and earnings inequalities are transmitted across generations" (Filippin & Paccagnella, 2011, p. 3). Social research has explored the ways in which subjects who have been born into financial security and have enjoyed the benefits of a good education, established social networks, and cultural capital develop personal confidence and even a sense of entitlement (Kendall, 2002; Dahrendorf, 2011). The reassurance that the resources of friendships, contacts, and capital will furnish a safety net for failure allows privileged subjects to take risks, to stand out, to stand alone, and to shine (Halpern, 2005). For the wealthy and well-supported, self-confidence is built on solid economic and cultural foundations. For the rest, there is another option—the aping of self-confidence.

The manufacture or faking of self-confidence, optimism, and drive has become a much-promoted strategy in Western culture. It has been advocated as a tactic to energize failing and disappointed subjects when employment is insecure and prospects look poor. In common parlance, you should "fake it until you make it." Barbara Ehrenreich (2009, p. 205) has argued that this "cult" of positive thinking has become the solution to hard times:

> How can we expect to improve our situation without addressing the actual circumstances we find ourselves in? Positive thinking seeks to convince us that such external factors are incidental compared with one's internal state or attitude or mood . . . coaches and gurus dismiss real-world problems as "excuses" for failure.

When complaints about tangible obstacles to success, many of these arguably rooted in class difference, become reconfigured as "excuses" for poor personal performance there is little recourse but to adopt a mode of robust individualism. In their influential discussion of societal processes of individualization Ulrich Beck and Elisabeth Beck-Gernsheim (2001) argue that individual self-fulfilment and personal achievement have become the driving imperative of the present era, and the self-made subject has become its leading character. In late capitalist social and political fields, the prevalent uncompromising message is: "Your own life—your own failure" (Beck & Beck-Gernsheim, 2001, p. 24; see also Harvey, 2005). Hence, in the corporate motivation industry every failure must be re-conceptualized and even welcomed by the right-thinking individual as an opportunity (Ehrenreich, 2009). I suggest then the manufacture of confidence, and the *presentation* of the confident self, is supposed to arm subjects in their "struggles in the social field," to use Andrew Sayer's phrase. As Sayer (2005, pp. 96–7) explains in his analysis of the moral judgments articulated around social class, these struggles need not even be understood, any longer, in traditional class terms. They involve the competition for resources, for sure, for employment, for income, and for security, but they also involve a competition for recognition, inclusion, positionality, and advancement. As he indicates, in some domains this competition is deadly serious because it is a zero-sum game; after all there are only so many positions and opportunities available at any one time. Again, this is implied by our news story above. Workers might be "great" but where both have equal ability the quiet ones will surely be overlooked in favor of their more gregarious "look at me" peers, those who have confidence or who can manufacture it.

But even confidence may not be enough. Individual ambition cannot, in itself, guarantee economic survival in job markets where contracts are short, hours are unpredictable, agencies call the shots, and self-employment is precarious. If a personal passion for work, promoted by popular entertainment, life coaches, and human resource departments, is the hallmark of employability, then this may not be sustainable over the longer term. The language of meritocracy as articulated in popular culture has suggested to the millennials, above all, that if they are passionate about what they do they should be certain of future success. But Jean Twenge's (2014, p. xiii) hotly debated book *Generation Me* argues that "everyone told them that they were special and didn't need anyone else, and then adulthood shows them . . . that these things just aren't true."

Career Selfies: Positivity, Play, and Passion

Much of the discourse around workplace selfies emphasizes employee positivity. Individuals and teams are encouraged to celebrate their jobs and to publicly exhibit their enthusiasm and energy. AGENT, an online media site for entrepreneurs, for example, curates workplace selfies, declaring: "Mark your professional accomplishments, hitting targets, and the team spirit in the your [sic] office by celebrating Workplace Wednesday."[6] Its pages collate worker selfies taken by employees in public and private sectors including charities, hospitals, TV studios, and banks. A typical example is a group selfie featuring head-and-shoulder portraits of three employees, smiling broadly up at the camera from behind their desks and computers. Underneath is posted: "The award-winning Receipt Bank converts bills, invoices and receipts into data that you, and your company, can use. Some of the staff at the Washington, DC branch made use of their selfie stick to take this work selfie at their office in December 2016." Another image shows eight coworkers in evening attire looking up from a central table covered with food and wine. Their grins signify their pleasure in the occasion. The text reads "Arcus is a planning, environmental and engineering company. . . . In December 2016, employees of Arcus took this work selfie whilst at a Scottish Renewables Dinner."

The value of these kinds of images to company branding is publicly acknowledged. Blogger and "creative strategist" Sophie Andrews (2017, February 1) advises:

> Do you want your customers to fall in love with your brand? Help them connect with you by providing them with a glimpse into the inner heart and soul of your company. Rather than lining everyone up for a group photo, choose candid shots of you and your crew at work. . . . Include playful images that show just how much fun work can be.

The association of selfies with spontaneity and fun, together with the conventional Western expectation that the camera requires the subject to smile, can be harnessed to mask the power relationships between capital and labor, which form the basis of paid work. The soft power of selfies helps to personalize companies and brands. Companies use employee selfies to showcase initiatives, to recruit staff, and to attract clients and consumers. In other words, selfies have become part of both human resource management and external marketing and public relations (PR).

I suggest that PR agencies are especially attuned to the potential use value of selfies to the enhancement of a company's image and corporate vision. After all, PR has been in the vanguard of the neoliberal project through its association with consumerism, celebrity branding, and individualization. Alongside accountants, lawyers, and consultants, PR naturally supports the elites on whose fortunes it depends (Hall, Massey, & Rustin, 2015).[7] As a profession, PR refreshes itself and continues to be relevant through its hybridization with popular cultural forms such as reality TV (Deery, 2012), blogging, and selfie culture. The hugely influential firm M&C Saatchi PR, for example, includes a digital selfie board on its website. The selfies are of various sizes, they seem to be in no particular order, and, at first glance, suggest a collegial, creative, and anti-hierarchal collective. The ancillary signs (the settings and the clothes, hairstyles, jewelry, and quirky accessories) seen in the photos build up a summative picture of fashionable, well-turned-out, middle-class professionals. There is no visible text. The selfies portray mainly younger, mostly white faces and are visually united because they are reproduced in monochrome. But when the cursor hovers over these faces it turns out that while the smaller portraits are anonymous, the larger ones are named and these people represent key personnel in the organization. Floating text offers succinct biographies and pithy sayings, which fog over the boundaries between work and home personas such as: "Account Director. Live to learn and learn to play" or "Director. Magazine junkie. Mother. Media hound" or "Director. Dog lover. Work lover. Considerate lover." These images and profiles appear to substantiate Saatchi's overall message: "We have happy, connected people based in 10 markets worldwide . . . all with one thing in common: We're driven by passion."[8] The selfie does an important job on the Saatchi platform because it signifies that the agency's workers are indeed happy, connected, independently minded, and passionate about what they do.

A similar chain of signification to that just described is also harnessed by training academies in their campaigns to attract students and apprentices. For example, TAFE NSW, an Australian vocational education and training provider, whose slogan is "Be Ambitious. Be whatever you want to be," invited young people to post their "career selfies."[9] Likewise, in the UK, the British government launched a campaign called Get In Go Far to show "young people how an apprenticeship can give them the skills and experience they need to land their dream job." Apprentices were invited to share selfies to "celebrate the campaign." One shot reposted by the campaign depicts a busy scene at a National Apprenticeship Event in Derby, North of England. This selfie shows two casually dressed young men at an information fair. In the background, a poster instructs: "Reinvent yourself." Selfie culture is arguably at the heart of this mandate to reinvent the self and it supports the dubious promise of dream jobs and workplace self-actualization.

These various uses of the selfie culture blur the lines between private and public, between corporate publicity and social networking, and as such they testify to the erosion of distinctions between the personal self, the laboring self, and the branded self. This chimes with the wider rhetoric of performance management that maintains that workers need to be fully present in the workplace—body and soul. Facebook's Chief Operating Office Sheryl Sandberg's (2013) makes this much clear. Indeed, in her much-vaunted everywoman guide to success in the workplace she seems to suggest that we have little option:

> I am now a true believer in bringing our whole selves to work. I no longer believe that people have a professional self for Mondays through Fridays and a real self for the rest of the time . . . in today's era of individual expression, where people constantly update their Facebook status and tweet their every move it makes even less sense. . . . I think we benefit from expressing our truth, talking about personal situations . . . (Sandberg, 2013, p. 89)

While Sandberg is seeking to connect the private emotional self with the public self to arrive at a work/life balance solution that works for women, in particular, it is notable that she cites social media usage as the reason why it no longer makes sense for workers to simply do their jobs. For her, social media postings seem to present a "truth" about ourselves and if this truth is already out there then it can't be put back in the box when work demands. If this is right, then workers will increasingly find themselves in a post-Goffman (1959) world where they no longer have recourse to a "back stage" behind the "front stage" performance of work. The selfie and the career selfie, the private self and the public self, would somehow be one and the same. The merging of both would arguably represent a further evolution of the neoliberal subject whose success or failure in the world can only be explained in terms of individual performance across the public–private divide.

Of late, capitalism patterns of employment have shifted from the "job for life" to a lifetime of jobs requiring workers to take responsibility for updating their skills, adapting to change, and marketing themselves on a regular basis. We are encouraged therefore to undertake regular "career selfies," a phrase now used to describe a self-audit of skills and goals (Wilen, 2015) or committed self-engagement with an employer. For example, Kevin Sheridan (2014), blogging at the Association for Talent Development, advocates taking an "engagement selfie." In his column, headed with what appears to be a stock image of a smartly presented, conventionally attractive young white woman taking a selfie, he asserts:

> New situations pose new challenges. Acceptance of a new challenge begins with choosing an attitude of dealing with it. Instead of choosing the road to victimhood and disengagement, we can empower ourselves and choose positivity and engagement. Try it . . . this free "engagement selfie" survey . . . will . . . reveal the extent of your own engagement as an employee, as well as offer useful tips on what you can do on your own to become more engaged at work. (Sheridan, 2014)

The survey tests statements such as "My company/organization inspires me to 'go above and beyond' my normal job duties to help the company succeed." If the survey decides that you are "disengaged," action points are suggested to remedy the situation. These suggest individual tactics around networking, self-promotion, and so on. The message here is that the worker is largely on their own but he or she has *choices* and that one's *attitude* towards the threat of change is paramount. If subjects regard change in the workplace as a problem then they risk being positioned as a loser or a moaner. Like the other discourses already discussed, it amplifies the neoliberal message that the resistant, questioning, or resentful worker is out of step with the times. These discourses implicitly dismiss collective action as a viable mode of engagement with the world of work unless it refers to the mobilization of the workplace team. Trade union membership and workplace lobbying for change or recognition is never mentioned. Social media and the discourse of the selfie, in particular, reinforce the directive to stand out from the crowd.[10] Hence co-workers or other freelancers are styled as competitors in the race for advancement. Natasha Miller Williams' (2015) blog "The Career Selfie: 7 Ways to Get Noticed at Work" thoroughly blurs workplace career development and social media tactics in various ways which I can only briefly indicate here due to space limitations.

> Taking a snapshot of the work you're doing is essential to being noticed at work and ultimately moving up—a kind of career self-promotion. The best professional advice I ever received sounded something like this: "No one

> else is going to look over your career like you can. Don't be too modest to talk about what you're doing around here." What I heard was: *Go on. Take a career selfie. Shamelessly self-promote* [Miller Williams' emphasis]. So I did . . . Do something extra. In what ways can you add to your day-to-day role? Think of this as a special effect, like an Instagram filter. Taking on a side project at work is a great way to get more visibility. (Miller Williams, 2015)

Miller Williams' choice of image underlines the playful, aspirational, and empowering attitude that selfie culture encapsulates. It features a small black child seated behind a large desk taking a selfie. She wears her hair pinned back, is dressed in a smart suit and chunky pearls, and is surrounded by the paraphernalia of individual workplace success: a globe, a laptop, and an engraved work trophy. She is not "playing grown-up" in the usual sense because her clothes are perfectly cut to fit her tiny stature. She is a mini work-ready subject already learning how to take her neoliberal calling card. Miller Williams', Wilen's, and Sheridan's (above) use of social media metaphors adds a contemporary gloss to well-known career development advice. More importantly, from the perspective of this chapter, their messages and the way these are framed chime with the broader regulatory discourses of selfie practice already outlined above. These discourses are reinforcing cultural norms about the conduct of the self. Looked at together and cumulatively they function to attribute blame and redirect responsibility to the individual and to manage our expectations about recognition in the workplace. As such they exclude capital–labor relations and the class politics which underpins them from public conversations; after all, how can these conversations even be relevant when the solution to job market turbulence lies in the hands of the individual?

Conclusion: Idols of Self-production

To conclude, let's briefly situate the selfie culture discussed above in the context of longer historical debates about the heroes of mass culture and how these relate to the politics of class. To this end, I turn to sociologist Leo Lowenthal's much-cited 1944 content analysis of "entertainment" biographies in the popular American magazines of the 1940s. Here Lowenthal (2006) identified a significant, measurable proportional shift in magazine coverage away from people in the "serious" professions such as business and politics (designated by him as "idols of production") to those in the world of entertainment, media, and sport ("idols of consumption"). Lowenthal's research observed the tremendous increase in biographies that took the form of celebrity autobiographical sketches, résumés, biographical feature articles, and books. The argument was made that this swing also represented a decline in popular interest in public figures connected to history, to the forces of production, and to work and a growing curiosity about celebrities' private lives, consumer practices, and leisure. In other words, leisure and consumption rather than work increasingly formed the primary matter of public interest (Granter, 2009, p. 163). Now we would recognize Lowenthal's new idols, whom he regarded as somehow *misrepresenting* the real relations of production and of social mobility, as the heralds of a new information age and the most visible outliers of the expanding cultural industries. Their status as celebrities and media stars was bound up with new kinds of economic mechanisms that generated wealth and opened the field for new kinds of workers (Illouz, 2003, p. 96). The ubiquity, success stories, and charismatic appeal of celebrities intersected with and amplified neoliberal messages of individualism (Williamson, 2016).

The mass communications model that Lowenthal develops, its categorization of "idols," and the moral judgments attached to them, is open to challenge on the grounds, as noted above, that he misreads celebrities as distractions from economic relations when we might now say that they are, in fact, the essence of them. Eva Illouz's astute critique of his work also makes the point that the consumer and leisure culture that Lowenthal condemns as trivial and hedonistic is in reality a new site of labor. She remarks: "In consumer capitalism, the body has become the object of constant hard work, and the glamour and fun are undergirded by a fundamentally anxious attitude vis-à-vis one's self" (Illouz, 2003, p. 97). Along with Illouz, however, I suggest that this emphasis on biography, the attention to popular culture, and the consideration of the changing characterisation of success and failure in the public realm give this work longevity and relevance. As she also notes, Lowenthal's work continues to illuminate the complex relationship between culture and the economy and between capital, biography, and selfhood.

As already noted elsewhere, in our own time the binary opposition between the serious idols of production and the trivial idols of consumption has dissolved as politicians, business leaders, and innovators have increasingly been personalised, packaged, and celebritized (Biressi & Nunn, 2013). Business leaders and entrepreneurs undertake charitable work, they appear on television in entertainment formats, they write inspirational cross-over books about struggle and success, and they become our elected political representatives. Conversely, there are also many examples of celebrities from the entertainment and leisure industries who have contributed to public life through politics, charity work, or social entrepreneurial activity. Bearing these transformations in mind and the discursive regimes outlined above, I have made the case for developing a new category of media role model, one that is fitting and theoretically useful for the current moment, namely the idol of self-production. This idol of self-production sits alongside these other figures and, of course, intersects with them. He/she is expected to be self-made in the realm of work but also self-made in the media sphere. Moreover, the contemporary self-produced idol represents him or herself through the idiom of celebrity, via their engagement with selfie culture. This new idol seemingly attests to the conviction, maintained by some, that class history, affiliation, and the social conditions into which one is born need not hinder social mobility, job security, or prospects for promotion. This emphasis on selfie production in work cultures suggests that we can make ourselves over, as mini-celebrities or stars of our own lives, and like celebrities transcend our class origins. In the examples I have considered, *successful* practitioners of selfie culture are being endorsed as idols of self-production and as society's rightful winners, not only socially but also materially. This works to close off urgent debates about class injury, material inequality, and social failure. In sum, it belies the real forces of competition for resources and jobs.

Although "influencers" such as Sheryl Sandberg may maintain that our social media presences have rendered the division between the public and private spheres obsolete, competition means, of course, that individuals are ever more alert to the importance of the perfect profile. Job seekers are advised to shape, "curate," and maintain their professional online personas to present "their best public self" (Trauth, 2017, p. 223). This usually involves removing inappropriate selfies, checking one's privacy settings, and managing one's online persona to give the best possible impression. The selfie connects to profile-based social media platforms (Meikle, 2016, p. 96), and each time we register with a new interface we are invited to write a mini-biography similar to the ones described above on the Saatchi Board. These publicly available profiles must be managed and subjects are advised to anticipate the damaging consequences of displaying the self in ways that are offputting to employers, clients and contacts. Indeed, Alice Marwick's (2013) study of celebrity and public branding in the context of Web 2.0 deploys a Foucauldian approach to make the case that the values promoted by social media directly echo those developed by entrepreneurial business culture. In her discussion of technology workers, she observes that:

> . . . an online presentation must quite literally be "safe for work" to accrue status and benefit its creator. Whether this entails promoting one's image as a company would promote a brand or celebrity, or adhering to a single verifiable identity . . . people follow online norms that will increase their status. (Marwick, 2013, p. 17)

Here the very mechanisms of social media, its rules, and commonly accepted practices filter out people "who are not effective neoliberal subjects" (Rettberg, 2014, p. 23).

William Brown's (2014) filmic meditation on selfie culture theorizes the connection between selfies as a self-sustaining, capillary disciplinary practice (in his terms a "virus"), filtering (de-tagging images which do not conform to dominant ideals), and the politics of class. He contends, "The term we can best use to describe the aesthetic dimension of the image virus is money. The more we look like, or want to look like, money the more the image virus has its grip." The selfie is more often a *performance of social success* than a socially grounded self-document. In fact, the real material conditions of class difference and social disadvantage are usually repressed or occluded in a practice which presents the self as individualist, effective, and untethered to the anchor of class origins. The hallmarks of social class are wiped away by selfies which display the nicely attired, smiling, aspirational neoliberal subject. But, as cultural historians have long argued, that which has been established as socially marginal often becomes symbolically central (Stallybrass & White, 1986). Selfies, and the self-work involved in their production, strenuously seek to overcome or deny the material and symbolic obstacles to social mobility. As such they are a ubiquitous and mundane reminder that such obstacles exist.

Notes

1. There is another essay to be written on overtly politicised selfie culture, where selfies are mobilised to expose injustice or create change (Kuntsman, 2017). These are practices which connect more directly to the political mobilisations of social class discussed in the introduction.
2. Available at https://blog.google/products/photos/google-photos-one-year-200-million/ (report for 2015)
3. Available at http://selfiecity.net/
4. Available at www.facebook.com/thejobfactorynewzealand/posts/1490922007852346
5. Available at www.thestate.com/news/business/article13911254.html
6. The AGENT website available at www.agent.media/
7. Available at www.lwbooks.co.uk/soundings/kilburn-manifesto. It was posted in 2013. Printed in Hall et al. (2015).
8. Available at http://mcsaatchipr.com/agency/
9. TAFE NSW twitter feed available at https://twitter.com/tafensw
10. It is important to stand out only in ways which chime with the values of companies and recruiters. There is evidence that unappealing social media content can damage the prospects of job-seekers and even university applicants (see Brake, 2014).

Works Cited

Andrews, S. (2017, February 1). Selfies in the workplace. *The Huffington Post*. Retrieved from http://www.huffingtonpost.com/sophie-andrews/selfies-in-the-workplace_b_14558572.html

Baym, N., & Senft, T. (2015). What does the selfie say? Investigating a global phenomenon. *International Journal of Communication, 9*, 1588–1606.

Beck, U., & Beck-Gernsheim, E. (2001). *Individualization*. London, UK: Sage.

Biressi, A. (2011). The virtuous circle: Or helping people to help themselves in British lifestyle programming. In H. Wood & B. Skeggs (Eds.), *Reality television and class* (pp. 144–155). London, UK: British Film Institute.

Biressi, A., & Nunn, H. (2013). *Class and contemporary British culture*. London, UK: Palgrave Macmillan.

Biressi, A., & Nunn, H. (2014). "I'm passionate, Lord Sugar": Young entrepreneurs, critical judgment, and emotional labor in Young Apprentice. In S. Panse & D. Rothermel (Eds.), *Critique of judgment in film and television* (pp. 90–107). Basingstoke, UK: Palgrave Macmillan.

Brake, D. (2014). *Sharing our lives online: Risks and exposure in social media*. Basingstoke, UK: Palgrave Macmillan.

Brown, W. (2014). *Selfie*. UK: Beg, Borrow, Steal Films.

Burns, A. (2015). Self(ie)-discipline: Social regulation as enacted through the discussion of photographic practice. *International Journal of Communication, 9*, 1716–1733.

Dahrendorf, R. (2011). *The modern social conflict: The politics of liberty* (2nd ed.). Piscataway, NJ: Transaction Publishers.

Deery, J. (2012). *Consuming reality: The commercialization of factual entertainment*. New York, NY: Palgrave Macmillan.

Ehrenreich, B. (2009). *Smile or die: How positive thinking fooled America and the world*. London, UK: Granta.

Elias, A.S., & Gill, R. (2016). Beauty surveillance: The digital self-monitoring cultures of neoliberalism. *European Journal of Cultural Studies*. Retrieved from http://openaccess.city.ac.uk/15704/

Filippin, A., & Paccagnella, M. (2011). *Family background, self-confidence and economic outcomes*. Bonn, Germany: The Institute for the Study of Labor. Retrieved from https://papers.ssrn.com/sol3/papers.cfm?abstract_id=1965134

Giddens, A. (1991). *Modernity and self-identity*. Cambridge, UK: Polity Press.

Gilbert, J. (2008). *Anticapitalism and culture: Radical theory and popular politics*. Oxford, UK: Berg Publishers.

Gilbert, J. (2013). What kind of thing is "neoliberalism"? *New Formations, 80*, 7–22.

Goffman, E. (1959). *The presentation of everyday life*. New York, NY: Anchor Books.

Granter, E. (2009). *Critical social theory and the end of work*. Farnham, UK: Ashgate.

Hall. S., Massey, D., & Rustin, M. (Eds.). (2015). *After neoliberalism: Analysing the present*. London, UK: Lawrence and Wishart.

Halpern, D. (2005). *Social capital*. Cambridge, UK: Polity Press.

Harvey, D. (2005). *A brief history of neoliberalism*. Oxford, UK: Oxford University Press.

Illouz, E. (2003). Redeeming consumption: On Lowenthal's "The Triumph of the Mass Idols." In E. Katz, J. D. Peters, T. Liebes, & A. Orloff (Eds.), *Canonic texts in media research* (pp. 90–102). Cambridge, UK: Polity Press.

Kendall, D. E. (2002). *The power of good deeds: Privileged women and the social reproduction of the upper class*. Oxford, UK: Rowman and Littlefield.

Kuntsman, A. (Ed.). (2017). *Selfie citizenship*. London, UK: Palgrave Pivot.

Littler, J. (2017). *Against meritocracy: Culture, power and myths of mobility*. London, UK: Routledge.

Lowenthal, L. (2006). The triumph of mass idols. In P.D. Marshall (Ed.), *The celebrity culture reader* (pp. 124–152). London, UK: Routledge.

Lupton, D. (2015). *Digital sociology*. London, UK: Routledge.

Marwick, A. (2013). *Status update: Celebrity, publicity, and branding in the social media age*. New Haven, CT: Yale University Press.

Meikle, G. (2016). *Social media: Communicating, sharing and visibility*. London, UK: Routledge.

Miller Williams, N. (2015, April 20). *The career selfie: 7 ways to get noticed at work*. Retrieved from https://www.linkedin.com/pulse/career-selfie-7-ways-get-noticed-work-natasha-miller-williams

Negra, D., & Tasker, Y. (2014). Gender and recessionary culture. In D. Negra & Y. Tasker (Eds.), *Gendering the recession: Media and culture in an age of austerity* (pp. 1–30). Durham, NC: Duke University Press.

Nunn, H., & Biressi, A. (2010). Shameless? Picturing the "underclass" after Thatcherism. In L. Hadley & E. Ho (Eds.), *Thatcher and after: Margaret Thatcher and her afterlife in contemporary culture* (pp. 137–157). London, UK: Palgrave Macmillan.

Ouellette, L., & Hay, J. (2008). *Better living through reality TV: Television and post-welfare citizenship*. Oxford, UK: Blackwell.

Pakulski, J., & Waters, M. (1996). *The death of class.* London, UK: Sage.

Palmer G. (Ed.). (2008). *Exposing lifestyle television: The big reveal.* Hampshire, UK, and Burlington, VT: Ashgate.

Price, S., & Sabido, R. S. (2015). *Contemporary protest and the legacy of dissent.* London, UK: Rowman & Littlefield International.

Rettberg, W. J. (2014). *Seeing ourselves through technology: How we use selfies, blogs and wearable devices to see and shape ourselves.* Basingstoke, UK: Palgrave Macmillan.

Sandberg, S., & Scovell, N. (2013). *Lean in: Women, work, and the will to lead.* London, UK: W. H. Allen.

Sayer, A. (2005). *The moral significance of class.* Cambridge, UK: Cambridge University Press.

Sheridan, K. (2014, August 19). Take an employee engagement selfie. *Association for Talent Development.* Retrieved from https://www.td.org/Publications/Blogs/Management-Blog/2014/08/Take-An-Employee-Engagement-Selfie

Stallybrass, P., & White, A. (1986). *The politics and poetics of transgression.* Ithaca, NY: Cornell University Press.

Stover, C. (2014). "Divulging the eat deets": Postfeminist self-surveillance on women's fitness blogs. *Thinking Gender 2014.* UCLA Center for the Study of Women. Retrieved from https://escholarship.org/uc/item/7rv4v26h

Trauth, E. (2017). Curating the public self: Helping students present an authentic professional persona via LinkedIn. In K. Bryant (Ed.), *Engaging 21st century writers with social media* (pp. 221–230). Hershey, PA: IGI Global.

Tyler, I. (2013). *Revolting subjects: Social abjection and resistance in neoliberal Britain.* London, UK: Zed Books.

Twenge, J. (2014). *Generation me: Why today's young Americans are more confident, assertive, entitled—and more miserable than ever before.* New York, NY: Atria Books.

Wilen, T. (2015). *Career selfie? It might be time to upgrade.* Retrieved from www.linkedin.com/pulse/career-selfie-might-time-upgrade-dr-tracey-wilen

Williamson, M. (2016). *Celebrity: Capitalism and the making of fame.* Cambridge, UK: Polity Press.

10

RICH TV, POOR TV: WORK, LEISURE, AND THE CONSTRUCTION OF "DESERVED INEQUALITY" IN CONTEMPORARY BRITAIN

Jo Littler and Milly Williamson

Introduction

In January 2017, the UK ITV show *This Morning* featured a woman, Deborah Hodge, who had recently appeared on the Channel 5 reality TV show *On Benefits*. Phillip Schofield, one of the show's presenters, told Hodge that it "quite frankly got my back up" that she had spent £10 on two bottles of Prosecco (fizzy Italian wine) at Christmas and was filmed saying "cheers to the taxpayer for my gift." The incident was widely reported as Schofield losing his temper, with headlines including "Schofield blasts *This Morning* guest" and "Schofield hits out at mum" (Minn, 2017). The story and its wider amplification in the media worked on a number of discursive levels. It concertedly stoked pre-existing debate and moral panic about "benefits scroungers." The arrival of this motif on a show previously distanced from such moral condemnation was itself an event marking the further encroaching of such discourse into the mainstream. Meanwhile, left commentators—relatively marginalized in the UK media landscape—pointed out that such "fauxrage" enabled moral posturing about the fecklessness of the poor. In the memorable words of *Guardian* columnist Phil McDuff, "even if they hung old sacks at their window in lieu of curtains and ate cold beans by the light of recycled candles" to save money, any pleasurable consumption would be considered frivolous waste. Such indignation, he writes, "is a vicious reaction against the poor's presumptuous insistence on experiencing life as if they were as fully human as the rest of us" (McDuff, 2017). It was also pointed out that while the presenter Philip Schofield was castigating the unemployed about how they spent ten pounds, he was being paid a two-million-pound salary by ITV and had a private net worth valued at twelve million pounds (Singh, 2009; The Richest, 2017).

The benefits "scrounger" and the celebrified but abject reality TV performer are two central contemporary media images of working-class people in the UK media. Both are frequently depicted as "morally repugnant" (Tyler, 2013) and their construction resurrects elements of long-standing classed social types that are part of a "continuous morality play" through which the media reasserts dominant social values (Golding & Middleton, 1982, p. 238). The current resurrection of the welfare "scrounger" type has been joined by a new social type—the feckless, leisured "ordinary" celebrity—and we suggest that they are two sides of the same coin. Both have ideological taproots that extend back at least into the 19th century and are contemporary mediated manifestations of older discourses of the workshy, spiv, or shirker. Both are ideological responses to a broader economic and political crisis extending back to the 1960s; both are also the main fodder of reality TV today because they are cheap-to-make formats in the context of rising costs, declining audiences, and declining advertising revenue. Television production companies and broadcasters have utilised reality TV since the late 1990s as a cost-cutting mechanism through the exploitation of ordinary people in the media and a means by which to attack the conditions of workers in the television industry (Collins, 2008; Williamson, 2016). Both of these "social types" of reality TV feature working-class subjects who do not work and who are demonised, vilified, and depicted as amoral and/or excessive, although in different ways, as a result. While those on benefits are usually depicted as deviant and pathological, working-class celebrities on shows such as *Love Island* (ITV2, 2015–), *Ex on the Beach* (MTV, 2014–), and *Geordie Shore* (MTV, 2011–) are regularly shown as "bad subjects" for taking part in conspicuous leisure as part of the labour of reality TV, often fuelled by excesses of alcohol and sex. Both figures were elided together in the case of Deborah Hodge, Schofield's guest on *This Morning*, given her role as a mother of four who had given up her job as an art teacher in order to try to "make it" on reality TV and buy the house she was currently renting. Hodge was featured in a number of stories in the press, particularly *The Daily Mail*, which interviewed her about her plans while simultaneously viciously castigating her for her foolishness and recklessness (Waterlow, 2016).

This chapter will examine both representations of working-class "lack," contrasting them with forms of glamorous "overwork" recurring in representations of the rich, and connecting both to the political and cultural economy of their televisual production. For while configuring the working class as an underclass through "poverty porn" has expanded in this neoliberal era of a viciously widening gap between rich and poor, so too has the extravagantly favorable representation of the super wealthy. In Britain this has particularly taken the form of lavish costume heritage dramas about aristocratic culture such as *The Crown* (Netflix, 2016–), *Downton Abbey* (ITV, 2010–2015), and *Victoria* (ITV, 2016). In contrast with the shoestring production values and exploitative payment of celetoid reality TV stars, these programmes are opulent productions which package British upper-class life for a global, and particularly a transatlantic, market. In contrast with the depiction of working-class leisure as irresponsible and reckless, aristocrats are today recurrently depicted as hardworking and responsible. While both these tropes have, to be sure, very long-standing histories, their particular visibility at the present time and the specificities of their contemporary cultural expression are important. The juxtaposition of the "hardworking" rich and the "lazy" poor on British television works as an ideological justification for the continually extending chasm between wealth and poverty. At the same time their significantly different production values offer material evidence of classed investment in television production. In this short piece we unashamedly operate on a broad canvas by selecting salient examples of the rich and the poor on TV in contemporary Britain in order to provide a form of class and media analysis through what we consider to be eclectic but important juxtaposition. To begin with, we will look at the figure of the "scrounger."

The Return of "Scroungerphobia"

The benefits "scrounger" is as much a staple on British reality TV as the "ordinary" celebrity. Indeed, sometimes they are one and the same, as participants in benefits "documentaries" are in effect temporarily celebrified. "White Dee," for example, a key character on *Benefits Street*, was the subject of extensive media commentary (Allen, Tyler & de Benedictus, 2014). At a time when the Conservative government in Britain is making £12 billion cuts in welfare payments in the service of austerity, leading politicians and their allies in the media have demonized welfare claimants by stigmatising them and linking them to criminal and antisocial activity, and to already demonized and criminalized sections of the population—immigrants, gypsies, and single mums—further vilifying those groups. As Peter Golding and Sue Middleton argue in their landmark analysis of images of welfare, "The poor have been a nuisance, a threat and a financial burden throughout our history, and explaining their continuing and irritating presence has been a persistent problem of the ideologists of capitalism" (Golding & Middleton, 1982, p. 186).

The benefits "scrounger" is an important figure in the project and is not a new media phenomenon. It made a spectacular appearance in the British media in the 1970s as the "welfare scrounger" in order to explain, or rather, explain away, rising poverty. Three tropes were mobilized in the mid 1970s—individualism, moral pathology, and efficiency—in order to blame the poor for the crisis of capitalism by explaining broader economic problems (and in particular the fiscal crisis) as the outcome of a bloated and overly generous welfare state being exploited by "welfare scroungers" (Golding & Middleton, 1982, p. 226). The media created a sense of moral outrage between the "law abiding majority and the deviant claimant" (p. 83) in order to supply a set of explanations and rationalisations that shifted attention away from rising unemployment and refocused, and individualised, social problems and issues. The news media played a key role in this regard. By the mid-1970s, stories of welfare abuse managed to shift the narrative from one of concerns about benefit fraud into a more general suspicion of the welfare apparatus and the values that underpinned it, as part of a process of ideologically dismantling the welfare consensus (Golding & Middleton, 1982).

The image of the scrounger has been deployed by large sections of the UK media in order to popularise "opposition to the welfare system based on the twin themes that it was both unnecessary and an excessively costly burden" (Golding & Middleton, 1982, p. 109). Golding and Middleton (1982, p. 109) suggest that "scroungerphobia" developed in the 1970s in order to "remoralise the workless millions to ensure the continued vitality of the work ethic and the preservation of law and order" in the context of economic crisis and, by 1980, the largest increase in unemployment since the 1930s. But the fiscal crisis (the blame for which was being dumped at the door of the "welfare scrounger") was in fact the manifestation of wider structural problems facing British capitalism. Throughout the 20th century the private sector in the UK faced a crisis of accumulation, which was lower in Britain than in most major industrial nations. Capital investment was low throughout the post-war period (mostly hidden until the 1960s) and continues to be low, creating a long-term, ongoing crisis in productivity. Consequently, the "seeds of the neo-liberal attack on the welfare state have long been germinating in the soil of post-war economic uncertainties, even though not finally transplanted into the sunlight of popular debate until the 1970s" (Golding & Middleton, 1982, p. 224).

That crisis has only deepened in the subsequent decades, as Britain became the test-bed for neoliberalism in the Global North after the government made a deal with the IMF in 1976 (Hall, 1998; Harvey, 2005; Klein, 2008).[1]

Neoliberalism vigorously promotes corporate power, the marketization of collective forms of public provision, and the idea that competition is a ruling principle for all areas of life. This formation attempts to push forward and colonize new ground wherever it can; and just as the culture of Thatcherism tapped into pre-existing beliefs about welfare and poverty at a moment of economic crisis, so too has the economic crisis and political uncertainty of our time found right-wing expression in a new demonization of the welfare "scrounger."

In 2013, Conservative politicians reanimated longstanding motifs of a "division between those who apparently reap the comfortable benefits of welfare dependency and those whose inadequately rewarded labours finance them" (Golding and Middleton, 1982, p. 107), by suggesting, as did the then Prime Minister David Cameron, that claiming benefits was a "lifestyle choice." On the eve of announcing draconian cuts in welfare payments, Cameron claimed that "No-one wants to work hard every day and see their hard-earned taxes being used to fund things they themselves cannot afford or keep generations dependent on welfare."[2] However, while in the 1970s it was the tabloid press that amplified these views, today it is reality TV which has been at the forefront of this endeavor, with all five terrestrial channels in the UK churning out "documentaries" and docusoaps about people on benefits. From Channel Four's notorious format pioneering

Benefits Streets (2014) to the BBC's *We All Pay Your Benefits* (2013), Britain's broadcasters have whipped up anger and resentment at those depicted on "handouts" in the service of audience ratings. The tabloid press both feed off and cash in on this demonization by running stories about the characters from these shows. However, while earlier incarnations of the welfare scrounger were put into service to *hide* poverty, or deflect attention away from it (Golding & Middleton, 1982), one of the key ideological planks in the current construction of the "welfare crisis" is the view that welfare itself is one of the major causes of poverty rather than say, zero-hours contracts and greater job insecurity, falling wages, redundancy, and the contraction of traditional manufacturing industries (see Jensen & Tyler, 2015; McRobbie, 2018). The construction of welfare dependency as a cause of poverty circulates around "bad subjects" who are constituted as abject, and as Angela McRobbie demonstrates, these representations are often focused on women (McRobbie, 2018). Jensen and Tyler suggest that this is mediated through notions of intergenerational worklessness, drug dependency, antisocial behaviour, troubled families, teenage pregnancy, single mums, the workshy, and "benefits broods"—the portrayal of people who have large families ostensibly to increase their benefits (Jensen & Tyler, 2015). Both McRobbie and Jensen and Tyler argue that the production and repetition of "revolting subjects" is a central mechanism through which today's anti-welfare common sense is crafted. These shows combine a longer-standing construction of welfare claimants as "taking advantage" and as chaotic, with the more recent idea that welfare recipients are trapped in poverty *because* they receive benefits. The overall impression they engender is that welfare claimants are either undeserving and manipulative, or will be better off if their money is taken away or cut.

While all channels have indulged in this form of "poverty porn," it is Channel Five that dominates the field in this kind of diet. Channel Five's most recent offering, *The Great British Benefits Handout* (2016), was preceded by at least 16 shows of this kind, each with "benefits" in the title, each of which tackled the motifs of welfare dependency outlined by Tyler and Jensen above. But, unlike the BBC or Channel Four, Channel Five is an independent broadcaster whose regulatory remit is closer to ITV, so we must ask why it seems to be the channel that most enthusiastically pushes the Conservative government agenda in its aberrant construction of welfare claimants. Part of the answer has to do with the fortunes of the channel and its strategies for revenue generation in what has been a flat advertising environment for UK TV from the beginning of the 21st century. Channel Five emerged in the combined regulation-lite and increasingly commercial policy environment of the late 1990s. This policy environment (which promoted deregulation, increased competition, and commercialisation) occurred simultaneously with the introduction of new technology, channel proliferation, and media convergence. The result was an international crisis in the television industry with rising broadcasting costs and a simultaneous loss of revenue (Raphael, 2004; Deery, 2014; Williamson, 2016). The television industry responded in several ways to this crisis, including a series of cost-cutting exercises (Raphael, 2004; Williamson, 2016) and commercialising programmes as fully as possible (Deery, 2014).

In the UK, the result was the Communications Act of 2003, which lifted cross-media ownership caps and enabled non-European organisations to entirely own a British television company. The logic of Channel Five in this context primarily worked to offer a commercial diet of entertainment built on a developing business model of buying cheap production formats and already tried-and-tested series in order to maximise advertising revenue. Even so, this strategy did not initially pay off for the relatively small entity that was Channel Five in an atmosphere of mergers and acquisitions that had resulted from deregulation, and which produced the growth of enormous media giants. In 2010, Channel Five was operating at a loss of £48 million (Sweney, 2016). That year the channel was acquired by Richard Desmond (owner of the media group Northern Shell) for £103 million with promises of investment in new programmes and programme development (Knight, 2012). Instead, Desmond and Northern Shell set about making the company a profitable investment for shareholders and future possible acquisitions. This involved beefing up its advertiser-friendly programming, including its reality TV offerings, by acquiring shows like *Big Brother* from Channel Four, as well as poaching the life-on-benefits format from Channel Four.[3] Although the channel still lost £13 million under Desmond's ownership in the nine months to September 2014, it demonstrated that it was the kind of commercial entity ripe for acquisition by a multinational conglomerate interested in increasing the bottom line. And in 2014, enabled by the 2003 legislation, it was bought by Viacom for £463 million—more than triple its sale price to Desmond just four years earlier. Desmond reportedly paid himself and his top executives £100 million in bonuses, and Viacom set about using its size and strength to effect a 40% increase in ad revenue for the channel within the first year. Its first step was to shut down Channel Five's own sales operation, with a loss of almost 100 jobs (Sweney, 2016) and outsource its £300m-plus TV ad sales business to Sky until 2020 (Channel Five Annual Report, 2015). Linking up with Sky enabled Viacom to negotiate better advertising deals with media agencies because of its size in the market. Channel Five cites *Benefits Britain: Life on the Dole* as one of the channel's highlights for ad revenue (Channel Five Annual Report, 2015, p. 215).

Through these economic and cultural channels, Channel Five has engaged in a form of right-wing populism, of giving expression to "common sense," of voicing "what everyone knows" by reanimating longstanding images of welfare abuse and dependency and thus itself helping to re-create the mythology of welfare scroungers that it seeks to evoke, and it does so as a central plank in a programming strategy that is less concerned with the quality of its content than it is with the business of attracting as much advertising revenue as possible for as little outlay as possible. These images come at a time of increased marginalisation of working-class people from public culture, the decline in the numbers of working-class actors, the decline of thoughtful, multifaceted narratives of working-class experiences, and the decline of pride in working-class identity and collectivity (Skeggs, 2004; Friedman, O'Brien & Laurison, 2016; Jones, 2016). We have seen the winnowing of the space for participation of working-class people in the British media both behind the screen and in front of it, and an increase in 21st-century "poverty porn" where they are subject to ridicule, denigration, and abjection—in short "scroungerphobia."

Celebrity and Class in Reality TV

But this sub-format of reality TV is not the only one which benefits from the manipulation of images of working-class "worklessness" to cash in on unacceptable versions of leisure. Today, reality TV is populated with working-class reality celebrities who perform a version of "leisure" which is depicted as "hedonistic, irresponsible and raucous" (Kay, 2017), and which, at the same time, denies the *labour* of these performances (Turner, 2010; Wood et al., this volume) and hides the profitable surplus value extracted from them (Williamson, 2016). Wood, Kay, and Banks argue that the construction of disgust is very much a classed phenomenon that is dependent upon the denigration of working-class performances of leisure as "illegitimate labour." They argue that the work of ordinary celebrities in reality TV is considered "not real work" and that reality celebrity "has come to symbolise the antithesis of commitment to a career—rather, it signifies a particular kind of narcissistic worklessness" (in this volume; see also Skeggs & Wood, 2011, 2012).

In the UK, the three most popular of these shows are *Geordie Shore*, *The Only Way Is Essex*, and *Ex on the Beach*. These shows are filmed in spaces that might be more closely associated with the conspicuous consumption of Thorstein Veblen's traditional "leisure class" than with the *mise-en-scene* of working-class "graft"[4]—Mediterranean beaches, yachts, exclusive resorts with swimming pools and bars, nightclubs, and restaurants. However, these settings and the participants who populate them are framed as imbued with a sense of repugnant excess—showing too much flesh and emotion, too much interest in sex, drinking, and swearing, and too little middle-class cultural capital. Traditional spaces of leisure are also invaded by the visibility of intimate "backstage" spaces such as the bedroom and the toilet, and the "private" activities that occur in such spaces, including sexual intercourse, vomiting, and defecation, contributing to a sense of these celebrities as abject. But there is also a sense of troubling anxiety, as reality celebrities have become what Jilly Kay terms a new working-class-based "illegitimate leisure class" (Kay, 2017) that, while it is denigrated in the wider media and commentariat, also provides working-class viewers with an "opportunity structure" (Allen & Mendick, 2013, p. 87) at a cultural and historical moment when the creative arts are increasingly closed to the working class. These shows and the celebrities that perform on them are denigrated because they offer a version of conspicuous consumption to working-class audiences in images that may be the inverse of Veblen's leisure class, but are considered no less ripe for emulation.

Nonetheless, celebrities on reality TV are usually unpaid or badly paid for their performances (Williamson, 2016) and instead they must generate a precarious income by promoting products online or at appearances at nightclubs (Wood, 2016). Wood and colleagues (in this volume) point out that this precarity is gendered, and it takes a particular toll on female working-class bodies. For example, female reality celebrities put on weight prior to the release of a fitness DVD in order to be photographed as "overweight," so that they can later appear trim and "fit" to promote the DVD. Rather than an "easy paycheck" this gendered labour involves "intensive corporeal toil" (Wood et al., this volume). The character and terms of celebrity promotional labour differ between upper-middle-class celebrities and working-class celebrities. The wealthy celebrities of E4's *Made in Chelsea* are less dependent on selling their labour through promotional work than are their working-class counterparts in *Geordie Shore*, and at any rate "tend to get more lucrative, enduring and less ad-hoc endorsement contracts," such as *Made in Chelsea*'s Binkie Felsted gaining a contract as the new face of Reebok (Kay, 2017). Unlike their working-class counterparts, the worklessness of the upper-middle-class celebrities of *Made in Chelsea* is "normalized" as appropriately performed leisure through their knowledge of proper class-based conduct in the glamorous venues of leisure.

Reinventing the Rich: Aristocrats "Learning to Labour"

Working-class subjects on reality TV, a genre related to a specific and exploitative mode of television production, are then today insistently being presented as the undeserving poor, feckless in their leisure. By contrast, the marked trend in televisual presentations of the British rich occupies very different symbolic and economic terrain and has been expanded by a recent spate of extremely popular lavish TV period dramas devoted to the aristocracy, including the ITV dramas *Downton Abbey* and *Victoria* and the Netflix dramatic serial *The Crown*. The latter was widely reported as being "the most expensive TV show ever made" with a reported budget of $100 million for two series (Lewis, 2016; Loughrey, 2016).

Such shows clearly build on a longer tradition of British heritage drama, including *Upstairs/Downstairs* in the 1970s and the enthusiastic embrace of historical aristocrats by the 1980s silver screen, particularly in Merchant-Ivory films such as *Chariots of Fire* (1981) and *Howard's End* (1992). The latter have been frequently and accurately read in the context of the rise of a 1980s neoconservative Thatcherite agenda that promoted and sold a reactionary version of the past to legitimate its present via what came to be termed "the heritage industry," a complex that also includes new forms of heritage experience attraction as well as "heritaged" lifestyle brands (Hewison, 1987; Higson, 2001; Littler & Naidoo, 2004; Harvey, 2005). Just as these earlier visual texts worked hard to celebrate aristocratic culture, so too do these current versions, which have mushroomed in appeal, cost, and reach to an extent not seen since the 1980s. Given this symbiosis it could also be noted that alongside the continuation of the neoliberal agenda of marketization and competitiveness, Prime Minister May's combination of a populist, demotic appeal made explicitly to the working class with an extremely punitive agenda and eager embrace of authoritarian despots in pursuit of financial profit is more than a little reminiscent of Thatcher's regime.

In terms of our interests in classed dynamics of work and leisure, there are several interesting features operating in these recent aristocratic dramas which seem to be part of an extended cultural continuum since the 1980s and to offer something qualitatively new and specific both in terms of cultural production and representational dynamics in this different conjuncture. In the process of depicting aristocrats who have extensive leisure time, many of these programmes are extremely keen to emphasise the story that they work very hard: that they are tireless "grafters" in the service of the common good. *The Crown*, for instance, starts this process early on in its first episode, where the future queen is learning from her dying father about the graft and craft of monarchy. Their talking point is the sheer volume of papers that the king has to read from his government, a task he is presented taking very seriously, and conducting in a far more adroit manner than those in the cabinet ("I turn them over so I see the ones they don't want me to see" he says of the large box of files left for him by the prime minister).

Indeed the whole series is in many ways the story of aristocrats *learning to labour*, focalized through an invited identification with the queen's neck-twitching repressed emotional life and no-nonsense stoicism which are necessary attributes of the job. We are encouraged to admire the extent of this emotional labour as part of, and alongside, a wider repertoire of skills the queen is depicted acquiring. (It is notable that this largely sympathetic, dramatic portrait includes a sympathetic and romanticised framing of its relationship to imperialism, reducing imperial subjects to sentimental storyline fodder). Being monarch is portrayed as such a weighty burden it killed George VI; "the responsibility of becoming king killed your father!" says the Queen Mother in the third episode.

As Michael Billig put it, when we are talking of the royal family we are talking of other issues too (Billig, 1992), including nation, community, family, and inequality. The favorable presentations of the monarchy might be part of a longer tradition which ebbs and flows, but its marked resurgence, and the lavish effort and expenditure on it at this time of expanding plutocratic power, when eight people own the same wealth as half the world, is no accident (Oxfam, 2017). The wealth of the monarchy is of course hereditary, accumulated over centuries, and the strategies of cultural legitimation for such power have a long and undistinguished history (Clancy, 2015). Nonetheless, the monarchy is used to validate the accumulated wealth of other plutocratic elites. Even the reporting of the lavish budget in the tabloid press is couched in terms of class deference—the *Mirror* online tells its readers that *The Crown* may be the most expensive television show ever made—"but we think it might just be worth every penny" because of the "attention to detail" and "award winning" performances. The paper reports with glee the £200k cost of a 30-second scene of a train (Jeffries & Methven, 2016). The justification of the expense of depicting the on-screen royals has distinct echoes of those deployed on the cost of the actual royals, and in the former case, this is funded by one of the top streaming services, Netflix, which is using its strong market position and resources to establish their "quality" credentials through narratives of the monarchy in order to consolidate that market position. There are what we might term "feedback loops of cultural validation" between the monarchy, the aristocracy, plutocrats, and capitalists. On a practical material level, this occurs when Conservative governments agree to make the queen exempt from tax or donate £370 million to refurbish Buckingham Palace in a time when the amount of homeless people living on the streets has risen by 16% (Davies, 2016; BBC, 2017). Crucially, on a cultural and symbolic level, it works to validate the principle of inherited wealth. As Andrew Sayer argues in *Why We Can't Afford the Rich*, obtaining income from *existing assets* that yield rent, interest, or capital gains is unearned income, and people who gain this income are *rentiers* (Sayer, 2016; also see Lapavitsas, 2013). It is a form of wealth extraction, but it becomes packaged as, and confused with, wealth creation. A neoliberal political system supports, above all, *rentier* interests, in which the 99% become increasingly indebted to the 1%. Because contemporary plutocrats, like aristocrats, often leverage their inheritance through unearned income (like Donald Trump in the US, or the Duke of Westminster in Britain), becoming *rentiers* in the search for more wealth, there is a vested interest in their mutual validation.

The wildly popular TV drama *Downton Abbey* (ITV/PBS, 2015) is instructive here. A joint US/UK production, it depicted a British stately home in the early decades of the 20th century and the varied, interwoven lives of its inhabitants, from cooks to ladies, butlers to lords. Fashioning British heritage for the domestic and international export market, it had extremely and at times unprecedentedly high ratings across a wide range of countries including China, Brazil, Singapore, Denmark, Israel, Belgium, and Iceland (Egner, 2013). Like *The Queen*, *Downton* displayed lavish aristocratic lifestyles, while similarly offering some contextual historical background that depicted key events within a very conservative narrative. The key difference is of course the greater amount of screen time devoted to the working-class members of the household; although in tune with the dramatic, conservative tenor, they are overwhelmingly depicted as knowing and being happy with their social station (Littler, 2017).

While *Downton* includes a variety of depictions of the rich, it overwhelming presents them as *extremely* hard-working subjects. The Earl of Grantham and his American heiress wife Cora (again, symbolizing the mutual marriage of aristocracy and plutocracy) are hard-working paternalists who construct hospitals for their village and act like kind parents nurturing their subjects. One of their daughters becomes a hard-working "new woman" and magazine editor; another expends extensive effort branching out into the pig farming business. The majority of these aristocrats are not depicted as leisure-class scroungers but rather as noble, industrious (and proto-feminist) subjects. In the process, these social and economic elites acquire the patina of cultural worth through their association with "hard work." Hard work is an attribute with classed connotations which has become wrenched from the working classes and re-gifted to the rich, and it is notable that plutocrats across the spectrum use such imagery and language to justify their privilege (Khan, 2010; Littler, 2017). *Downton* also depicts the changing historical landscape as one where some social change is considered impossible for that moment (notably, combating racism—a "mixed race" relationship is deemed impossible), while other kinds of change are embraced and depicted as inevitable, particularly that of aristocrats becoming businessmen/women and developing "enterprise initiatives" around, for example, housing, car dealerships, and pig farming (Littler, 2017). In the process, the cultural and symbolic traffic between inherited wealth and capitalism becomes revalidated.

The Contemporary Construction of "Deserved Inequality"

Through these engaging dramas and shaming shows the divergence between rich and poor becomes validated as a historical truth and justified present. Both construct the image of contemporary inequalities as being, above all, *deserved*. The dream of a "life of leisure" may be expanding in the context of neoliberal "austerity," of growing precarious working conditions and longer hours for less pay, but reality TV recurrently turns leisure into labour for the predominantly working-class contestants of such shows (and their audiences), whose convincing performance of leisure (often highly sexualized and gendered) is being exchanged for a shot at fame. Those who already *have* ample leisure are being insistently presented as hardworking, while those who have nothing must work at convincing performances of a leisured existence.

There are of course many other classed representations and subjects we have not discussed whose presence feeds into this wildly unequal economic order: the "good" working- or middle-class neoliberal subject, who works hard, goes the extra mile, works beyond what they are supposed to. This is part of the core message of the iconic morality play of *The Apprentice* (Littler, 2007; Couldry & Littler, 2011), whose mobile neoliberal meritocratic subjects validate the divergent social order and rampant inequality; they present the dream of social mobility as a possibility rather than horrendously difficult and improbable in Britain's stagnant economy. Just like the representations of rich and poor we have considered in this chapter, these depictions connect to a much wider issue of the neoliberal self in which the "good" subject is one who overworks. Of course, the irony is that workers in the UK work longer hours for less pay than their European counterparts, and a smaller proportion are unemployed. It is not insignificant that at a time when depictions of supposed working-class fecklessness abound, in contrast to portrayals of aristocratic and upper-middle-class hard work and prudence, British workers are working harder for less pay while the unearned income of the rich rockets.

These symbolic inversions of work and worklessness serve to further discipline an already overstretched working class in an economy of declining productivity, which is due, not to a lack of "graft," but to lack of investment and increased exploitation.

Notes

1. The much bloodier test-bed in the Global South being Chile, where the democratic socialistic government of Salvador Allende was violently deposed with US backing.
2. www.france24.com/en/20130407-uk-cameron-welfare-lifestyle-choice-budget-cuts-unemployment, accessed February 25, 2017.
3. Much to the annoyance of Channel Four chief executive David Abraham, who was more concerned about the fact that Channel Five had cloned the successful format than he was about the 1800 complaints received by the regulator Ofcom about *Benefits Street*.
4. In the UK, "graft" refers to tireless hard work and a "grafter" is one who is industrious.

Works Cited

Allen, K., & Mendick, H. (2013). Young people's uses of celebrity: Class, gender and "improper" celebrity. *Discourse: Studies in the Cultural Politics of Education*, *34*(1), 77–93.

Allen, K., Tyler, I., & de Benedictus, S. (2014). Thinking with "White Dee": The gender politics of "austerity porn". *Sociological Research Online*, *19*(3), 2. Retrieved from www.socresonline.org.uk/19/3/2.html

BBC News. (2017, January 25). Rough sleeping rises at appalling rate, charity says, as figures show 16% rise. *BBC News*. Retrieved from www.bbc.co.uk/news/uk-england-38719087

Billig, M. (1992). *Talking of the royal family*. London, UK: Routledge.

Channel Five Annual Report. (2015). Retrieved from http://ar2015.itvplc.com/assets/pdf/ITV_2015_Annual_Report.pdf

Clancy, L. (2015, May 2). Baby's first photo call: How the royals learned to act normal. *The Conversation*. Retrieved from http://theconversation.com/babys-first-photo-call-how-the-royals-learned-to-act-normal-40809

Collins, S. (2008). Making the most out of 15 minutes: Reality TV's dispensable celebrity. *Television and New Media*, *9*(2), 87–110.

Couldry, N., & Littler, J. (2011). Work, power and performance: Analysing the "reality" game of *The Apprentice*. *Cultural Sociology*, *5*(2), 263–279.

Davies, C. (2016, November 18). Buckingham Palace to undergo "essential" £370 million refurbishment. *The Guardian*. Retrieved from www.theguardian.com/uk-news/2016/nov/18/buckingham-palace-to-undergo-370m-refurbishment

Deery, J. (2014). Mapping commercialization in reality television. In L. Ouellette (Ed.), *A companion to reality television* (pp. 311–28). Chichester, UK: Wiley Blackwell.

Egner, J. (2013, January 3). A bit of Britain where the sun never sets: Downton Abbey reaches around the world. *New York Times*. Retrieved from www.nytimes.com/2013/01/06/arts/television/downton-abbey-reaches-around-the-world.html?_r=2

Friedman, S., O'Brien, D., & Laurison, D. (2016). "Like skydiving without a parachute": How class origin shapes occupational trajectories in British acting. *Sociology*, *19*, 1–19.

Golding, P., & Middleton, S. (1982). *Images of welfare: Press and public attitudes to poverty*. Oxford, UK: Martin Robertson.

Hall, S. (1988). *The hard road to renewal*. London, UK: Verso.

Harvey, D. (2005). *A brief history of neoliberalism*. Oxford, UK: Oxford University Press.

Hewison, R. (1987). *The heritage industry: Britain in a climate of decline*. London, UK: Methuen.

Higson, A. (2001). Heritage cinema and television. In D. Morley & K. Robins (Eds.), *British cultural studies: Geography, nationality and identity* (pp. 249–260). Oxford, UK: Oxford University Press.

Jeffries, M., & Methven, N. (2016). *The Crown* is most expensive TV series ever made at £100 million – but it's worth it. *Mirror*. Retrieved from www.mirror.co.uk/tv/tv-news/crown-most-expensive-tv-series-9141199

Jensen, T., & Tyler, I. (2015). "Benefits broods": The cultural and political crafting of anti-welfare commonsense. *Critical Social Policy, 35*, 4.

Jones, O. (2016). *Chavs: The demonization of the working-class*. London, UK: Verso.

Kay, J. B. (2017). #Sponsored selves: Reality celebrity and the labour of "worklessness" (Unpublished paper).

Khan, S. (2010). *Privilege: The making of an adolescent elite at St Paul's School*. Princeton, NJ: Princeton University Press.

Klein, N. (2008). *The shock doctrine*. Harmondsworth, UK: Penguin.

Knight, J. (2012). Channel Five recovers with £26 million profit despite advertising slowdown. *The Independent*. Retrieved from www.independent.co.uk/news/business/news/channel-5-recovers-with-26m-profit-despite-advertising-slowdown-7799815.html

Lapavitsas, C. (2013). *Profiting without producing: How finance exploits us all*. London, UK: Verso.

Lewis, H. (2016, November 5). *The Crown* creator disputes "most expensive show ever made" rumors. *Hollywood Reporter*. Retrieved from www.hollywoodreporter.com/live-feed/crown-not-expensive-show-ever-made-creator-says-as-peter-morgan-matt-smith-claire-foy-talk

Littler, J. (2007). Celebrity CEOs and the cultural economy of tabloid intimacy. In S. Holmes & S. Redmond (Eds.), *A reader in stardom and celebrity* (pp. 230–243). London, UK: Sage.

Littler, J. (2017). *Against meritocracy: Culture, power and myths of mobility*. London, UK: Routledge.

Littler, J., & Naidoo, R. (2004). White past, multicultural present: Heritage and national stories. In R. Phillips & H. Brocklehurst (Eds.), *History, nationhood and the question of Britain* (pp. 330–341). London, UK: Palgrave.

Loughrey, C. (2016, January 25). *The Crown*: The Netflix show is the most expensive TV series ever. *The Independent*. Retrieved from www.independent.co.uk/arts-entertainment/tv/news/the-crown-netflix-most-expensive-show-ever-matt-smith-a7392911.html

McDuff, P. (2017, January 6). What's wrong with spending your benefits on Prosecco? Nothing. *The Guardian*. Retrieved from www.theguardian.com/commentisfree/2017/jan/06/spending-benefits-prosecco-feckless-poor-phillip-schofield

McRobbie, A. (2018). *Feminism and the culture of neoliberalism*. Cambridge, UK: Polity.

Minn, H. (2017, January 4). Phillip Schofield blasts *This Morning* guest who bought Christmas Prosecco with benefits: "You got my back up". *Daily Mirror*. Retrieved from www.mirror.co.uk/tv/tv-news/phillip-schofield-blasts-benefit-scounger--9561308

Oxfam. (2017). *An Economy for the 99%.* Retrieved from http://policy-practice.oxfam.org.uk/publications/an-economy-for-the-99-its-time-to-build-a-human-economy-that-benefits-everyone-620170

Raphael, C. (2004). The political economic origins of reali-TV. In S. Murray & L. Ouellette (Eds.), *Reality TV: Remaking television culture* (pp. 119–134). New York, NY: New York University Press.

The Richest. (2017). Phillip Scofield: Net worth. Retrieved from www.therichest.com/celebnetworth/celeb/phillip-schofield-net-worth/

Sayer, A. (2016). *Why we can't afford the rich.* Bristol, UK: Policy Press.

Singh, A. (2009, January 25). Quitting over Schofield's salary? That's b★★★★s says TV Fern. *Evening Standard.* Retrieved from www.standard.co.uk/news/quitting-over-schofields-salary-that-s-bs-says-tv-fern-6898729.html

Skeggs, B. (2004). *Class, self, culture.* London, UK: Routledge.

Skeggs, B., & Wood, H. (2011). *Reacting to reality television.* London, UK: Routledge.

Skeggs, B., & Wood, H. (Eds.). (2012). *Reality television and class.* Basingstoke, UK: Palgrave.

Sweney, M. (2016). Chanel 5 back in black as almost 100 jobs are cut following Viacom takeover. *The Guardian.* Retrieved from www.theguardian.com/media/2016/jul/06/channel-5-back-in-black-as-almost-100-jobs-are-cut-foollowing-viacom-takover

Turner, G. (2010). *Ordinary people and the media: The demotic turn.* London, UK: Sage.

Tyler, I. (2013). *Revolting subjects: Social abjection and resistance in neoliberal Britain.* London, UK: Zed Books.

Waterlow, L. (2016, November 10). "I'm not too proud to clean toilets": Single mother on benefits who quit her teaching job to pursue fame is now looking for menial work after her dream of stardom failed. *The Daily Mail.* Retrieved from www.dailymail.co.uk/femail/article-3924012/Single-mother-benefits-admits-defeat-bid-famous.html

Williamson, M. (2016). *Celebrity: Capitalism and the making of fame.* Cambridge, UK: Polity.

Wood, H. (2016). The politics of hyperbole on Geordie Shore: Class, gender, youth and excess. *European Journal of Cultural Studies*, 20(1), 39–55.

PART IV

Digital Cultures

11

WHEN LEFT THEORY "LEAVES BEHIND THE DREAM OF A REVOLUTION": CLASS AND THE SOFTWARE ECONOMY

Rob Wilkie

First introduced in Lev Manovich's *The Language of New Media* (2001), and developed by such writers as N. Katherine Hayles (2005), Alexander Galloway (2004), Benjamin H. Bratton (2016), Geoff Cox and Alex McLean (2013), and Mathew Fuller (2008), the field of "software studies" proposes we have entered "a new computer culture" that is "a blend of human and computer meanings, of traditional ways in which human culture modeled the world and the computer's own means of representing it" (Manovich, 2001, p. 46). From search engines to social networks, and cloud storage to self-driving vehicles, software studies takes as its starting point the notion we increasingly live in a "virtual" reality in which the rise of digital technologies and, more specifically, the immaterial labor creating the software that runs them, means "code now conditions existence in the West" (Kitchin & Dodge, 2011, p. 260). It is not accidental that Elon Musk, the Internet's favorite billionaire, made headlines by speculating that the odds we are not already living inside a computer-coded software simulation are "one in billions" (Boult, 2016). Musk's musings on the possibility that material reality is defined by the immateriality of code reflect a broader notion connecting high theory and popular culture in which the "software revolution" said to be driving contemporary capitalism is a deconstructive "double-code." It refers not only to technological advances in how we produce, store, transmit, and access information, but more importantly to the belief that the significant role software plays in everything from manufacturing and finance to communications and entertainment represents a fundamental shift that "de-codes" the basis upon which capitalism is organized, bringing about the end of divisions between production and consumption, the material and the immaterial, and above all the class divide between owners and workers. Code, in short, has become the theoretical language through which class critique is deleted from the analysis of network capitalism.

Code theory is symptomatic of broader assumptions undergirding cultural theory today, for which class is either erased completely in favor of "power" and "inequality," or has become a "political concept" in which "our understanding of labor cannot be limited to waged labor but must refer to human creative capacities in all their generality" (Hardt & Negri, 2004, p. 105). As such, I want to mark from the start that when I use the concept of class I am referring not to a cultural theory of class—that is, class as a series of shifting and amorphous political and cultural identities defined by a relation of "affinity" and "difference"—but rather to the objective economic division between owners and workers within capitalism that ultimately determines all other relations in society. Class, in other words, not in terms of the type of work that is done, or the way that people might perceive their own social position, but as the effect of "the specific economic form, in which unpaid surplus labour is pumped out of direct producers" and which "determines the relationship of rulers and ruled, as it grows directly out of production itself and, in turn, reacts upon it as a determining element" (Marx, 1998, p. 778). While cultural theories of class blur the divisions between owners and workers either by promoting illusions of a commonality of Weberian lifestyle practices, or by dividing people into innumerable classes based upon employment type or income, I argue for a historical and material theory of class which brings back to the forefront of cultural theory the "hidden abode of production" (Marx, 1996, p. 186) that shapes all other social relationships and explains why all of the contradictions of contemporary life—from rising poverty amidst increasing wealth, to the "digital divide" and "precarity" of work despite technological advances—are effects of the mode of production.

According to dominant readings of software in code theory, network capitalism is not defined by class divisions between owners and workers, but by oscillating and opposing antagonisms operating within structures of "power." Here I am referring to the Foucauldian argument that the exploitation of labor by capital has been replaced by the diktats of "biopower," or "a mode of production that makes life itself the site of valorization" (Galloway, 2012, p. 136). According to the biopolitical reading of contemporary capitalism, surplus value "comes from the cognitive and immaterial product of a creative action" (Negri, 2008, p. 19) and cannot be reduced to any particular activity or class. As such, the social ceases to be the space of class conflict and instead becomes a space of play between repressive forces which try to discipline eruptions of creativity in order to control any vital energies produced and the "disorganized, differential, and powerful multiplicity" whose creative acts ultimately resist all forms of control (Negri, 2008, p. 22).

It is through this framework that the software revolution is read as a two-fold process that displaces the economics of class exploitation in favor of an oscillating cultural politics of "control" and "resistance." First, contemporary capitalism is said to represent what Deleuze and Guattari (1983) theorize as the "decoding" economy (p. 246), or the idea that the production of profit under capitalism no longer rests on a clearly defined exploitation of labor by capital. Instead, capitalism is depicted as structured around an endless cycle of releasing and recapturing excessive creative energies generated by all social practices, not just those traditionally considered "work." In this post-labor, post-work form of network capitalism, profit depends upon capturing and selling the life activity of "users" whenever and wherever they log on to programs like Facebook or Snapchat, such that "the boundaries between work time and spare time, labour and play, become fuzzy" (Fuchs, 2014, p. 126). Second, because of software's enabling of the capturing of creative energies through the continual tracking, recording, and shaping of user behavior, network capitalism supposedly dismantles the class division between owners and workers in favor of a series of constantly shifting assemblages that defy "reductive" class categorizations. Instead of the class binary of owners and workers, code theorists substitute the concept of "immaterial labor" in which the production of surplus value is "not completely confined to a specific class formation," but instead "is a form of activity of every productive subject within postindustrial societies" (Terranova, 2013, p. 41). According to the theory of immaterial labor, class becomes an outdated concept the moment when everyone, regardless of whether they are at home or at work, turns out to be a producer of the information that is "data mined" by the Internet corporations who "accumulate profit by exploiting the play labour of users" (Fuchs, 2014, p. 126). When all of us, actively or passively, are producing information commodities every time we log into our email, play a game, or even just turn on our phones, there is no longer an easy way of classifying who is an "owner" and who is a "worker." As Maurizio Lazzarato (2004) puts it,

> in the era of immaterial labour and cooperation between minds it is not possible to think social conflicts in terms of the friend/enemy dichotomy or in terms of the conflict between two classes, nor in terms of liberal (private/public) or socialist (individual/collective) traditions (p. 187).

The emerging code economy is thus taken to represent a spontaneous "communism of capitalism" (Virno, 2004, p. 110) in which the elimination of traditional class contradictions between owners and workers through technological advances means the only remaining barrier to social equality is freeing life from the cultural homogenization of the network economy. In turn, social change is redefined as "exodus" from the instrumentality of work (Dyer-Witheford & de Peuter, 2009, p. 218), rather than ending a system of private ownership of the means of production so that labor can be put to meeting the needs of all.

The idea that "software structures and makes possible much of the world" (Fuller, 2008, p. 1), and that the "hard" work of commodity production is being replaced by the "soft" labor of coding information, upending in the process all social barriers between production and consumption, human and nonhuman, material and immaterial, and, above all, the class division between owners and workers, is said to mark the end of the history of social transformations. Manuel DeLanda (2016) argues, for instance, "Left" theory can only survive today if it "leaves behind the dream of a Revolution that changes the entire system" (p. 48). On the contrary, I argue that the narrative of a code economy in which "labor is becoming even more informational and communicative" such that "all activities have been turned into production" (Cox & McLean, 2013, p. 49) is the latest version of the desire for a post-class form of capitalism in which surplus value is created by the generation of new ideas, rather than the exploitation of labor. This ideological fantasy obscures the need for social transformation, since "there is no longer an outside to the relations of production" (Roggero, 2010, p. 161), but instead celebrates "acceleration" in which "the liberation of the potentiality of labor against the blockage determined by capitalism must happen within the evolution of capitalism itself" (Negri, 2014, p. 366). In contrast to the dominant reading of software as ushering in an era of post-class network capitalism, I argue new technologies such as software do not eliminate class but sharpen it. Software is the product of labor and thus, like all technologies under capitalism, a mechanism used by the owning class to extend rather than extinguish the exploitation of productive labor of the working class that is at the heart of the capitalist system. When examining the consequences of the software revolution, a historical and materialist theory of class, defined by Marx (1998) as one's position in the "direct relation between the owners of the conditions of production and the direct producers" (p. 778), is necessary if we wish to bring about real social transformation and not just prepare a new generation of workers with the cultural and technological "skills" required by global capitalism.

Erasing Class: The "Life" of Software Assemblages

Software studies emerges as a challenge to capitalism's instrumental rationality which, through brutal technological efficiency, is said to turn the immeasurable singularity of "life" into "quantifiable metrics that are now visible and amenable for computation and processing" (Berry, 2011, p. 2). Writers such as Lev Manovich (2013), Wendy Hui Kyong Chun (2011), and Matthew Fuller (2008) argue software is not simply a neutral series of algorithms—a passive object waiting for human agency—but an active assemblage, capturing of all aspects of life through the mechanisms of code while simultaneously creating "lines of flight" (Deleuze & Guattari, 1987, p. 21) that undermine quantitative reduction and open a space of resistance from within. Software studies is thus located, on the one hand, within the philosophical tradition of Heidegger's (1977) anti-instrumentalist poetics, which attempt to linguistically dematerialize the material world in order to naturalize class inequalities while nonetheless challenging the reduction of life to "standing-reserve" (p. 17), and, on the other, Foucault's (1978) theory of "biopolitics," in which capitalism is understood as shifting from labor exploitation to technics of power in order "to administer, optimize, and multiply [life], subjecting it to precise controls and comprehensive administrations" (p. 137). As such, it is part of a series of new philosophical movements, including "new materialism" (Bennett, 2010), "thing theory" (Brown, 2015), "speculative realism" (Shaviro, 2014), and "object-oriented-ontology" (Harman, 2016), which claim to challenge capitalism's instrumental logic by recognizing the agency of all "actants" (Latour, 2004, p. 75)—whether human or nonhuman, material or immaterial—in shaping the existing in unknown ways. Calling into question the representation of software as "realized instrumentality" (Fuller, 2008, p. 3) and "a universal language through which the world speaks, and a universal engine on which the world runs" (Manovich, 2013, p. 2), software studies proponents argue code represents a posthuman vitality that, as an expression of nonhuman forms of life, resists capture as "a hybrid assemblage that is contingent, relational, productive, and made in the moment" (Kitchin & Dodge, 2011, p. 246). In other words, software is an embodied metaphor for the attempt by humanity to reduce life to "means to an end" and the ability of life to exceed humanity's instrumental reason.

In *Programmed Visions: Software and Memory*, for example, Chun (2011) argues computing has been "central to the management and creation of populations, political economy and the apparatuses of security" and that "without [computers] there would be no government, no corporations, no schools, no global marketplace" (p. 7). She writes that the role of software under neoliberalism has been to create the appearance of "the *seemingly* sovereign individual, the subject driven to know, driven to map, to zoom in and out, to manipulate, and to act" (Chun, 2011, p. 8). However, the "sovereignty" of the individual, she continues, remains dependent upon "individuating us and also integrating us into a totality" defined by the terms of the global market. Yet, while Chun (2011) challenges the neoliberal idea of "empowerment" offered by software as giving the user "control" over things like access to market information that enables "better decisions" (p. 8), her challenge is limited to exposing capitalism's inability to ever fully control the effects of software and thus incorporate it entirely within the structure of commodification. Software, in her analysis, remains a "ghostly presence" that "produces and defies apprehension" (Chun, 2011, p. 3). Going back to Heidegger's (1971) theory of the "thing" as a Kantian materiality which exists by means other than those of human labor and beyond human reason (p. 179), Chun (2011) writes "software as thing cannot be reduced to software as a commodity" because a thing is simultaneously ambiguous and specific (p. 6). She claims, despite the "dream" of complete and instantaneous access to information promised by neoliberalism, "our computers execute in unforeseen ways, the future opens to the unexpected. Because of this, any programmed vision will always be inadequate, will always give way to another future" (Chun, 2011, p. 9). Similarly, Kitchin and Dodge (2011) argue "software is the product of a sociotechnical assemblage" (p. 247), which means "the relationship between people, material technology, time, and space is contingent, relational, productive, and dynamic" (p. 16) and thus forever "open to rupture" (p. 19). The sense that code inherently resists capture reflects a belief that "neither the agency of human programmers nor the description of code fully accounts for the complex and rich ways that code creates a world (*welt*) beyond human design" (Holmes, 2016, para. 1). Software "glitches" are read not as errors or failures, which would presume the existence of a normalized "operational" state, but a form of what Henri Bergson (1983) describes as *élan vital*, or spontaneous eruptions of "life force" that cannot be reduced to an "on/off" binary. When our computers fail to operate in expected ways, this argument goes, we are exposed to the limits of human intention in controlling life's flows, guaranteeing a "space for profound and unfinished imagination" (Fuller, 2008, p. 7). In this sense, software becomes an expression of life's vitalism, which repels the intentionality of control and design. As software studies proponents argue, the "possible and often unpredictable actions that result when a program runs" (Cox & McLean, 2013, p. 63) mean that the creativity of life, even if that life is the post-life of software, "is not simply reducible to market principles" (Cox & McLean, 2013, p. 51).

The depiction of software as one agent in a series of "hybrid assemblages" (Kitchin & Dodge, 2011, p. 16) which "tie humans and non-humans together into new aggregates" (Berry, 2011, p. 2) draws heavily upon Deleuze and Guattari's (1983) reworking of Bergsonian vitalism in their claim that the transformation of capitalism can only happen from within, by "accelerat[ing] the process" of decoding and deterritorializing—that is, the explosion of schizophrenic desires which exceed attempts of re-coding and control—that capitalism inevitably unleashes upon itself (p. 240). Arguing that "Marxist economists too often dwell on considerations concerning the mode of production" (p. 230), what has made Deleuze and Guattari's (1983) work so influential is not their ability to effectively explain anything about capitalism, but the way in which they blur the material basis of class divisions in the private ownership of the means of production, while nonetheless appealing to a sense of frustration and hostility toward an increasingly homogenizing and instrumental capitalist culture. The rhetorically "crude" and "disruptive" aspects of their writings—repeated uses of "shit" and "fuck," for example—situate them as the "hipster" opposition to "staid" corporatizing forces that stunt the possibilities of everyday life, while at the same time promising workers that challenging the banality of corporate culture requires nothing more than fully acceding to one's desires. The celebration of their work by those claiming to resist corporate culture reflects the extent to which the capitalist ideology that surplus value comes from sources other than exploited labor has taken hold in contemporary "Left" theory.

According to Deleuze and Guattari (1983), history is defined by the emergence and resistance of life forces to that which attempts to capture these "flows of desire, to inscribe them, to record them, to see to it that no flow exists that is not properly damned up, channeled, regulated" (p. 33). All societies operate as assemblages and, through the deployment of "codes" designed to structure the possibilities and limits available to all participants within the assemblage, attempt to tame the vitalism of desire and direct it toward maintaining unequal power relations. In this model, desire is that which exceeds attempts by the "socius" to contain it in order to extract value from it. Desire, they argue, is revolutionary because it represents an inherent and unconscious resistance to the intentionality of human design "by wanting what it wants" (Deleuze & Guattari, 1983, p. 116). It is, for them, a measure of *élan vital.* In displacing the analysis of production under capitalism in favor of a system they claim is based upon the generation and controlling of desire, Deleuze and Guattari (1983) argue "the theoretical opposition" within capitalism "is not between two classes," but rather "between, on the one hand, the decoded flows that enter into a class axiomatic on the full body of capital, and on the other hand, the decoded flows that free themselves from this axiomatic" (p. 255). By declaring all production is desiring-production, and proposing all are subject to the "axiomatic" of control of capitalism's desire-capturing assemblage, there is no basis upon which to differentiate between owners and workers. Property in Deleuze and Guattari (1983) instead becomes a post-class potential for "creativity," expressed by anyone regardless of their objective position in the division of labor.

The influence of Deleuze and Guattari's post-class theory of "desire" is engrained in the way in which software studies approaches the relationship between class and the labor that produces surplus value. In *Speaking Code: Coding as Aesthetic and Political Expression*, for example, Cox and McLean (2013) argue network capitalism is less about the exploitation of labor than "captur[ing] the creative and communicative capacity of the socialized labor force and turn it into information that can be marketized" (p. 49). According to their reading, the shift from material to immaterial production requires expanding the definition of labor "to involve cultural activities not traditionally considered to constitute work, including intellectual labor and artistic practices" (Cox & McLean, 2013, p. 51). Instead, "labor is no longer simply contained by the factory walls" (p. 48), but "is becoming even more informational and communicative, leading to a situation in which all activities have been turned into production" (Cox & McLean, 2013, p. 49). As a result, "the once straightforward distinction between waged and unwaged work, or work and nonwork (play), becomes even harder to establish" (Cox & McLean, 2013, p. 51). Once again, we are back to the notion that value creation is the effect of a post-class "assemblage" designed for extracting creative energies unleashed by practices of desire. According to this model, which they claim disrupts "orthodox conceptions of labor, value and agency" (p. 50), the shift from exploitation at the point of production to a generalized capturing of creativity means "neither labor time nor wage is considered to be the central issue under critique but technological skill and organizational forms defined by cultural, informational factors and knowledge" (Cox & McLean, 2013, p. 50). In turn, insofar as all social acts are deemed productive of new value, "class antagonism is transformed into a broader dynamic" that is "no longer simply between workers and capitalists" but instead operates between "communities and platforms" (Cox & McLean, 2013, p. 50). Class, in other words, ceases to be an objective matter of one's position in the division of labor, but rather becomes a fluid relationship between forces of control and resistance. Thus, Cox and McLean (2013) conclude, "Although capital tries to treat ideas as it would any other goods, it does not succeed in commodifying them altogether, because intellectual work is not simply reducible to market principles" (p. 54). Citing Franco Berardi, they state, "If neoliberalism attempted to capture the very essence of life, it will always ultimately fail, as it wrongly assumes 'that the soul can be reduced to mere rationality'" (Cox & McLean, 2013, p. 68). Just as in Deleuze and Guattari (1983), the limit of capitalism is life's inherent vitality that erupts from any attempt at capturing and controlling it, such that social transformation requires nothing more than "an even more indeterminate approach and openness to other transformative possibilities, such as the possible and often unpredictable actions that result when a program runs, including the return of errors" (Cox & McLean, 2013, p. 63). What better message for software companies than telling workers their liberation can be achieved through spontaneous and individual acts of creativity while nonetheless remaining within the system that exploits their labor.

Software and the "Hidden Abode" of Production

Couched in ethical language about "shifting from an emphasis on epistemologies to also encompass the way in which things are embedded with and produce certain kinds of knowledge and possibility of interaction with the world (and indeed make worlds)" (Fuller, 2008, p. 7), software studies proponents, concern with "life," "creativity," "desire," and "immateriality" dematerializes class by severing one's objective class position from private property relations. The underlying assumption of these concepts is that capitalism has shifted from the exploitation of "material" production to the capturing of knowledge and creativity produced by "immaterial" labor. As Yann Moulier Boutang (2011) declares, "The resource that capitalism seeks to prioritise today is collective intelligence, creativity distributed through the entirety of the population" (p. 34). Creativity, which is really another way of substituting "vitalism" for labor without appearing spiritualist, is a post-labor, post-class mystification of the production of surplus value under capitalism. While emerging as a cultural reaction to the extent to which everyday life has become commodified, the problem with such arguments is they obscure the extent to which all technology—whether the earliest flint tools or the code that runs the apps on your iPad—is a product of human labor in the past which is put to use by human labor in the present. As Marx and Engels (1975) write, the world around us is

> not a thing given direct from all eternity, remaining ever the same . . . [it is] the result of activity of a whole succession of generations, each standing on the shoulders of the proceeding one, developing its industry and intercourse, and modifying its social system according to changed needs (p. 39).

In other words, regardless of whether we are talking about a painting or computer code, knowledge is the form labor takes under advanced conditions of production. The scientific and technological advances manifest in the software revolution, which appear to replace the labor of humanity with the labor of machinery and promote immaterial value over material production, are, in fact, "the productive powers of social labour and the social powers of production in general" (Marx, 1994, p. 128). This "simple" fact—what appears to be a product of pure knowledge is, in actuality, stored labor waiting to be put to use—is not as simple as it first seems because it means that technology is a social object whose creation and use are determined by the social relations in which human labor occurs. In order to understand the software revolution, therefore, we cannot begin with the products of labor as they appear in the marketplace, but must consider the conditions under which they are produced.

Capitalism is a system in which private ownership of the means of production has the consequence that technological advances, which could be used to meet the needs of all, are used to increase the productivity of labor for the purposes of producing private profits instead. Class is the effect of capitalist property relations, not its cause. A worker, who has nothing to sell but their labor-power, must go to work for the capitalist and, for as much time as their wage has purchased, produce not just enough value to pay for their labor and maintain the workplace, but also create new value above and beyond these costs. As Marx (1994) explains,

> labour capacity is only bought because the labour it can perform, and enters into an obligation to perform, is greater than the labour required for the reproduction of this labour capacity, and is therefore represented by a value greater than the value of the labour capacity (p. 133).

For this reason, capitalism's fundamental goal is not the production of any particular product, as "the value of the product as such is a matter of indifference to capitalist production" (p. 110), but "the production of the greatest amount of surplus value" (Marx, 1994, p. 110). The capitalist does not care if their workers spend their labor-time writing code or constructing bombs, only that as much of the labor-power they have purchased with a wage is put to producing more value than they paid for it. This is why "immaterial labor" is a thoroughly fuzzy concept. It conflates everything from the type of work that is done, to the commodity produced, to the lifestyle of the person who consumes it, in order to claim that Marx's labor theory of value is "incapable of understanding the creative energy of labor itself" (Negri, 2008, p. 20). However, when Marx (1994) talks about the productivity of labor as critical to the profitability of capitalism, he is not referring to "what labor is productive in general," but explaining why it matters that "labor *which is converted directly into capital* is *productive*" (emphasis in original) (p. 128). Central to capitalism is not the type of work available or the kind of commodity produced, but whether the labor the capitalist has purchased results in the production of new capital beyond the costs of production. The more technology advances, the more productive labor becomes. In this sense, software is not an autonomous "actant" equally participating in the shaping of social relations, but the social labor of many workers consolidated into technologies that allow one worker to be as productive as several.

While Deleuze and Guattari's disciples claim "machines are not just a product of labor but, much more importantly, of engineering design and science" and that "design, both functional and aesthetic, also produces value, as does the organization of production" (DeLanda, 2016, p. 45), the consequence is that knowledge production is rendered autonomous from labor. This is where the figure of the "assemblage" comes in, as a means of addressing the complexity of contemporary circuits of production while obscuring deepening class divisions. The representation of the social as consisting of "unique historical entities" (DeLanda, 2016, p. 6) which include not only people, but things like "the architecture of the buildings that house them, the myriad different tools and machines used in offices, factories, and kitchens" as well as "the many symbols and icons with which they express their identity" (DeLanda, 2016, p. 20), redefines value as that which is created by the organization of different elements—from workers and desks to electricity and ideas—without having to account for the fact that all of these elements are the products of human labor. This representation of value as produced through the "dynamic" organization of the assemblage is a managerial theory of capitalism that attributes the source of value to entrepreneurs, administrators, bureaucrats, and even the buildings or computers, more than it does to workers. A building does not just appear, nor do ideas simply fall from the sky. The person who codes the app on your phone is a worker whose labor builds upon the labor of others who, among other things, create the computer they work on, write the software they use to develop the code, produce the electricity that runs the computer, educate them on how to code, built and maintain the building they work in, and produce and distribute the food they eat. At each stage in this process, capitalism seeks to reduce the time necessary to reproduce the costs of production in order to increase the time devoted to surplus value. The fact that capitalism obscures the "hidden abode" of production behind the illusion of a "free" market exchange means that, as Marx (1994) writes, new technologies appear as "independent of surplus LABOUR and SURPLUS VALUE, since these are presupposed to them as given" (emphasis in original) (p. 126). The extent to which capitalist labor relations dictate all other aspects of life means that the labor that produces life disappears behind the illusions of a culture of code.

The assertion that network capitalism's fundamental antagonism is between an outdated instrumental culture and an emerging playfulness of profound ambiguity that is always "open to rupture" (Kitchin & Dodge, 2011, p. 19) takes as its starting point the notion that we are entering a "code" economy built upon the encoding of life rather than the exploitation of labor. As Teresa L. Ebert and Mas'ud Zavarzadeh (2014) argue, the displacement of labor in the affirmation of "life" is "to, in effect, affirm the way things are as the way they ought to be (and thus always will be)" (p. 412). What I would call "software vitalism" reproduces a post-class ideology in which technology has supplanted labor to become the primary source of value. Rather than "freeing" humanity to concern itself with the (re)distribution of objects in the world, software vitalism furthers the reach of capitalism through the expansion of production. The rhetoric of an emancipatory code economy embraces the cultural logic of "disruption" that has become the centerpiece of the libertarian ethos of Silicon Valley, while normalizing (by disappearing) the exploitation of labor on which it is based. When writers such as Christian Fuchs (2014) claim that "on Facebook, YouTube, and Twitter, all consumption time is commodity production time" (p. 90) because "all human time of existence tends to be exploited for the sake of capital accumulation" (p. 91), they blur the boundaries of owner and worker by collapsing the production and the consumption of commodities into a single moment. While it is often said that companies like Facebook and Google "break" the labor theory of value because they "produce nothing," it is important to distinguish between accumulated capital and the source of that capital. While much of the internet economy does rely on monetized information—for example, in the form of targeted advertising—their massive capital reserves primarily represent the accumulation of surplus value produced elsewhere. For example, no new value is created when Facebook sells information that results in a viewer watching a film trailer. Rather, already existing capital in the form of money is transferred to Facebook from the film studio that bought the rights to this information. It was the exploitation of the labor during the film's production that generated the surplus value used to purchase targeted advertising. In fact, this is why there is increasing pressure on Google and Facebook to be more accountable for the effectivity of digital ads (Alba, 2017). The software industry, however, does create new value when it hires the labor of coders to create software that makes it possible to collect, categorize, and classify the information that can then be sold. In other words, while individual consumer habits help realize surplus value as profit, they are not its source. The source of new value in the software industry comes from exploited wage-labor that creates software commodities enabling consumer information to be accumulated.

Approached from a historical and material perspective, it becomes clear that technology is fundamentally dialectical. On the one hand, under capitalism technology represents the negation of the worker insofar as it is only used "as a means of exploiting to a higher degree the worker's powers of labor and the combination of workers" (Marx, 1994, p. 126). On the other hand, the potential of technology to meet people's needs—that is, to negate their negation as exploited workers—is a reflection of the deeply collective nature of production. As Marx (1994) explains, "That the worker delivers more of the product in the same time . . . is the result of cooperation, of the division of labor, and lastly of the association with machinery (natural forces) and methods of work (science)" (p. 126). The increasing alienation of the software revolution described in books like Sherry Turkle's *Alone Together* (2011) and Nicholas Carr's *The Glass Cage* (2014) reflect the fact that under capitalist relations of production,

> unity in cooperation, combination in the division of labour, the application of the forces of nature and science, as well as the products of labour in the shape of machinery, for the purpose of production, are all things which confront the individual workers themselves as *alien* and *objective*, as mere forms of existence of the means of labour which are independent over them and rule over them. (Marx, 1994, p. 123)

While capitalism negates the lives of individual workers, it nonetheless continues to move toward a social system of production that links workers all over the world and shows, however much it tries to kill the "dream of a Revolution," that humanity's future depends upon collectivity rather than the divisiveness of individualist desires. Social change will not come via a new app. The future cannot be "disrupted" or "accelerated" into difference. It is only by negating the negation of exploitation that capitalism can be transformed, class inequality brought to an end, and the full development of all can take place.

Works Cited

Alba, D. (2017, January 21). Under pressure to prove its ads actually work, Google opens up. *Wired*. Retrieved from www.wired.com/2017/02/pressure-prove-ads-actually-work-google-opens/

Bennett, J. (2010). *Vibrant matter: A political ecology of things*. Durham, NC: Duke University Press.

Bergson, H. (1983 [1911]). *Creative evolution* (A. Mitchell, Trans.). Lanham, MD: University Press of America.

Berry, D. M. (2011). *The philosophy of software: Code and mediation in the digital age*. Basingstoke, UK: Palgrave Macmillan.

Boult, A. (2016, June 3). We are "almost definitely" living in a Matrix-style simulation, claims Elon Musk. *The Telegraph*. Retrieved from www.telegraph.co.uk/technology/2016/06/03/we-are-almost-definitely-living-in-a-matrix-style-simulation-cla/

Boutang, Y.M. (2011). *Cognitive capitalism* (E. Emery, Trans.). Cambridge, UK: Polity Press.

Bratton, B.H. (2016). *The stack: On software and sovereignty*. Cambridge, MA: MIT Press.

Brown, B. (2015). *Other things*. Chicago, IL: University of Chicago Press.

Carr, N. (2014). *The glass cage: Automation and us*. New York, NY: W.W. Norton & Company.

Chun, W.H.K. (2011). *Programmed visions: Software and memory*. Cambridge, MA: MIT Press.

Cox, G., & McLean, A. (2013). *Speaking code: Coding as aesthetic and political expression*. Cambridge, MA: MIT Press.

DeLanda, M. (2016). *Assemblage theory*. Edinburgh, UK: Edinburgh University Press.

Deleuze, G., & Guattari, F. (1983). *Anti-Oedipus: Capitalism and schizophrenia* (R. Hurley, M. Seem, & H.R. Lane, Trans.). Minneapolis, MN: University of Minnesota Press.

Deleuze, G., & Guattari, F. (1987). *A thousand plateaus: Capitalism and schizophrenia* (B. Massumi, Trans.). Minneapolis, MN: University of Minnesota Press.

Dyer-Witheford, N., & de Peuter, G. (2009). *Games of empire: Global capitalism and video games*. Minneapolis, MN: University of Minnesota Press.

Ebert, T., & Zavarzadeh, M. (2014). The digital metaphysics of cognitive capitalism: Abandoning dialectics, the North Atlantic left invents a spontaneous communism within capitalism. *International Critical Thought*, *4*(4), 397–417.

Foucault, M. (1978). *A history of sexuality* (Vol. 1). (R. Hurley, Trans.). New York, NY: Pantheon Books.

Fuchs, C. (2014). *Digital labour and Karl Marx*. New York, NY: Routledge.

Fuller, M. (2008). *Software studies: A lexicon*. Cambridge, MA: MIT Press.

Galloway, A. (2004). *Protocol: How control exists after decentralization*. Cambridge, MA: MIT Press.

Galloway, A. (2012). *The interface effect*. Cambridge, UK: Polity Press.

Hardt, M., & Negri, A. (2004). *Multitude: War and democracy in the age of empire*. New York, NY: Penguin Press.

Harman, G. (2016). *Immaterialism: Objects and social theory*. Cambridge, UK: Polity Press.

Hayles, K.N. (2005). *My mother was a computer: Digital subjects and literary texts*. Chicago, IL: University of Chicago Press.

Heidegger, M. (1971). The thing (A. Hofstadter, Trans.). In *Poetry, Language, Thought* (pp. 61–184). New York, NY: Harper & Row.

Heidegger, M. (1977). The question concerning technology (W. Lovett, Trans.). In *The question concerning technology, and other essays* (pp. 3–35). New York, NY: Harper & Row.

Holmes, S. (2016). "Can we name the tools?": Ontologies of code, speculative techné and rhetorical concealment. *Computational Culture, 5*. Retrieved from http://computationalculture.net/article/can-we-name-the-tools-ontologies-of-code-speculative-techne-and-rhetorical-concealment

Kitchin, R., & Dodge, M. (2011). *Code/space: Software and everyday life*. Cambridge, MA: MIT Press.

Latour, B. (2004). *Politics of nature: How to bring the sciences into democracy* (C. Porter, Trans.). Cambridge, MA: Harvard University Press.

Lazzarato, M. (2004). From capital-labour to capital life. *Ephemera, 4*(3), 187–208.

Manovich, L. (2001). *The language of new media*. Cambridge, MA: MIT Press.

Manovich, L. (2013). *Software takes command: Extending the language of new media*. New York, NY: Bloomsbury Publishing.

Marx, K. (1994). Economic manuscripts of 1861–1863 (B. Fowkes, Trans.). In *Marx-Engels collected works* (Vol. 34). New York, NY: International Publishers.

Marx, K. (1996). Capital (Vol. 1) (B. Fowkes, Trans.). In *Marx-Engels collected works* (Vol. 35, pp. 7–247). New York: International Publishers.

Marx. K. (1998). Capital (Vol. 3) (B. Fowkes, Trans.). In *Marx-Engels collected works* (Vol. 37, pp. 5–794). New York, NY: International Publishers.

Marx, K., & Engels, F. (1975). The German ideology. In *Marx-Engels collected works* (Vol. 5, pp. 19–451). New York, NY: International Publishers.

Negri, A. (2008). The labor of the multitude and the fabric of biopolitics (S. Mayo & P. Graefe with M. Coté, Trans.). *Mediations, 23*(2), 8–25.

Negri, A. (2014). Some thoughts on the #accelerate manifesto. In R. MacKay & A. Avanessian (Eds.), *#Accelerate#* (pp. 363–378). Falmouth, UK: Urbanomic Media Ltd.

Roggero, G. (2010). Five theses on the common. *Rethinking Marxism, 22*(3), 357–373.

Shaviro, S. (2014). *The universe of things: On speculative realism*. Minneapolis, MN: University of Minnesota Press.

Terranova, T. (2013). Free labor. In T. Scholz (Ed.), *Digital labor: The internet as playground and factory* (pp. 33–57). New York, NY: Routledge.

Turkle, S. (2011). *Alone together: Why we expect more from technology and less from each other*. New York, NY: Basic Books.

Virno, P. (2004). *A grammar of the multitude: For an analysis of contemporary forms of life*. (I. Bertoletti, J. Cascaito, & A. Casson, Trans.). Los Angeles, CA: Semiotext(e).

12

CLASS IN "THE CLASS": CONSERVATIVE, COMPETITIVE, AND (DIS)CONNECTED

Sonia Livingstone and Julian Sefton-Green

We recently spent a year with a class of 13- to 14-year-olds in a fairly typical London school.[1] We followed 28 young people through their lessons at school, and in the corridors and playground moments of the school day, and then we spent time with them in their homes, meeting their parents, understanding their friendship groups, sharing their hobbies, discussing their social networks, going online together. Our interest lay in how this highly diverse group made sense of the world—what was expected of them, what gave them pleasure, and what problems they encountered. Our purpose was to grasp young people's own views of the world and how these intersected with the views of their parents, teachers, and the wider society. Avoiding a media-centric approach, a central thread through our ethnographic portrait was the young people's everyday use of media and, more profoundly, their experience of growing up in a so-called "digital age."

In *The Class: Living and Learning in the Digital Age*, we interrogate these views and experiences through the lens of late modern theories of selfhood, pedagogy, and sociality (Livingstone & Sefton-Green, 2016). More than ever before, people are charged with charting their own course through life and taking responsibility for their own risks to a degree that contrasts markedly with previous eras, when social convention and tradition had greater force. Yet in trying to cope with the stresses of modernity, people are beset by unprecedented levels of uncertainty—incomplete knowledge, conflicting experts, complex decisions, precarious alliances, untrustworthy institutions, too little time.

Socio-technological developments promise enticing solutions and enhanced life choices, but they demand complex calculations of risk that preoccupy and burden us. As Zygmunt Bauman (2002, p. xv–xvi) put it: "Modernity replaces determinism of social standing with compulsive and obligatory self-determination. . . . Let there be no mistake: now, as before, individualization is a fate, not a choice." From this perspective, each individual is on their own, since traditional networks of support or welfare provision are no longer reliable or ever present. Thus Ulrich Beck and Elisabeth Beck-Gernsheim (2002, p. 23) write of the necessity for individuals to become "actors, builders, jugglers, stage managers of their own biographies and identities and also of their social links and networks." Moreover, the unequally distributed resources of social, economic, and cultural capital that individuals have at their disposal are further exacerbated through the processes of social reproduction. As a result, "social inequality is on the rise precisely because of the spread of individualization" (Beck & Beck-Gernsheim, 2002, p. xxiv). But Beck and Beck-Gernsheim argue further that we must now recognize "the non-class character of individualized inequalities"—for while inequality is still with us, the disembedding "processes of individualization deprive class distinctions of their social identity" (2002, p. 39).

Somewhat problematically for our project, such theories of late modernity appear to speak for everyone yet they devote relatively little attention to the nature or specificities of children's experiences or of the key institutions of family and school that shape them. In this chapter, we contribute to this volume's analysis of the changing relations between media and social class in late modernity by reflecting on what we learned from our fieldwork about the lived realities of social class in the class (forgive the double use of "class"!), focusing on the young people's use of media and the wider processes of mediation in which their lives are entangled.

Conceiving of Class Difference

The contention that it is class consciousness rather than inequality that is fading in late modernity certainly rang true in our fieldwork. People still use the terms "middle" and "working" class, but the meaning of these terms is changing, no longer mapping neatly onto right and left wings of the political spectrum, or management and workforce, or even onto wealthy and poor but instead referring to a looser association between social status and forms of knowledge, social capital, and cultural tastes and habits. Social class, as several contributors to this volume have noted, involves an active process of identification and signaling ways of belonging to wider collectivities, not a deterministic process of positioning through socioeconomic factors.

In our study differences of social class (and indeed, racial difference) were publically effaced by the school, creating a seemingly "fair" neutrality despite the fact that students spoke multiple languages, practiced the breadth of the world's religions, and, while some lived in homes worth several million pounds, others lived in state subsidized council ("social") housing. Some of the students were migrants or refugees with educated parents who had held high-status jobs in their country of origin but now lived in far poorer circumstances. In about half the families, the mothers had higher education degrees, but in other cases, especially single-parent families, parents were working in low-paid precarious jobs. From economic, cultural, and social perspectives (Savage, 2015), the young people in our class were a microcosm of contemporary Britain, and they lived with the risk of conflict, misunderstanding, and prejudice also faced by the wider society.

While teachers, parents, and the young people themselves generally endorsed the idea that all should be equal, treated according to their individual merits, the class was hardly unaware of differences in social class. We saw this most clearly in the choice of friendships, enacted offline and online, where the young people self-assorted into relatively homogeneous groupings by socioeconomic position, ethnicity, and gender, albeit with interesting exceptions that we explore in the book. But while most of the young people preferred not to articulate this as anything other than a personal choice, Megan and Shane had a go at discussing differences of social class, drawing on a polarized discourse of "people like me" and "others." Megan, a popular girl from a middle-class family, gave a highly coded account, based on who lived where and which elementary school they went to. When asked to explain further, she admitted that:

> I'm not really friends with—this sounds bad—any poor people. But that's not because I'm not friends with people who are poor. It's just that just happens to be who I'm friends with.

We thought this comment suggested a commitment to holding on to these social distinctions, but Megan did not welcome our pushing her on this point. Indeed, when we next asked whether the mix of backgrounds at the school was problematic, Megan was glad to explicate the democratic vision of the whole class:

> No, I don't really think that's an issue, like, because we all go to the same school, so we're not that different. . . It's not like we're going to have fights: "You're not as rich as me. I don't like you." So I don't think it matters. I think it's good because you can always meet someone who's, like, different to you.

Shane, whose family was not well off, was more willing to explain how social class divided the students:

> In our year, we've got the posh people. There's the people that play pat ball, football, and the people that chat about rubbish.

While Shane had no trouble identifying "the posh people," he found it hard to explain why they merited such a label: "They're not posh, but we just call them posh, I don't know why." Although it may not have been obvious from his initial classification, Shane was not keen on those who "play pat ball," preferring those who play football (soccer) or "chat about rubbish"—meaning, "not chat about rubbish but, like, the people, like, always having a laugh."

The wealthier parents had chosen to live in a mixed neighborhood and to send their children to the local school rather than to bring them up in a more privileged context. Some of the less well-off parents had worked hard to give their child this chance to benefit from a "good school." Shane lived on the edge of the catchment area, and his mother told us of her efforts to get him into the school as a way of extricating him from the more problematic environment of his primary school, and was glad that his new friends were, as she told us, "lovely boys, all well-mannered kids." This did not necessarily provide Shane with a straightforward route to "success." As he explained, "When I was younger, I wanted to be a footballer. But it's not as easy as people think it is." Later, he reflected: "I'm basically guaranteed a job with my uncle, but if not, I'd rather be a carpenter or like something designing stuff, making wood."

Although Shane was from a poor background and Megan from a relatively privileged one, both were more able to identify privilege than poverty. In our sociologically informed efforts to classify members of the class, we faced a similar hurdle: identifying who was middle class was fairly straightforward but, with the exception of Shane himself (who bore a remarkable resemblance to Paul Willis' lads "learning to labour"; see Willis, 1978), none of the class could be neatly labeled as working class, with several having more cultural capital than one might expect from their economic resources, for reasons of migration or divorce.

Mediated Imaginaries

Schools are expected to fulfill more roles than simply providing and accrediting learning. They are organized in ways that promote a particular way of being. Given that members of a class are brought together not exactly by accident but by processes over which they have little control, they have to learn to manage their relations with each other and with the wider community of the school. Recognizing the wide diversity of backgrounds accommodated within the class, the school in our study had good reason to emphasize a narrative about the students as a collectivity. As their class teacher Catherine explained, "They have a real sense of, you know, an identity as [the class] and I think that, for the most part, they're quite proud of that." Another teacher added, when asked about the relations among the wealthier and poorer students, "I don't think it affects, necessarily, the way they interact with each other." Or, as Megan explained, in justifying the school's seemingly arbitrary rules on uniform and appearance, "It's like being a community, because everyone is the same." While some may read the efforts of the school critically as imposing middle-class social norms on the potentially unruly mass, civility can also connote positive ideas of tolerating or getting on with others (Elias, 2000). As Susanne Wessendorf (2014, p. 392) observes of highly urban multicultural neighborhoods, such as that of our school, these are "super-diverse" and thus demand "civility towards diversity" as a daily strategy of their inhabitants—for survival, and for effective functioning.

Stanton Wortham (2005, p. 1) argues that not only do the "social identification, power relations and interpersonal struggles" of daily life occur in the classroom as anywhere else but they also intersect with the academic learning that necessarily occurs there. Wortham was particularly interested in the "common pedagogical strategy of building an analogy between students' actual or hypothetical experiences and the curricular topic" (2005, p. 2). Since building these analogies is doubly hazardous—both because the teachers know little of the students' lives at home and because these are themselves very diverse—popular culture is often positioned as a shared body of experience by which teachers can bridge what students are presumed to know already and what they need to learn. To motivate students in physical education, the teacher observed that they would do the same warm-up exercises as celebrity footballers. To advertise the science club in the year group assembly, students were enjoined to find out "how an iPhone works." To explain graphs in math, the exercises were to plot data on mobile phone tariffs or Hollywood film profits. To judge work in geography, students were invited to act as judges on *X Factor*, a popular reality television show. These popular culture references far from matched the actual interests of the students, and at times they actively masked significant differences between them, skating over potential conflicts. So, while to the teachers, references to television programs or listening to music offered a kind of common culture (see Jones, 2009 on how popular culture has come to stand in for common culture) that enabled both teaching and civility, the limitations of this approach were never far away.

Meanwhile, in their leisure time the young people exploited the potential of media to imagine more individualized alternatives to the shared imaginary constructed by the school. For example, Abby, from a poor, mixed-race home, loved music because:

> I think music, kind of, describes a person really. So like, if there was like. . . if you listen to that type of music they're kind of, they've got their own type of personality kind of, like that music and I think if you, like, listen to, like R&B type music, you're not exactly like [unclear] or nothing, but you kind of, have the same type of personality as the music.

And Megan, from a more privileged and artistic home, said:

> All Tumblrs are different so you can have some which is just writing or some that is just pictures . . . I used to have a Kawaii blog, which is like . . . although if I Tumblr it's just a random [thing]—if I thought something was nice I'd re-blog it. Then I went to Kawaii which is flashing images and now it's gone to Hipstar, sort of indie.

To these girls, their choices are highly individual, however outsiders might interpret them. Building on her choices, Abby imagines how her interest in music could lead her first to an elite music school and then to a musical career, though when we talked again a few months later, she had already given up on that idea. Dilruba, who lived in a low-income, mixed-ethnicity family of four girls and a single-parent mother, dreamed of a career in fashion, which she expressed partly through being an early adopter of Twitter—as a way of "keeping up-to-date. Just, like, looking, like, seeing celebrity lives."

At that time, Twitter permitted entry to an adult world, allowing first steps in following, contributing, and trying things out, even if little noticed by others. Abby, too, had also worked out that Twitter could bring her closer to the music world that she hoped to join as a career. And so had Dominic, from a far wealthier home: as a footballer and football fan, he would join in Twitter conversations among professional footballers and commentators, enjoying the chance to be part of something that he cared about but which was beyond his normal reach as a young teenager.

By contrast, the whole class used Facebook. While once exciting as a space of identity work (Livingstone, 2008), this was used by the young people in a remarkably parallel manner to the school's civil space, as an online domain in which banal but significant phatic and identity tasks could be played out. Almost everyone was "friends" on Facebook with everyone else, rendering this meaningless for the construction of strong ties or for more intimate explorations of selfhood but meaningful in terms of weak ties (Granovetter, 1983; Hampton & Wellman, 2003) and the generalized construction of a common social belonging.

In short, consumption of media represents a key site for young people's identity work (Buckingham, 2008), both providing a visible way of marking the acceptance or rejection of taste cultures (Thornton, 1995) and also because, in ways young people may relish more than adults, media consumption affords easy and active experimentation with possible identities. Insofar as "taste classifies and it classifies the classifier" (Bourdieu, 1984), our fieldwork revealed young people's lives lived between the social conservativism of family and school life and the mediated imaginaries made possible through media connections. These mediated imaginaries served to reinforce a kind of conservative progressiveness—an enlightenment notion of civility—while also offering the flexibility for individualized escape routes.

Educational Aspirations and the Digital Home

At home, we saw a similar oscillation being played out between the shared experiences of family life—often with the family on the sofa around the television set for at least some part of each day, usually at the instigation of a determined parent, irrespective of social class—and the desire of family members to pursue individual pursuits in their own time and spaces (for children, usually in their bedrooms and/or online). But in one crucial respect digital media were co-opted into a highly classed practice, namely, that of supporting school learning and, thereby, children's imagined futures. In this regard, perhaps unsurprisingly given a context of considerable anxieties over precarious futures, we saw parents (as well as school) tending to see children less in terms of who they are or what they do than in terms of who they could become (Qvortrup, Bardy, Sgritta, & Wintersberger, 1994; Corsaro, 2011). Crucially, digital media are being co-opted into the future-oriented effort to ensure children "keep up" or "get ahead" (Blum-Ross & Livingstone, 2016), with an emphasis on the provision of curricular knowledge in ways that promise competitive academic achievement and, perhaps, social mobility.

Yet the evidence shows that social mobility—the chance for young people to improve on the material conditions of their parents—has ground to a halt in recent decades, to the point where developed countries can no longer promise future generations increased prosperity or quality of life (Brown, Lauder, & David, 2011; Cribb, Hood, Joyce, & Phillips, 2013; Putnam, 2015). Rather, as Basil Bernstein (1990) argued, education "re-contextualizes" knowledge so as to ensure success for young people from middle-class homes compared with those who are less privileged. In effect, education is a key instrument for the social reproduction of inequality, notwithstanding that it professes "fairness." This intensifies the felt burden on parents as they struggle to ensure that their child can be included among school's beneficiaries.

Social reproduction occurs as much, if not even more, at home than at school as families with already-greater economic and cultural capital work competitively to sustain their social advantages (Bourdieu, 1984). These processes, too, appear intensified in late modernity. In the UK, Valerie Hey (2000) wrote of the "offensive" sociality (or "pushy individualism") of the new middle class by contrast with the "defensive" sociality of the disadvantaged (with their reliance of the traditions of hierarchy). In the US, Annette Lareau (2011) contrasted the rigorous schedule of adult-organized out-of-school enrichment activities ("concerted cultivation") practiced by middle-class families with working-class families' assumption of "natural growth," arguing that the former breeds a cumulative sense of entitlement in children which helps them get ahead in institutionalized settings such as the school. Meanwhile, in working-class families, "the cultural logic of child rearing at home is out of synch with the standards of institutions" (Lareau, 2011, p. 3), and thus "social class dynamics are woven into the texture and rhythm of children and parents' daily lives" (Lareau, 2011, p. 236) to the disadvantage of the already disadvantaged.

In our study we focused on the relationship—imagined and practiced—between learning at school and at home. In a host of different ways, digital media promised to undergird this relationship in progressive ways, improving mutual understanding, overcoming dysfunctional boundaries, building on spontaneous interests, and supporting personalized pathways. Yet the realities more often supported processes of social reproduction. In our book, we traced this in two main ways. One was how families acquired and deployed home computing technology so as to support their children's homework, arranging a corner of the home and devoting time in the daily routine to ensuring its "proper" use. A second was the way in which some of the families supported their children's music learning, variously providing instruments, lessons, and social and other forms of support. We have only space here to illustrate the first of these, with two vignettes.

Yusuf's parents, Muslim immigrants from East Africa, took the idea of supporting learning in the home a step further. They had invested in an expensive but unaccredited set of CDs containing a curriculum in math and English for their four children to improve their educational outcomes working individually in an especially kitted-out bedroom at home. The father, originally a trained nurse but now working as a railway ticket inspector, acted as the head teacher (school principal), charting the children's progress on a series of complex wall charts. Yusuf's teachers were unaware of this domestic investment in technology and effort, and it was unclear whether it brought educational benefits—especially as Yusuf was withdrawn for language support at school. Indeed, we saw a rather reserved boy with little time to relax or identify and pursue his own interests.

By contrast, Giselle's educated and artistic parents supported a host of creative learning practices in their daughter, including a mother who took sketchbooks, paints, and an easel on holiday to teach her children art, and child-led rather than grade-led music lessons with an "alternative" teacher. A similar structure of support framed Giselle's technological pursuits. For example, her father told us unprompted of how her *Minecraft* play developed technological fluency and social skills to participate in a virtual social world. Giselle had learned to conceive of her gameplay as part of her interest-driven artistic practice, contrasting with the school's hard distinction between art lessons, ICT lessons, and, excluded from school entirely, playing computer games.

Unlike Yusuf's home, which mimicked school routines, testing, and outcomes, for Giselle it was home that was seen as superior in providing creative and flexible opportunities to learn, and school that failed to match up. As Giselle's father said:

> I don't know what happens in the school really . . . when it comes to music I think it always sounded like music is a bit chaotic generally at school, and isn't really the place to really . . . the music classes aren't really the place to do much at all. . . .

Our book offers more such examples, further complicating any simple conclusions about digital media use in relation to social class. But we do want to stress that it wasn't the working-class families just leaving their children to grow up as they might, while middle-class families push theirs ahead. Rather, we saw most if not all parents strive for some degree of "concerted cultivation," to borrow Lareau's terminology, or for some "curricularization" of leisure time (Buckingham

& Sefton-Green, 2004), but their differential starting points in terms of cultural capital made for differential outcomes. Supporting and going beyond the accounts of Hey, Lareau, and others, we observed, first, that some middle-class parents deliberately eschewed competitive pressures by seeking alternative approaches which, since they were often built around artistic endeavors, we decided to call "bohemian." Second, since many of our poorer families belonged to minority ethnic cultures, the pedagogic support they provided at home tended either to misrecognize the values of the majority culture (and, thereby, the school's values) or to result in outcomes that could not be converted into those valued or even recognized by the school.

Mediated Disconnections

While parents often used digital media as part of their efforts to build a bridge between home and school, albeit sometimes unsuccessfully, a further theme emerging from our study of media use was the desire for positive disconnections. As we saw in a host of apparently disparate but thematically linked ways, children, parents, and teachers all had good reasons to try to keep the spaces of their lives distinct. And, in a highly mediated age, this often meant subtly undermining the extraordinary capacity for digital networks to connect previously unconnected people, activities, or experiences in an effort to preserve privacy and autonomy.

In one such episode, we saw how digital connections could work against the interests of those with something to lose, even as they might, in other circumstances, aid those with something to gain from the greater visibility of their private lives. Aiden, an Afro-Caribbean boy in the class, had been expelled from a previous school for violent behavior, and his family was, we were told, "known to social services," meaning that the family was in receipt of a range of state interventions. At school we observed him to be generally polite but reserved, seemingly anxious to avoid trouble, and to make a success of this new opportunity. However, he brought a somewhat dangerous air of what he termed "the street" into the social world of the class, and on several occasions we witnessed his good behavior disintegrate as he became drawn into disruptive exchanges.

One day we arrived at school to learn that it was no longer prepared to try to integrate Aiden into mainstream education; he had, in effect, been expelled again. The trigger was an incident on Facebook, but as so often, behind the amplification of conflict on Facebook lay a "real-life" (offline) incident, which he described to us in these terms:

> Basically some girl Facebooked me and said, "How did you get out at lunchtime?" And I said, "I'm allowed to go." And then she said, "Oh, I'm going to come with you." And I'm like, "Okay, cool, but if you get caught, don't bring my name into it." And then she came with me, and we were in… some chicken and chip shop. And then we were playing about: she was

> grabbing me as a little play thing, and I punched her in her leg. And then she told her friend. And then her friend started hyping [acting "over the top"] to me on Facebook, and I replied back. And then I don't know how the school found out or what it had to do with them . . . She told her friend, who was a boy, and then he started hyping to me. And then I retaliated, and I don't know how the school got involved.

Reflecting on this incident, both Aiden and his mother acknowledged that he was at fault, but Aiden was adamant that this incident was not a matter for school. In his view, such peer interactions—on Facebook, on the street—were played out according to social codes that adults did not understand, nor were they meant to. He put a lot of effort into managing life at school so as to keep it quite separate from life with his tight group of friends "on the street," and so he felt the school's decision was unjust.

When we visited Aiden's Facebook profile, we found that the seemingly reserved boy we had met at school had more "friends" than anyone else in the class (over 1,000) and low privacy settings, and he chatted daily with much vigor and interest. These communications revealed a curious mix—for the most part, he presented himself as a tough guy, strutting, flirting, threatening, and swearing. Yet there were also some photos of a "good boy," along with happy birthday messages, suggesting (to us) a curious switching between seemingly incompatible identity performances.

Most interesting was the way in which Aiden sought to manage the boundary between personal and public through his use of language. Quietly well-spoken at school to adults, online he relished the linguistic repertoire of black London English along with contemporary forms of hip-hop culture (in this case, variants of British "Grime," London-centric rap). On Facebook, nearly all expressions were in this argot, often involving highly sexist and sexual observations about women, violence, and anger, as well as solidarity with other oppressed black youth. The very frequency and intensity of these interactions revealed Aiden's investment in asserting particular identity practices, in contrast with the largely banal yet civil online interactions of most of the class. For Aiden, unlike others in the class, Facebook offered a closed and peer-directed space for important personal expression and subcultural solidarity.

Had such interactions remained "on the street," it is possible that Aiden could have maintained the boundaries between different parts of his life. Interestingly, his teachers tended to share Aiden's view that in-school and out-of-school spaces should be separate. But as they explained to us, once Facebook had made the out-of-school visible within school, they could not fail to take action. Indeed, several teachers had complained to us that social networking incidents increasingly opened up an unwelcome and troublesome window onto the mess and muddle (as they saw it) of some of the students' lives out of school, forcing them to deal with problems that they regarded as outside their remit. As one teacher said,

"I honestly think that some students become something quite different when they are online." Then, compounding the problem,

> unfortunately often that home matter spills into school, and that's where ... that's where that tension and that difficulty lies, because we then have to call home and say, "There's been this incident. Part of the investigation has shown that it stemmed from ..." And then you're into home territory.

Over and again, teachers told us of incidents in which events in one location had spilled over and continued online and then all through the day, to the point that they felt they had to intervene in life out of school in order to protect school standards. One problem was the way in which Facebook interactions leave "hard traces," making them difficult to ignore: as one teacher commented in the middle of a longer story of student conflict—"then one of the parents showed me the evidence, the rock-solid, watertight evidence, of the Facebook exchange which definitely proved [what had been claimed]." Yet these teachers knew that they could be presented with edited highlights, so that disentangling what had really happened in an out-of-school exchange might prove both technically challenging and highly time-consuming. In short, although Aiden's story is a sadly familiar one of social disadvantage reproducing itself across generations, digital media have complicated matters—on the one hand, creating a new space for at times rapid-fire transgressive peer interaction, while on the other, undermining long-established boundaries of authority dividing home and school in ways that can become troubling for all concerned.

Conclusions

Our analysis of the relation between media and social class in the lives of a class of 13- to 14-year-olds began by questioning the continued relevance of the contrast between middle- and working-class families, given that the class included educated families with little money, minority ethnic families with strong subcultures but lacking majority-cultural capital, female-headed households difficult to classify in traditional class terms, and few, if any, traditional working-class households at all. Our ethnography went on to show how social class could not predict family responses to the demands of late modernity. For instance, some of the middle-class families were content to endorse the authority of the school while others sought more "bohemian" alternatives, and some of the migrant families prioritized values and practices characteristic of their home cultures (and local subcultures) rather than those endorsed by the school or wider society. These alternative or subcultural pathways were rather quietly trod, with rich subcultural knowledge gained outside the school sometimes making little impact on or even being recognized by the bounded life of the school.

In contrast to earlier studies of school life (see Giroux, 1983; Willis, 1978), we weren't struck by either "hidden curricula" or the processes of "learning to labour" that implicitly validate middle-class children while working-class children are allocated to the factory floor or seek tactics of resistance. This is not because the school was as fair as it claimed, but rather because the discourse of individual competition and success was made explicit rather than tacit. Differences in opportunity or achievement were not seen as either controversial or unfair—quite the contrary. Thus, it seems that a sense of collective classed identity is giving way to an uncertain and ambivalent recognition of status differentials, understood as a matter of individual talent or luck, good or bad. The long-term outcome—that social advantage and disadvantage persist, with little social mobility evident—is little changed from 20 years ago, but the means by which it comes about and the implications for identity and social relations are being reconfigured.

What can schools or families do about the determining influences of social class? How could different conceptions of learning alter such seemingly over-determining social structures? These questions have haunted almost every study of childhood and youth and, with varying degrees of explicitness, they underpin most countries' education and family policies, as well as those for digital inclusion and educational technology. While investigating young people's lives in the round might seem only to deepen our knowledge of these challenges, we also believe that it reveals some chinks in the processes of social reproduction, at least for some young people in some circumstances. As we argue in more depth in our book, paying attention to the ways that young people develop and enact their identities within particularly enabling or constraining contexts, often mediated, enabled us to reveal not so much cruel fate as society's lack of imagination and resources for creating alternatives. By imagining and investing in alternatives that can expand young people's vision of future opportunities, by establishing new pathways by which such opportunities might be reached, perhaps their prospects could be altered. But our year with the class has also taught us that such a project can only work if it engages with people's identity commitments to how things have been until now, and with their often-justified fears about a risky or threatening future.

Note

1. This chapter draws on research supported by the John D. and Catherine T. MacArthur Foundation under Prime Award no. 10-97572-000-USP and the Regents of the University of California. It draws on material published in Sonia Livingstone and Julian Sefton-Green, *The Class: Living and Learning in the Digital Age* (New York, NY: New York University Press, 2016).

Works Cited

Bauman, Z. (2002). Foreword. In U. Beck & E. Beck-Gernsheim (Eds.), *Individualization* (pp. xiv–xx). London, UK: SAGE.

Beck, U., & Beck-Gernsheim, E. (2002). *Individualization*. London, UK: SAGE.

Bernstein, B. (1990). *The structuring of pedagogic discourse: Class, codes and control* (Vol. 4). London, UK: Routledge.

Blum-Ross, A., & Livingstone, S. (2016). Families and screen time: Current advice and emerging research. *LSE Media Policy Project Media Policy Brief 17*. London, UK: LSE. Retrieved from http://eprints.lse.ac.uk/66927/

Bourdieu, P. (1984). *Distinction: A social critique of the judgement of taste* (R. Nice, Trans.). London, UK: Routledge.

Brown, P., Lauder, H., & David, A. (2011). *The global auction: The broken promises of education, jobs, and incomes*. New York, NY : Oxford University Press.

Buckingham, D. (2008). Introduction. In D. Buckingham (Ed.), *Youth, identity, and digital media* (pp. 1–24). Cambridge, MA: The MIT Press.

Buckingham, D., & Sefton-Green, J. (2004). Structure, agency and pedagogy in children's media culture. In J. Tobin (Ed.), *Pikachu's global adventure: The rise and fall of Pokemon* (pp. 1–33). Durham, NC: Duke University Press.

Corsaro, W.A. (2011). *The sociology of childhood* (3rd ed.). London, UK: SAGE Publications.

Cribb, J., Hood, A., Joyce, R., & Phillips, D. (2013). *Living standards, poverty and inequality in the UK: 2013*. London, UK: Institute for Fiscal Studies.

Elias, N. (2000). *The civilizing process* (2nd ed.). Oxford, UK: Wiley-Blackwell.

Giroux, H.A. (Ed.). (1983). *Hidden curriculum and moral education: Deception of discovery*. Richmond, CA: McCutchan Publishing Corporation.

Granovetter, M. (1983). The strength of weak ties: A network theory revisited. *Sociological Theory, 1*, 201–233.

Hampton, K., & Wellman, B. (2003). Neighboring in Netville: How the internet supports community and social capital in a wired suburb. *City & Community, 2*(4), 277–311.

Hey, V. (2005). The contrasting social logics of sociality and survival: Cultures of classed be/longing in late modernity. *Sociology, 39*(5), 855–872.

Jones, K. (2009). *Culture and creative learning: A literature review*. London, UK: Creativity, Culture and Education.

Lareau, A. (2011). *Unequal childhoods: Class, race, and family life* (2nd ed.). Los Angeles, CA: University of California Press.

Livingstone, S. (2008). Taking risky opportunities in youthful content creation: Teenagers' use of social networking sites for intimacy, privacy and self-expression. *New Media & Society, 10*(3), 393–411.

Livingstone, S., & Sefton-Green, J. (2016). *The class: Living and learning in the digital age*. New York, NY: New York University Press.

Putnam, R.D. (2015). *Our kids: The American dream in crisis*. New York, NY: Simon & Schuster.

Qvortrup, J., Bardy, M., Sgritta, G., & Wintersberger, H. (1994). *Childhood matters: Social theory, practice and politics*. Aldershot, UK: Avebury.

Savage, M. (2015). *Social class in the 21st century*. London, UK: Pelican.

Thornton, S. (1995). *Club cultures: Music, media and subcultural capital*. Cambridge, UK: Polity Press.

Wessendorf, S. (2014). "Being open but sometimes closed." Conviviality in a super-diverse London neighbourhood. *European Journal of Cultural Studies, 17*(4), 392–405.

Willis, P.E. (1978). *Learning to labour: How working class kids get working class jobs*. Aldershot, UK: Ashgate.

Wortham, S. (2005). *Learning identity: The joint emergence of social identification and academic learning*. Cambridge, UK: Cambridge University Press.

13

FOR THEMSELVES AND FOR THEIR COMMUNITIES: ALTERNATIVE MEDIATIONS OF DIGITAL NATIVES

Vicki Mayer and Aline Maia

Do a Google search for "digital native" in the US or "nativo digital" in Latin America and the images are strikingly similar. White babies and toddlers are shown dressed in the latest fashions at the shopping mall and clutching some form of internet-enabled screen technology. Most are boys as well. If there is a group of connected teens, there may be some more variation in skin colors, but the visual evidence of the relationship between media technology uses, age, race, and social class is unmistakable. The mental gestalt of the digital native contradicts any of the numerous empirical studies of who uses media technologies and how. Yet it permeates popular culture and thus reproduces a digital divide in theoretical, if not in practical terms. For many young North and South Americans face precarious futures as the global economy has all but closed the prospects that this diverse and educated generation will earn as much as their parents did (Thompson, 2015). What the Brazilian journalist Gilberto Dimenstein (1991) called a state-led war on poor, Black youth two decades ago has become a feature of all contemporary political economies structured to maintain extreme racial and class inequality. As the education scholar Henry Giroux (2016) summarizes, young people of color in the US are subject to a neoliberal war in which they "are treated as criminals and increasingly deprived of decent health care, education, food and housing." Against this severe backdrop of class conflict and social control, the whitewash of digital natives in media images seems all the more dangerous.

Our objective—and goal from our privileged perches as a White and a Black member of the academy—is to challenge what Walter Lippmann (1922), speaking of wartime news coverage a century ago, called these "pictures in our heads" by introducing some alternative images of digital natives from young people located in the African diasporas of the US and Brazil. We have gotten to know them both through their online productions—their blogs, videos, and regular social media postings—as well as through participant observation in the places where they reside. *Favela em Dança* and *Noirlinians* are projects that combine digital media with popular performances and Afro-urban cultures in Rio de Janeiro, Brazil and New Orleans, USA, respectively. We analyze these projects using the sociocultural insights of Dell Hymes and Jesús Martín-Barbero around the importance of mediating alternative racial and class worldviews through popular media. This is the intervention we feel is still needed in the study of media regarding both its materiality and its messages. For until we change the scripts around who produces digital media, and what kinds of content they make, we are perhaps bound to reproduce the racial and class biases that now seem part of a transnational imaginary for media production.

What Is a Digital Native?

Whereas the term "native" was central to colonial economies' identification of non-White peoples as utilitarian objects of exchange value, the phrase "digital native" relates to the continued commodification of those without a political voice. The latter phrase stems from the merger of business consulting strategies with the expansion of e-learning in high tech markets directed at mostly affluent young people. Marc Prensky, who coined the term in 2001, for example, brands himself as an "internationally acclaimed thought leader, speaker, writer, consultant, and designer in the field of education" (2016) who is available to help school managers dedicate more of their scarce resources to more screens, software packages, and proprietary online resources. In the past 15 years, marketing campaigns have constructed the digital native as the most desirable segment of consumer markets, referencing those millennials with high levels of social capital and disposable income within their home and school environments. Michael Serazio's (2015) interviews with youth marketing executives reveal a "media logic" that constructs digital natives as technically savvy, managing and making little distinction between their online and offline lives. Digital natives in this discourse demand interactivity with media that stresses "networked hypersociality and participatory exhibitionism"—two characteristics that advertisers attempt to exploit through their media platforms and campaigns. Serazio (2015) argues that the discourse about the digital native is instrumentally invested in positioning young people as both hyper-consumers and an audience to be sold, rather than focusing on a generation that has been "burdened with massive amounts of personal debt" (p. 612). In this way, the digital native communicates class inequalities by refocusing our attention on media users with buying power but without political power.

Despite the hype, and for our purposes, we think the idea of a digital native can still be useful in thinking about what it means to be "native" within a space, digital or not. Anthropologically speaking, to be native is to share what Dell Hymes

(2003) calls a distinct "narrative view of the world" (p. 80). This definition refers to stories, grounded in everyday experiences and lay knowledge of a culture that is shared among members of a group. For Hymes (2003), all humanity is based on the stories people can tell about themselves, but not all stories have equal status in social worlds.

> In sum, if one considers narrative to be a mode of thought, and indeed that narrative may be an inescapable mode of thought, then its differential distribution in society may be a clue to the distribution of other things as well—rights and privileges having to do with power and money, to be sure, but also rights and privileges having to do with the fundamental functions of language itself, its cognitive and expressive uses in narrative form. (p. 81)

In other words, to be native to a space is to be adept in wielding the rights and privileges of its assumed linguistic codes and narrative forms. Studies of educational systems, for example, have demonstrated that competency is attained less through creative self-actualization and more through the adaptation of the appropriate and the exclusion of alternative ways to tell stories (Bernstein, 1971; Labov, 1972; Gee, 1991). Stories then play a fundamental role in social reproduction when the narrative patterns of one's home are subordinated to those in schools and other formal educational settings. As if prescient about the dominant class narrative embedded in the school-based discourse of the digital native, Hymes (2003) wrote that all stories are patterned in ways that reveal the unequal distribution of power and wealth in society, recognizing "class as not just a diagnostic attribute, but an active specifiable force" (p. 126).

To be a digital native in this more critical framework acknowledges the ways media users are *not just stratified* via access to digital technologies and their material infrastructures. These digital divides in the United States and in Brazil continue to play an important role in the distribution of resources to young people, in terms of both the personal wealth needed for basic internet access at home and the income-based models for funding schools and educational opportunities (Leite & Rezende Nunes, 2007; Seiter, 2007). Beyond this, a digital native must be able to use media in a way that reproduces the narrative patterns considered appropriate to the members of the community where those stories circulate. In this sense, there seems to be an implicit understanding that digital natives will create media that represents themselves through the class-structured grammars of those media worlds.

This presents a challenge to any school-based media program that claims at once to promote creative self-expression while teaching professional norms for telling one's story in a particular medium. The utopian dreams associated with the popular crowdsourcing of knowledge via online encyclopedias and wikis (e.g., Firer-Blaess & Fuchs, 2014) can be easily frustrated when the authors must abide by the expressive constraints of those genres. Similarly, academic programs that aim to foster more diverse voices in media production professions find that the liberal call for diversity can only be answered by students who know and heed the narrative rules for stories as perpetuated within those organizational cultures (e.g., Caldwell, 2014). The creative potential of digital storytelling, for example, has been tempered by technical and generic limits which afford its audiences only "partial powers of story constitution and authorship" (Kaavoori et. al., 2017, p. 1059). Neither digital humanities nor digital media production programs are outside of the hidden curriculum that Henry Giroux and Anthony Penna (1979) so long ago identified as a key mechanism for ensuring social reproduction (see also Losh, 2015 for a critique of the ways digital learning projects reproduce existing social inequalities).

An alternative to this conception of digital natives would seek to look at how the generational access to new media technologies has enabled the production and distribution of other narrative views of the world. Young people, roughly those born after 1990, have come of age with the popularization of ever-smaller and more portable computers, from the laptop to the smartphone. Through these devices, roughly a generation in Brazil and the US has become accustomed to representing themselves to their peers. Here Jesús Martín-Barbero's (1987) theory of mediations is a useful guide to understanding how new processes of making and consuming media content operate in tandem with the construction of one's identity. Tracing the history of Latin American melodrama from newspaper serials of the 1850s to the telenovelas that dominate prime-time broadcasting today, Martín-Barbero (1987) has argued that each new medium integrated and enunciated ways of seeing society based on the material conditions of the working-class masses. In this hegemonic process:

> The new communication technologies adopted their formats in the sense of a *mediation*, a change of their technical materiality to achieve a new potential for social communication [As invenções tecnológicas no campo de comunicação acham aí sua forma: o sentido que vai tomar sua *mediação*, a mutação da materialidade técnica em potencialidade socialmente comunicativa]. (p. 191)

Since the 1990s, Martín-Barbero (2008) points to popular Colombian drug ballads [narcocorridos] as a genre that expresses the narrative worldviews of marginalized youth throughout Latin America. The songs, which lionize those young people that society has deemed "disposable [descartável]," demonstrate how each new medium incorporates emerging sensibilities (Martín-Barbero, 2008, p. 10). In all places where young people lack jobs and social mobility, Martín-Barbero (2008) argues that they speak in a generational and class-based idiom, from their dress codes and tattoos to their performances of themselves via popular media. He writes:

> Technology today is one of the most powerful metaphors for understanding the weaving—as in networks and interfaces—or the constructing one's

> subjectivity [A tecnologia é, hoje, uma das metáforas mais potentes para compreender o tecido—redes e interfaces—de construção da subjetividade]. (2008, p. 20)

By considering each medium in terms of its technical and social capacities to afford people without class power a means to construct their own identities, Martín-Barbero (2008) creates a path for understanding digital natives less in terms of their buying power and more in terms of how they construct their identities via the medium.

By refocusing the conception of the digital native away from only the most privileged young people, we hope to show how digital media made by and for young Black audiences in Rio de Janeiro and New Orleans are mediations of their social locations and subjectivities. In each of these African-American majority cities, Blackness is understood as an identity of less privilege than Whiteness. This perception reflects the sharp contrast in income and other sociological indicators of social class, such as education and mortality rates. The fact that so much popular culture in both places—from stories and song to fashion and dance—are mediations of both Black and working-class cultures shows their close connections in terms of narrative views of the world. This is not to say that race and class are irreducibly the same in either place. Yet among the young Black media producers we met, all of them hoped to use media technologies not just as forums for self-expression but also as tools of social mobility. Even if not statistically likely, the class-based aims embedded in being a digital native created an inevitable tension between representing oneself and self-exploitation.

Favela em Dança

Translated as the "Favela Dance Festival," *Favela em Dança* (www.favelaemdanca.com.br/) has brought together young people to dance and compete in the Cantagalo neighborhood since 2013. Cantagalo is located on a hill sandwiched between two of the most famous and elite neighborhoods of Rio de Janeiro. Called a "favela," Cantagalo has had a reputation of being an impoverished slum or a working-class community, depending on the class standpoint of the observer. Per 2010 statistics, nearly 5,000 residents called Cantagalo their home ("Pavão/Pavãozinho/Cantagalo," 2016). There, the average income was about two-thirds of the median in the rest of the city, and young people were particularly challenged to stay in school. Most adults in 2009 had left school before finishing their seventh year; only 80 percent of teens, aged 15 to 18, were in school ("Diagnóstico Sócio-Econômico Comunidades com Unidades de Polícia Pacificadora do RJ," 2010). Participants in the dance project hail from many favelas in the city and even surrounding states to counter negative images of the dark-skinned youth in favelas as dangerous, unskilled, and uneducated. For three days, they perform highly localized versions of Black urban styles, such as hip hop, breakdancing, krump, funk, and passinho—which spread as a global phenomenon on television and on the internet during the 2016 Olympics. The rest of the year, the organizers maintain a strong presence promoting the project and its young participants across online platforms and social media.

The website claims *Favela em Dança* is "in the favela, by the favela, and for the favela," a statement that refers to the social and class location of favela residents throughout Brazil. In an interview, executive director and co-founder of the group Ronaldo Marinho said the principle objective of the group was to "leave a legacy within the community" ["deixar um legado dentro da comunidade"] by reinforcing a local favela economy based on dance and the local vendors that sponsor and support it through regular events. This legacy has included training and supporting young people to create their own media images which can then be used to promote young people as creative artists and cultural producers. The YouTube channel for the group has offered regular "virtual battles" between collectives of young people in professionally staged productions. Personal videos of the past winners offer commentary on the meaning of passinho—a Brazilian hip-hop style—to international dance history. For example, in a two-minute clip dance teacher and mentor Rodrigo Soninho explains that passinho in the last decade has been a movement, like hip hop in urban US centers before it, involving "trade and improvisation to create a new vocabulary based on an integration of styles" ("Favela em Dança | Rodrigo Soninho," August 20, 2014). Shot at the beach, the video produced by a fellow project participant demonstrates a number of professional camera movements and editing techniques, including panoramas, split-screen performances, and continuity cuts. The unequal sound levels and need for a windscreen when recording Soninho beachside suggests the lack of a professional mixer and microphone rather than a lack of skills in media production. The video's seamless matching of the dancer's moves and voice shows Soninho as an organic intellectual who is speaking for his generation through his body and his image. Soninho says that the project was important for him, as the creator of his own dance studio, not because it showed elites in Rio "ghetto" culture, but because it showed "every community has culture." This sentiment resonates with Raymond Williams' (1989) theory that culture is ordinary, reflecting not just a few privileged individuals or the discourses in the Cambridge tea houses, but the dialectics between "the known meanings and directions" of a community and the "new observations and meanings" of its members (p. 93). While Williams lamented the loss of working-class cultures in Britain in mass mediated forms, the videos by participants in *Favela em Dança* demonstrate the ways national Brazilian culture has benefitted from the non-mediated creative contributions of working-class communities.

At the same time, the young people involved in *Favela em Dança* saw themselves as revitalizing their economically depressed community. The website boasted in 2016 that over 120 workers have been employed in businesses that work with the project. During the festival, eateries and lodging facilities have seen a 30 percent boost in business. Students who visit the project also receive a free "tour" of the neighborhood. While these businesses were still part of a precarious service economy, the solidarity between informal and formal workers in the community, whether they be students or servers, producers or performers, aimed to lift all futures. By being the protagonists of their own online images and their communities instead of marginal or even criminal youth, Martín-Barbero (2008) writes that young people become the agents of change displaying "an alternate sense of sociability that permeates as much their political attitudes as their cultural practices, their moral standards, and their aesthetic tastes" (p. 13) ["as alternativas de sociabilidade que permeiam tanto as atitudes politicas quanto as pautas morais, práticas culturais e gostos estéticos"].

Noirlinians

Created in July 2015 as a blog that explores fashion, local Black history, and African diasporic cultural identities, *Noirlinians* (https://noirlinians.wordpress.com/) is primarily the project of two women. Denisio Truitt, the child of Liberian-Americans, came to New Orleans after living abroad and around the US. Mwende "FreeQuency" Katwiwa moved to New Orleans from Kenya. Both attended elite colleges on predominantly White campuses, but afterwards decided to live in predominantly African-American neighborhoods in what they call on the blog "the most African US city." Truitt designs clothes for a fashion brand she co-owns. Katwiwa works for reproductive social justice at a nonprofit organization. Both compose spoken word poetry. For them, the aims of the blog have been equally creative, entrepreneurial, and political.

The two creators have editorial control of the blog though they collaborate specifically with Black-identifying photographers living in the city. Together, Katwiwa and Truitt saw themselves as conversation starters between Black people globally about race and identity. Katwiwa said it was a conversation that developed naturally out of their own backgrounds: "We asked ourselves, 'Who am I in this context, as immigrant bodies in a diasporic space?'. . . We agreed to start a blog." Each blog entry focuses on race, identity, and the geography of New Orleans as a diasporic place. The women work together in all creative aspects of the site: designing the layout, modeling clothes, having other young people photograph them, and writing the essays. "We are both writers, creators and creative," said Katwiwa. While some of the clothing was personally designed by them, some was resurrected from their own closets or borrowed from friends. They selected aspiring young photographers who helped in finding local settings that have been significant to African-American history. In these ways, their digital images blended new and old. "We wanted this project to explore our identities with New Orleans as a historically Black city," she added.

Playing on both the rhetorics of Black Pride and the local vernacular, *Noirlinians* claims to represent "street style," both verbally and visually. Posts weave together personal reflections about strength and resilience in the wake of contemporary social movements, such as Black Lives Matter and the Black Feminisms Forum, lessons on the slave trade, segregation, and disfranchisement of local Black neighborhoods in the name of "development." Each post begins with a suggested "soundtrack," emphasizing that the words and photos are meant to have a rhythmic flow. Complementing this flow, the creators also maintain an active presence on Instagram and Facebook, providing more connections between New Orleans and current events in the global African diaspora. A post entitled "We Are Family" (December 2, 2016) begins with a statement by photographer Malik Bartholomew about the razing of a Black business district to make way for a freeway in 1966. Set to the eponymous song by Sister Sledge, Bartholomew's words about "Tha Bridge" merge into a photo series with Truitt and Katwiwa that begins with a photo that at once references the structure of the bridge and John Carlos and Tommie Smith's Black Power Salute at the 1968 Olympics. Truitt wears her own creation: an elegant grey wrap gown with an ermine collar placed on her shoulder. Katwiwa wears leggings under an indigo tie-dyed dashiki she "found [. . .] while raiding my grandma's closet." Their essays never mention class but focus on their social location as members of families who ate mac-n-cheese meals but were still more fortunate than their kin who were still in Africa. Private family photos are public on the site, blurring the lines at once between personal expression and public activism.

Digital media technologies have both enabled and challenged the project, said Katwiwa in an extended interview.

> **Katwiwa:** I don't like social media, I hate social media, I think it takes a lot of time.
>
> **Aline Maia:** But you use a lot of it . . .
>
> **Katwiwa:** Yes, I use a lot. I learned to use social media. If you actually go back to my, like, Facebook two or three years ago, you will see I used to barely post anything. I didn't even have a wall because I didn't like people saying things to me. I got it because people, like, need a way to keep in touch with you. [. . . but] I do not like technologies.

Contrary to the marketers' assumptions that digital natives naturally adopt new technologies to be hyper-connected, the co-creator of *Noirlinians* described social media as a self-taught effort and a form of work. Yet she embraced using the technologies regularly to have "more power [and] to be in charge of the stories getting out":

> **Katwiwa:** [V]oice is a very important part of a person, and for kids too—for finding their best place to fit in, for abilities that people don´t think about. I discovered that not only my voice, but my body could do things, even though I didn´t like computers, etc. People here in New Orleans, they did not have many options [at school or at home] for learning these things,

so they discount themselves. It might even seem to some that if you are just in a marching band, you are not artistic really. And [to that thought] I say "What?!?" Kids don´t see themselves as natural writers because they are taught so. [. . .]

Maia: And what about mass media? In your opinion, how can the media work in favor of or marginalize young people?

Katwiwa: Now it is better because media is becoming smaller and smaller so it allows people to show themselves, allows people to have their platform. So people get out there, you know, without your parents' permission or your school's permission, or anyone´s permission. So they can say whatever they want.

Putting *Noirlinians* in the same universe of artistic practices as spoken word poetry jams, fashion designing, and marching bands, Katwiwa also put herself in a network of young African Americans, using media to have control over her own representation and to speak up against the structural inequalities that hinder creative expression.

In these ways, Truitt and Katwiwa are digital natives whose narrative views of the world encompass a hybrid sensibility of being both media producers and consumers, creative professionals and dedicated activists, all the while speaking the language of a generation of Black youth who are seeking class mobility and resisting oppression. Henry Jenkins et al. (2016) use the phrase "precarious publics" to describe the gap that exists between the ability to use one's voice through media channels and the lack of influence those voices have in the public sphere. For the women behind *Noirlinians*, the precarity of young Black voices in the public sphere is connected to the economic precarity that keeps African-American communities marginalized in all markets. In addition to giving other young aspiring creatives a voice on the website through their photos and clothing designs, the website encourages people to buy products from fellow Black entrepreneurs both locally and in the diaspora. "All the links are there, so you can purchase the stuff 'cause the blog is about supporting other creative Black folks here and across around the globe," said Katwiwa, adding, "because if you are going to commodify something, at least you can buy from the people you know and from who you know who can make profit from this commodifying." This class sensibility in controlling the ways Black creative production is ultimately commodified is one thing that bonds the young media producers of *Noirlinians* with those of *Festival de Dança*. By leveraging their media content to ultimately attempt to lift the precarious economic prospects of an entire community, they show the trade-offs between commodifying one's identity and using it to lift the community's collective class status.

Concluding Observations

"Like it or not," writes digital education scholar Michael Thomas (2011), "'Digital Natives' has retained a powerful and enduring if, albeit, problematical resonance since Prensky popularized it in his essay" (p. 3). Thomas attributes the resonance of the term to an economy that prizes digital natives as a lucrative segment of technology markets. These social class implications around technology uses and economic value have been compounded within racialized social structures that further hinder seeing how young people of color are media creators. While our comparison of these two projects and their dynamic organizers are not meant to be representative of all young people of color, much less youth in general, we present them as an alternative to the images that marketers circulate. Indeed, our experiences have shown us that digital natives are frequently those in our midst who are using technology to mediate themselves and their communities in new and creative ways. To be a digital native is to have a consciousness about the ways technical skills and tools are situated in the contexts of everyday life, and to incorporate this knowledge in the process of mediating oneself. The digital natives in our studies are representing themselves always in dialogue with imagined communities both online and in the areas where they live. We hope this initial consideration of these media worlds provokes future research questions.

In terms of media and social class, for example, the term digital native has to be diversified to account for material differences in terms of technological access and education in order to see the diversity of digital native cultures. Just access to regular broadband service and professional recording equipment is a formidable barrier to most young people without considerable income or financial means. At the same time, we concur with Sonia Livingstone and Julian Sefton-Green's (2016) assessment that social class in the digital age is as much about the socialization of dispositions towards new technologies as it is about income or job futures. As they have also shown, school is a place where these dispositions are socialized, often in tension with parents' dispositions in the home. The digital natives involved in *Noirlinians* and *Favela em Dança* also straddle different worlds, not only between school and home but also in terms of neighborhood, city, and country. The participants in these projects have some college education, but they also embrace "the street," the dispositions of Black urban and global citizens. These hybrid sensibilities are mediated through their digital texts and images, guiding them to be inspired creatively and politically, but also careful and ambivalent towards the technologies that would commodify their images without supporting the local economies and class prospects in their multiple communities. Their critical dispositions, rooted in the intersections of class with race, are important if we are to see how young people from diverse social locations navigate a precarious digital future.

Works Cited

Bernstein, B. (1971). *Class, codes, and control*. Vol. 1, *Theoretical studies towards a sociology of language*. London, UK: Routledge and Paul Kegan.

Caldwell, J.T. (2014). Para-industry, shadow academy. *Cultural Studies, 28*, 720–740.
"Diagnóstico sócio-econômico comunidades com unidades de polícia pacificadora do rj." (October 2010). Retrieved from www.firjan.com.br/
Dimenstein, G. (1991). *Brazil: War on children*. London, UK: Latin American Bureau.
Firer-Blaess, S., & Fuchs, C. (2014). Wikipedia: An info-communist manifesto. *Television & New Media, 15*, 87–103.
Gee, J.P. (1991). A linguistic approach to narrative. *Journal of Narrative and Life History, 1*, 15–40.
Giroux, H. (2016, October 19). The United States' war on youth: From schools to debtors' prisons. Truthout. Retrieved from www.truth-out.org/news/item/38044-america-s-war-on-youth-from-schools-to-debtors-prisons
Giroux, H., & Penna, A. (1979). Social education in the classroom: The dynamics of the hidden curriculum. *Theory and Research in Social Education*, 7, 21–42.
Hymes, D. (2003). *Ethnography, linguistics, and narrative inequality: Toward an understanding of voice*. London, UK: Taylor & Francis.
Jenkins, H., et al. (2016). *By any media necessary: The new youth activism*. New York, NY: NYU Press.
Kavoori, A., Lashley, B. & Creech, B. "Voices for a New Vernacular: A Forum for Digital Storytelling." International Journal of Communication, 11, 1057–60
Labov, W. (1972). *Language in the inner city: Studies in black English vernacular*. Philadelphia, PA: University of Pennsylvania Press.
Leite, A.M.A., & Rezende Nunes, M.F. (2007). Juventudes e inclusão digital: reflexões sobre acesso e uso de computador de da internet pelo jovens. In M. Abramovav et al. (Eds.), *Juventudes: outros olhares sobre a diversidade*. (pp. 197–227). Brasília, Brazil: UNESCO.
Lippmann, W. (1922). *Public opinion*. New York, NY: Harcourt, Brace and Company.
Livingstone, S., & Sefton-Green, J. (2016). *The class: Living and learning in the digital age*. New York, NY: NYU Press.
Losh, L. (2015). *The war on learning: Gaining ground in the digital university*. Cambridge, MA: MIT Press.
Martín-Barbero, J. (1987). *De meios às mediações: comunicação, cultura e hegemonia*. Rio de Janeiro, Brazil: Editorial Gustavo Gili.
Martín-Barbero, J. (2008). A mudança na percepção da juventude: sociabilidades, tecnicidades e subjetividades entre os jovens. In S. Borelli & J. Freire Filho (Eds.), *Culturas Juvenis no Século XXI* (pp. 9–32). São Paulo, Brazil: EDUC.
"Pavão/Pavãozinho/Cantagalo." (2016). Rio + social. Retrieved from www.riomaissocial.org
Prensky, M. (2016). "Bio." Retrieved from http://marcprensky.com/marcs-bio/
Seiter, E. (2007). *The internet playground: Children's access, entertainment, and mis-education*. New York, NY: Peter Lang.
Serazio, M. (2015). Selling (digital) millennials: The social construction and technological bias of a consumer generation. *Television & New Media, 16*, 599–615.
Thomas, M. (2011). Technology, education and the discourse of the digital native: Between evangelists and dissenters. In M. Thomas (Ed.), *Deconstructing digital natives: Young people, technology and new literacies* (pp. 1–14). London, UK: Routledge.
Thompson, D. (2015, January 31). Millennials: $2,000 poorer than their parents were at the same age. *The Atlantic*. Retrieved from www.theatlantic.com/business/archive/2015/01/young-adults-poorer-less-employed-and-more-diverse-than-their-parents/385029/
Williams, R. (1989). Culture is ordinary. In R. Gayle (Ed.), *Resources of hope: Culture, democracy, socialism* (pp. 3–14). London, UK: Verso.

14

BIG DATA IS TOO SMALL: RESEARCH IMPLICATIONS OF CLASS INEQUALITY FOR ONLINE DATA COLLECTION

Jen Schradie

Introduction

Digital technology has enabled researchers to access massive amounts of online data and analyze it almost instantaneously. Often this data comes from public and private Internet repositories that hold so many information bytes that a colloquial term is not just data, but "Big Data."[1] This data may be mined, scraped, or downloaded from online sources for social research. Never before has so much data been available to so many people. Many types of researchers are enthralled with this goldmine. Corporations track, amass, and sell information on demographics and habits of consumers. Media organizations track eyeballs and clicks. And social scientists use online data with unprecedented high speed and low cost, whether it's using just a sliver of computer code to access millions of tweets for a social network diagram, online news sites for automated text analysis, digital labor platforms for online surveys, or online communities for ethnography 24/7.

There are many critiques of using online data for research, such as not focusing enough on the offline world, not sharing it publicly with academic researchers, or not using the scientific method. The more mass utopian hype over Big Data also faces criticism. After all, it isn't *that* new. The Romans and the Nazis amassed huge amounts of data on their populations. And then, of course, there is the creepy, Big Brother aspect. Another gaping hole in this digital cloud, I argue, is that online data analytics can leave out those excluded from the digital realm. This persistent sampling problem of online data threatens generalizability in social science research.

This paper received support from the Jacob K. Javits Foundation and the Berkeley Center for New Media. Support through the ANR Labex IAST is gratefully acknowledged. Additional guidance provided by Abigail Andrews, Mike Hout, Laura Robinson, Jeremy Schulz, and Kim Voss, but the author is solely accountable for any omissions or errors.
Please send any comments to Jen Schradie at jen.schradie@gmail.com

Despite assertions that the "digital divide" is passé, inequality persists between those who can afford consistent and high quality Internet connectivity and those who cannot. But Big Data isn't just gleaned from those who have *consumed* online content but also from those who have *produced* it. When it comes to creating publicly available online content, such as blogs, videos, and social media posts, digital creators are still dominated by those with more income, education, and class power. While age is still a factor, class persists as one of the most significant determinants of online data production, especially as to how it intersects with gender, race, or ethnicity (Hassani, 2006; Selwyn, 2006; Hargittai, 2008; Segev, 2010; Schradie, 2012).

In other words, Big Data is too small. Those who cannot afford consistent connectivity, let alone have the resources for content creation, are often absent from online analytics. Our samples, therefore, are too small, not in sample "n" size, but in generalizability. What mistakes, therefore, do Big Data studies make by ignoring data not visible online?

In this chapter, I introduce this question and describe what's at stake in the research context, explain the state of digital inequality, offer a social class critique of using online data for research, as well as make suggestions for addressing these weaknesses. I then propose that social class be more thoroughly studied as a concept in these and other digital studies, as well as included as part of any study using Big Data analytics.

Class is a contested term in the study of stratification. Many studies of (or incorporating) digital inequality examine socioeconomic divisions like income or education, rather than class power differences (Vanneman & Cannon, 1987; Wright, 1997; Zweig, 2001). Nonetheless, not being able to control the digital means of online content production or experiencing disempowerment in using digital technology—can both reduce how and how much poor and working-class people contribute to online data metrics (Robinson, 2009; Schradie, 2011; Sims, 2014).

The implications for this hole in the cloud are as vast as the deepening digital divide. Big Money is going into Big Data. Policymakers increasingly rely on online data for political decisions, so the concerns of the poor and working class may be left out of the equation (Hargittai & Jennrich, 2016). For instance, relying on Internet-based survey panel data for election predictions is less accurate without the incorporation of marginalized communities. For social scientists, our theories may hold true only for the digitally literate, and in some cases the digital elite.

Every study has limitations in terms of its applicability to the general population. But if researchers increasingly rely on data culled from the Internet, empirical findings and subsequent theories will increasingly be skewed away from marginalized communities and toward those who can afford, know how, and are empowered to post online.

Big Data and the Scientific Method

In 2008, Chris Anderson, editor-in-chief of *Wired Magazine*, wrote a provocative article entitled "The End of Theory: The Data Deluge Makes the Scientific

Method Obsolete" (2008). He argued that hypothesis testing is no longer necessary with Google's petabytes of data. Rather than needing first to come up with research questions, hypotheses, and *then* collect data, patterns would organically emerge from massive data sets that would guide social scientific discoveries. The data would provide all of the answers to how society works. Correlation would "supersede" causation:

> This is a world where massive amounts of data and applied mathematics replace every other tool that might be brought to bear. Out with every theory of human behavior, from linguistics to sociology. Forget taxonomy, ontology, and psychology. Who knows why people do what they do? The point is they do it, and we can track and measure it with unprecedented fidelity. With enough data, the numbers speak for themselves.

An easy strawman, Anderson's piece generated a host of articles in academic journals decrying his claim. The overall consensus, to no one's surprise, was that the scientific method, such as hypothesis testing, is far from over (e.g., Pigliucci, 2009). Some focused on the debate around "correlation is not causation" and that correlation can lead you in the wrong direction with spurious noise. Still, many implicitly pointed to what Box (1976) articulated so well pre-Big Data—that science is an iterative process in which correlation is useful in that it can trigger research that uses hypothesis testing. Most argued as Pigliucci (2009, p. 534) did:

> But, if we stop looking for models and hypotheses, are we still really doing science? Science, unlike advertising, is not about finding patterns—although that is certainly part of the process—it is about finding explanations for those patterns.

For many social scientists, this issue may simply seem like fodder for an undergraduate lesson in the scientific method. Yet what may unite all scholars is that throwing online data up in the air to see what lands fails to carry out the mission of academic work: to generate research questions situated in existing scholarly work—and in the process, challenge and build on each other's research to generate knowledge.

The problem is not simply the lack of hypothesis testing but the absence of social theory and normative value in research questions. In fact, the first part of the title of Anderson's *Wired* article was "The End of Theory." Is research driven by available Big Data from corporations or is it driven by theoretical questions of how society operates? The dearth of social theory in data science is a wider problem than this chapter can tackle, but inherent in evaluating how society operates theoretically, and in practice, is how inequality functions.

Some may simply fail to acknowledge its generalizability problems. The risk of taking online data at face value, without a broader societal and historical context, has only accelerated since Anderson's controversial article. First, online data permeate many academic disciplines, from new data science majors to digital humanities programs. In 2016, 95% of nationally ranked universities in the US had data analytics program (Tableau, 2016). Journals have even emerged on this specific topic, such as *Big Data and Society*. At the same time, it has become easier and faster to download, analyze, and visualize online data. But the digital divide has largely been overlooked with an increasing rate of scholarship that often analyzes publicly produced online data.

Since the initial firestorm over the scientific method, researchers have decried pitfalls that researchers face with Big Data. Some scholars have tackled the question of representation with online data, but the debate often focuses on whether or not it tells a better story than smaller, micro-level analog data. For instance, Karpf (2012) contended that what is happening offline and the context of Big Data are essential to understanding it, while Snijders, Matzat, and Reips claimed that the mathematical models used to mine data do not reflect actual online behavior (2012). Nonetheless, Hargittai and Jennrich did argue that policy needs to reflect inequalities derived from online data (2016). As a result, the focus on our "digital trace" does not tell a complete story of society. Despite these limitations of Big Data, scant attention has been paid to how social stratification may limit online data's representativeness in research.

Digital Production Inequality: What's Missing?

While the debate over scholarly Big Data is abundant, another critical area, I argue, is *who* specifically may be left out of research data: the poor and working class. They are less apt to be online content users and creators, which can bias the digital data that researchers collect. Therefore, scholarship using these data may result in theories skewed toward metrics from middle- to upper-class digital participants. If online data often captures both the public's consumption and production of content,[2] it is helpful to analyze these two critical areas of digital inequality to understand how, exactly, Big Data is too small.

First, consider consumption, or access, to the Internet. Data metrics may capture consumers' use of various platforms. Classic theories of diffusion (Coleman, Katz, & Menzel, 1957) suggest that successful innovations start with early adopters and eventually result in near universal adoption. Therefore, starting with early Internet adopters from the 1990s, one might expect that the digital connectivity divide would eventually disappear with most everyone online three decades later. Despite increasing adoption rates in the United States and in many countries, research shows a persistent class-based divide (Zhang, 2014; Anderson, 2017) of consumers. African-Americans, Latinx, and people with lower educational and income levels are less likely than non-Latinx, white, and college-educated Americans to go online and have connectivity, although the gap is closing slightly for Latinx (Hargittai & Walejko, 2008; Jones, Johnson-Yale, Millermaier & Seoane Pérez, 2009; Schradie, 2015). As of 2016, 13% of Americans did not use the Internet, with income and education as major contributors to that gap (Anderson & Perrin, 2016). But the likelihood that people with a high school education are online is half as much as those with more education, and scholars have found that stating in a survey that one has been online may only indicate occasional access (Robinson, 2009), rather than consistent high quality connectivity.

But who is creating and posting online content into the digital cloud? Specifically, are the poor and working class posting to Twitter, blogging or uploading videos at the same rate as people from higher socioeconomic classes? In a word, no. Inequality in connectivity also affects what people are able to *do* online, specifically production of digital content. Certainly, not all wealthy, privileged people compose social media posts. However, working-class and poor people are doubly disadvantaged. They are less likely to be online in the first place—and then among those who make it into the online pool, they are less likely to be content creators online. For instance, people with a high school education are half as likely to create online content than those with a college degree, *even among people who are online* (Schradie, 2011). Simply, consumption of online content does not automatically lead to production of it. Content may not always differ based on the social class background of the creator, yet a body of scholarship has demonstrated that class does shape media content (e.g., Kendall, 2005).

And this class-driven gap in online content creation shows persistence, rather than closing over time. The digital divide is not over, nor are there signs that it will ever completely disappear, given that new hardware and software applications are continuously introduced, so playing catch-up to the early adopters is a treadmill, rather than a finish line. Being able to afford and control digital gadgets and Internet connectivity are key, but it is also a question of having the skills, confidence, and empowerment to post online (van Dijk, 2005; Van Deursen & Van Dijk, 2011; Haight, Quan-Haase, & Corbett, 2014; Schradie, 2017). Certainly, the "leapfrog" idea of people using cheaper mobile devices, such as smartphones, and bypassing more expensive laptops or desktops, does exist, as studies do point to people with lower incomes relying on these types of gadgets (Pew Research Center, 2017). However, the consistent use of these gadgets still requires that someone can purchase a phone, pay for a data plan, is the only user of it, knows how and is confident in using it, and has time to do so. Fully controlling the means of digital production is key. Inexpensive mobile phones may be useful for consumption or making short online posts but not practical for longer or more complicated digital content creation.

But what of the intersection of class with race? On the one hand, in the United States, blacks are up to twice as likely to post to social media than whites

(Hargittai & Litt, 2011; Schradie, 2012). Like other media formats, scholars have found a racial divide in different forms of media (Watkins 2011; Murthy, Gross, & Pensavalle 2016). Given the prevalence of #BlackTwitter in which African-Americans use the platform for support, community, and other solidarity purposes (Clark, 2015), one might expect that poor African-Americans may be an exception to the class gap. On the other hand, while blacks may *produce* some forms of social media content more than whites, this is only true among those who are online, as they are less likely to *consume* online content in the first place. Simply, the intersection of race and class is critical—poor African-Americans are dramatically less likely to post online content than wealthy whites. African-Americans are less likely than whites to be online in the first place, and social class is a critical part of that gap.

How Is Big Data Too Small?

If social scientists consistently use Big Data samples with a blind eye toward generalizability, then we are heading down a non-robust path that favors simplicity over the messiness of understanding the weaknesses of online data that can leave out the marginalized. In the process, it weakens rigorous methodological and theoretical analysis. Social stratification, particularly class divisions, matter with Big Data, but how? Substantive methodological methods illustrate how class makes a difference in Big Data analytics.

Network Analysis

When Anderson wrote his article in 2008, conducting social network analysis required the use of clunky software. Twitter, for instance, was just emerging on the social media landscape. Now, with a touch of a button, a day's Twitter conversation is instantaneously displayed, creating a sociogram of people's network ties. But that Twitter data is only as robust as the people who are tweeting, favorite-ing, or replying. In 2016, 20% of Americans with a high school education (or less) *and* who are already online used Twitter while 29% of college-educated Americans did, but this does not account for the people who are not online at all, who are more likely to be more working class.[3] So the gap is even wider in the general population. And just like the class differences between consumption and production of content more generally, everyone who has a Twitter account (consumption) is not necessarily tweeting (production) to create nodes of tweets and retweets, for instance.

It is possible that digital inequality may not impact the robustness of any analysis of social structural networks with online data because social classes are already divided and siloed into their own stratum, but one cannot make this assumption without examining class differences. Furthermore, we are not seeing how particularly vulnerable and marginalized populations fit into our so-called network society. If an analysis is culled from online data, lower levels of working-class people who are online may only be perceived as "weak" versus "strong" ties. Central nodes may be missing, as well. If that is the case, then the results lose more than generalizability. They are simply not valid. To overcome these weaknesses in social network analyses with digitally derived data, one could do diligence in determining the social class background of the nodes in the network, or at least an approximation. This may require two levels of assessment. One is by general Internet use and the other is online participation on specific platforms under study. Obtaining social class information may require offline data collection or, perhaps, partnering with platforms, if one is able to access this data without compromising privacy concerns.

A generalizability limitation example is with digital activism networks. This type of analysis is common, such as how people are spreading information or communicating around protest events. Research has shown class inequalities with social media usage for activism, in general (Pickerill, 2003; Schradie, 2017), but less is known about digital activist network inequality. Therefore, if one uses Twitter data to analyze the network ties of a protest and working-class participants are present but not tweeting as much, or at all, then the network ties resulting from this Twitter analysis would skew toward more privileged users and fail to incorporate working-class network ties from that event. To continue with the Twitter example, social class is one of the least understood demographic variables of participants on the platform because it is difficult to identify based only on the platform's data. If social class does not impact the research question at all, then one could proceed without knowing this information, but only after eliminating this factor. Other platforms, such as Facebook, have more demographic data, such as educational background, so distinguishing between college- and high-school-educated people is one option to approximate class, but this may be difficult with the Silicon Valley company's increasing restrictions on researcher access to data through their Application Programming Interface (API). Analyses of social networks would benefit from a full examination of how the results might vary with different social classes, rather than in a footnote. If it is not possible to determine people's class identity, at the very minimum, scholars should acknowledge this limitation.

Automated Text Analysis

Automated text analysis evaluates content. With digitally produced content accelerating, the options for examining text appear to be boundless. Some approaches are basic sentiment analyses using predetermined ways to examine text. More sophisticated techniques employ topic modeling with a way to "teach" the algorithm with human intervention, often called machine learning. The general argument, like much of the digitally enabled research using online data, is that text mining for content analysis is now not only more efficient but more accurate than hand-coding (Mohr & Bogdanov, 2013). Just as with network analysis, a variety of disciplines use automated text analysis, from history and film studies to computer science and sociology. But whose voice (and whose text) is being analyzed? While some scholars, especially historians, have gone out of their way to digitize handwritten or non-computer-generated text (Nelson, 2014), the tendency is increasingly toward analyzing what is already online, as that is also more efficient. But at what cost when working-class people are less likely to post online content in the first place?

One example is the study of so-called citizen journalism. Scholars have extensively studied the digital news landscape as an example of what citizen journalists are now able to do outside the confines of traditional news outlets (Gilmor, 2004). Prior to social media adoption and diffusion, traditional news media did not accurately represent the poor and working class, and when they did it was often mediated by voices of so-called experts, rather than by the population itself (Kendall, 2005). In the early social media era, a common view was that professional journalists from traditional media outlets got in the way of average citizens reporting directly through the likes of social media feeds, blogs, and other online posts (Wall, 2015). In this way, a more pluralist journalism would emerge. Yet, it was not simply the onslaught of so-called "fake news" that got in the way of more working-class people having representation in these formats. Bloggers, for instance, tend to be of the same privileged social class as those of traditional reporters—there are just more of them (Hindman, 2009). And if scholars rely on citizen journalist data, they may find that the citizen skews toward the elite.

Before the dawn of digital technology, scholars studied the artefacts of the elite—from 16th-century books to the *New York Times*. However, there was little pretense that this was representative of all of society. A common view of Big Data and online data, however, is that this digital information is more egalitarian, yet without metrics and offline comparisons, it is difficult to make that claim.

Survey Data

This trend of using online data in research is not just limited to digital content creation. Scholars harness the Internet to conduct surveys and polls. For years, the robustness of traditional telephone polling data has been on the decline with the increase in unlisted numbers and mobile phone lines, as well as fewer landline numbers and less public trust in the participation of polling. Two trends have emerged in response. One is the use of self-selecting users of platforms like Mechanical Turk (MTurk), an online labor system. MTurk workers are paid a nominal fee for doing low wage tasks, including taking polls. Studies have shown that they tend to skew towards digitally savvy and slightly higher socioeconomic levels (Berinsky, Huber, & Lenz, 2012), although other studies of MTurk workers' demographics have not reported socioeconomic details well enough to evaluate, often focusing on other characteristics (Huff & Tingley, 2015). The other survey approach has been with panel data. This is also a paid survey system in which people agree to participate in polls over a lengthy time period, and researchers pay companies to manage the polls. Since these surveys are conducted via the Internet, the participants are not likely to be from lower income or educational levels. Digital inequality has been given scant attention with online panel data. One analysis comparing MTurk and panel data in terms of robustness said that these can be used by "anyone with Internet access" (Weinberg, Freese, & McElhattan, 2014), and it found little difference in outcome with the two approaches. The problem, though, is that not everyone has sufficiently regular and consistent access in order to participate. Moreover, research has shown that many non-responders to survey questions are from lower classes (Laurison, 2015). The skill level required may also be a challenge for people without substantial new media literacy.

Social scientists have a few ways to work around this problem, in general, with representation problems in survey data. First, they can use a stratified sample in that they can ensure that those less represented are sought after to be included in the sample. Related is an approach to "weigh" people who are less represented, to give their findings more emphasis so that the sample ends up being representative of the general population under study. But if one only gives more statistical weight to poor people who are online this technique does not address any differences between people who are and are not online to participate in the panel. For instance, it is possible that some "poor" participants are college-aged youth, more likely to be online, and therefore have a temporary low income, rather than those who come from a working-class background. All of these companies who employ digital workers, whether with MTurk-like platforms or with panel data, need more rigorous evaluation and transparency to ensure their representativeness of class divisions.

Online Ethnography

The use of online data is not just limited to quantitative analysis. Researchers use qualitative techniques such as digital ethnography as a way to understand thick descriptions of the online world. This can include participant observation in an online community, such as listservs or games. Qualitative studies have a different approach from quantitative analyses in that they offer in-depth mechanisms and explanations of how society operates. Qualitative researchers who zoom in for precision (Becker, 1998) and thick description (Geertz, 1973) on middle- to upper-class online users may inadvertently create findings only relevant to that class. Just as scholars have found that class differences shape how people interpret older forms of media (Press, 1991), social class differences are reproduced with online engagement. For instance, having an information habitus or social milieu that is more middle to upper class shaped how some youth sought information online, with higher income users being more playful online, what Bourdieu called "skhole"; lower income students, though, lacked the time and autonomy to do more than tasks set before them (Robinson, 2009).

Online ethnographies could benefit from digging in the direction of how social class differences may shape online dialogue, postings, or other content. And with online ethnography, like with any method, it is particularly important to acknowledge how reflexivity, or the class perspective and position of the ethnographer, may shape observation. Qualitative researchers who have overcome social class limitations have conducted both online and offline ethnography to go deeper into the everyday lives of the poor and working class in online engagement. For instance, Sims delved into the contextualized lives of students at a school designed to overcome technological inequalities in the first place, finding that even skill and access remedies resulted in less beneficial online use (2014). The result is that understanding class differences in an ethnographic online context is similar to the other methods—that inequalities can be incorporated into the research design stage.

Implications of Small Data

What is the upshot methodologically? Certainly, any data set is imperfect and has limitations as to its generalizability. The efficiency and other advantages to using online data are clear. However, digitally created online data almost *always* have the same limitation: the data do not include people who are not online or who do not post as frequently as others. Therefore, the data are rarely generalizable to the population as a whole.

Of course, if scholars are just interested in what is happening online, then the Big-Data-is-too small concept is not as relevant, but if we want to understand what is happening in all of society—both online and offline—we cannot just examine those who are online 24–7.

Ultimately, then, theory suffers from Big Data being too small.

A well-established debate within Science and Technology Studies is about ways to move beyond technological determinism (Fischer, 1992), which is an outdated theory that technology unilaterally shapes society and culture. Nonetheless, there is still an enthusiasm for using Big Data without incorporating measures to overcome its class-based and other structural limitations. We simply know little about how the reverse of technological determinism—how society determines technology. More precisely, we need further research on how societal differences, in the form of class divisions, shape how and how much the voices, nodes, or text within Big Data are derived from online sources. While these broad theoretical questions are not new, it would behoove the academy to push for class-based contextual understandings of online data collection. Castells said, "Of course, technology does not determine society . . . nor does society script the course of technical change . . . technology *is* society, and society cannot be understood without its technological tools" (2010, p. 10). Still, what is missing is a definition of society that recognizes and includes all social classes. Robust theories generated from online data need to incorporate more than digital influencers.

Castells (2010) also argued that new technologies and a ripe societal context (i.e., the right historical time) converged to create a new global network society, although he fluctuated between arguing that this is not a revolutionary shift to broader claims that this new era is more profound than the Industrial Revolution in terms of its effect on the economy, culture, and society. He and others (i.e., Raine & Wellman, 2012) have suggested that we now have a network society because of the digital age, yet the question remains, a network society for whom? Is it changing for everyone equally? Broader theories of digital society would benefit from including and analyzing all social classes, not just those who are digitally networked. Most of the theory building and knowledge production from scholars of digital media will sit in more meso-level (or smaller) theoretical contributions, but even then, it is critical to have the most accurate understanding of one's data—and what is lacking—to build theory in a contextual, rather than an acontextual, direction. For instance, with the citizen journalism example, a half-century earlier, Mills described the hierarchy of the power of the media in which the working class is largely left out of the equation (1958). Presented with the digital era, especially in light of heavily funded "fake" news, as well as the digital divide, Mills might be dubious about the power of working-class citizens in the digital era.

Simply, the relationship between inequality and Big Data needs further analysis and attention on its own, particularly by analyzing class relations, rather than only socioeconomic variables. Nonetheless, studies that do make broad theoretical claims about online data need to include questions of inequality and sampling limitations in more than a footnote. I am not arguing that Big Data, therefore, should be discarded. Quite the opposite. It is not only a literal goldmine of information for academia, but it is also fascinating and fun to analyze. Instead, we need to figure out ways to use information from the digital cloud in a methodological and theoretical way that represents all of society, not just those online, or at a minimum, recognize that it is smaller than we might have thought.

Notes

1. The word "data" is plural, but I use the term "Big Data" in its singular form to represent the concept.
2. Of course, Big Data is not limited to online data nor to online data that is only from the public's consumption or production of Internet content.
3. www.pewinternet.org/2016/11/11/social-media-update-2016/

Works Cited

Anderson, C. (2008). The end of theory: The data deluge makes the scientific method obsolete. *Wired Magazine*. Retrieved from www.wired.com/2008/06/pb-theory/

Anderson, M. (2017). Digital divide persists even as lower-income Americans make gains in tech adoption. Washington, DC: Pew Research Center. Retrieved from www.pewresearch.org/fact-tank/2017/03/22/digital-divide-persists-even-as-lower-income-americans-make-gains-in-tech-adoption/

Anderson, M., & Perrin, A. (2016). 13% of Americans don't use the internet. Who are they? Washington, DC: Pew Research Center. Retrieved from www.pewresearch.org/fact-tank/2016/09/07/some-americans-dont-use-the-internet-who-are-they/

Becker, H.S. (1998). *Tricks of the trade: How to think about your research while you're doing it.* Chicago, IL: University of Chicago Press.

Berinsky, A.J., Huber, G.A., & Lenz, G.S. (2012). Evaluating online labor markets for experimental research: Amazon.com's mechanical turk. *Political Analysis, 20*, 351–368.

Box, G.E.P. (1976). Science and statistics. *Journal of the American Statistical Association, 71*, 791–799.

Castells, M. (2010). *The rise of the network society.* West Sussex, UK: Blackwell.

Clark, M. (2015). Black Twitter: Building connection through cultural conversation. In N. Rambukkana (Ed.), *Hashtag publics: The power and politics of discursive networks* (pp. 205–218). New York, NY: Peter Lang Publishing Inc.

Coleman, J., Katz, E., & Menzel, H. (1957). The diffusion of an innovation among physicians. *Sociometry, 20*(4), 253–70.

Fischer, C.S. (1992). *America calling: A social history of the telephone to 1940.* Berkeley, CA: University of California Press.

Geertz, C. (1973). *The interpretation of cultures.* New York, NY: Basic Books.

Gilmor, D. (2004). *We the media.* Santa Rosa, CA: O'Reilly Media.

Haight, M., Quan-Haase, A., & Corbett, B. (2014). Revisiting the digital divide in Canada: The impact of demographic factors on access to the internet, level of online activity, and social networking site usage. *Information, Communication & Society, 17*(4), 503–519.

Hargittai, E. (2008). Whose space? Differences among users and non-users of social network sites. *Journal of Computer-Mediated Communication, 13*(1), 276–297.

Hargittai, E., & Jennrich, K. (2016). The online participation divide. In M. Lloyd & L.A. Friedland (Eds.), *The communication crisis in America, and how to fix it* (pp. 199–213). New York, NY: Palgrave Macmillan.

Hargittai, E., & Litt, E. (2011). The tweet smell of celebrity success: Explaining variation in Twitter adoption among a diverse group of young adults. *New Media and Society, 13*(5), 824–842.

Hargittai, E., & Walejko, G. (2008). The participation divide: Content creation and sharing in the digital age. *Information, Communication & Society, 11*(2), 239–256.

Hassani, S.N. (2006). Locating digital divides at home, work, and everywhere else. *Poetics, 34*(4–5), 250–272.

Hindman, M. (2009). *The myth of digital democracy.* Princeton, NJ: Princeton University Press.

Huff, C., & Tingley, D. (2015). "Who are these people?" Evaluating the demographic characteristics and political preferences of mturk survey respondents. *Research and Politics*, 1–12.

Jones, S., Johnson-Yale, C., Millermaier, S., & Seoane Pérez, F. (2009). U.S. college students' internet use: Race, gender and digital divides. *Journal of Computer-Mediated Communication, 14*(2), 244–264.

Karpf, D. (2012). Social science research methods in internet time. *Information, Communication & Society, 15*(5), 639–661.

Kendall, D. (2005). *Framing class: Media representations of wealth and poverty in America.* New York, NY: Rowman & Littlefield.

Laurison, D. (2015). The willingness to state an opinion: Inequality, don't know responses, and political participation. *Sociological Forum, 30*(4), 925–948.

Mills, C.W. (1958). The structure of power in American society. *The British Journal of Sociology, 29*(1), 29–41.

Mohr, J., & Bogdanov, P. (2013). Topic models: What they are and why they matter. *Poetics, 41*(6), 545–770.

Murthy, D., Gross, A., & Pensavalle, A. (2016). Urban social media demographics: An exploration of Twitter use in major American cities. *Journal of Computer-Mediated Communication, 21*, 33–49.

Nelson, L. (2014). *Enduring political logics as cultural "memory": Comparing women's organizations in Chicago and New York City*. Dissertation. UC Berkeley, Berkeley, CA.

Pew Research Center. (2017). *Mobile Fact Sheet*. Washington, DC: Pew Research Center.

Pickerill, J. (2003). *Cyberprotest: Environmental activism online*. Manchester, UK: Manchester University Press.

Pigliucci, M. (2009). The end of theory in science. *EMBO Reports, 10*, 534.

Press, A. (1991). *Women watching television: Gender, class and generation in the American television experience*. Philadelphia, PA: University of Pennsylvania Press.

Raine, L., & Wellman, B. (2012). *Networked: The new social operating system*. Cambridge, MA: MIT Press.

Robinson, L. (2009). A taste for the necessary. *Information, Communication & Society, 12*(4), 488–507.

Schradie, J. (2011). The digital production gap: The digital divide and Web 2.0 collide. *Poetics, 39*(2), 145–168.

Schradie, J. (2012). The trend of class, race, and ethnicity in social media inequality: Who still can't afford to blog? *Information, Communication & Society, 15*(4), 1–17.

Schradie, J. (2015). Silicon Valley ideology and class inequality: A virtual poll tax on digital politics. In D. Freelon & S. Coleman, *Handbook of digital politics* (pp. 67–84). Cheltanham, UK: Edward Elgar.

Schradie, J. (2017). The digital activism gap: How class and costs shape online collective action. *Social Problems*, Forthcoming.

Segev, E. (2010). *Google and the digital divide: The biases of online knowledge (Chandos internet series)*. Oxford, UK: Chandos Publishing.

Selwyn, N. (2006). Digital division or digital decision? A study of non-users and low-users of computers. *Poetics, 34*(4–5), 273–292.

Sims, C. (2014). From differentiated use to differentiating practices: Negotiating legitimate participation and the production of privileged identities. *Information, Communication & Society, 17*(6), 670–682.

Snijders, C., Matzat, U., & Reips, U. (2012). "Big data": Big knowledge gaps in the field of internet science. *International Journal of Internet Science*, 7(1), 1–5.

Tableau. (2016). *The state of data education in 2016*. Seattle, WA: Tableau Inc.

van Deursen, A.J.A.M., & van Dijk, J.A.G.M. (2011). Internet skills and the digital divide. *New Media & Society, 13*(6), 893–911.

van Dijk, J.A.G.M. (2005). *The deepening divide: Inequality in the information society*. Thousand Oaks, CA: SAGE Publications.

Vanneman, R., & Cannon, L.W. (1987). *The American perception of class*. Philadelphia, PA: Temple University Press.

Wall, M. (2015). Citizen journalism: A retrospective on what we know, an agenda for what we don't. *Digital Journalism, 3*(6), 797–813.

Watkins, S.C. (2011). Digital divide: Navigating the digital edge. *International Journal of Learning and Media, 3*(2), 1–12.

Weinberg, J., Freese, J., & McElhattan, D. (2014). Comparing data characteristics and results of an online factorial survey between a population-based and a crowdsource-recruited sample. *Sociological Science*, *1*(August), 292–310.
Wright, E.O. (1997). *Class counts: Comparative studies in class analysis*. New York, NY: Cambridge University Press.
Zhang, P.H. (2014). Digital divides and socio-demographic factors: A longitudinal quantitative study of internet users in U.S. from 2000 to 2010. Dissertation. Capella University, Ann Arbor, MI.
Zweig, M. (2001). *The working class majority*. Ithaca, NY: Cornell University Press.

CONTRIBUTORS

Mark Banks is Director of the CAMEo Research Institute for Cultural and Media Economies and Professor in the School of Media, Communication and Sociology at the University of Leicester. His work focuses on work in the cultural industries and on cultural policy. He is author of *The Politics of Cultural Work* (2007) and *Creative Justice: Cultural Industries, Work and Inequality* (2017), and co-editor of *Theorizing Cultural Work: Labour, Continuity and Change in the Cultural and Creative Industries* (2013).

Anita Biressi is Professor of Media and Society at the University of Roehampton. Her publications include *Reality Television* (2005), *The Tabloid Culture Reader* (2008), and *Class and Contemporary British Culture* (2013). Her research interests include the popular articulation of neoliberalism, representations of social class, and the relationship between the media sphere and social self. Anita's latest work is a feminist project exploring news, gender, and the governing of women's voices in the public sphere.

Richard Butsch is author of *The Making of American Audiences: From Stage to Television, 1750–1990* (2000), *The Citizen Audience: Crowds, Publics, and Individuals* (2008) and *Screen Culture: A Global History* (forthcoming), and he is editor of *For Fun and Profit: The Transformation of Leisure into Consumption* (1990), *Media and Public Spheres* (2007), and *Meanings of Audiences: Comparative Discourses* (2014, with Sonia Livingstone).

John Corner is Visiting Professor in Media and Communication at the University of Leeds and Professor Emeritus of the University of Liverpool. He has published widely since the 1970s in books and journals, including the monographs *Television*

Form and Public Address (1995), *The Art of Record* (1996), *Critical Ideas in Television Studies* (1999), and *Theorising Media* (2011). Film and television documentary has been one of his principal research interests.

June Deery is Professor of Media Studies at Rensselaer Polytechnic Institute and author of *Consuming Reality: The Commercialization of Factual Entertainment* (Palgrave, 2012) and *Reality TV* (Polity, 2015). Her latest work looks at reality TV and the campaign and early administration of Donald Trump.

David Hesmondhalgh is Professor of Media, Music and Culture at the University of Leeds. His books include *Why Music Matters* (2013), *Creative Labour* (2011, with Sarah Baker), and *The Cultural Industries*, a fourth edition of which will be published in 2018. He is also editor or co-editor of six further books, including *Media Production* (2006) and *The Media and Social Theory* (2008, with Jason Toynbee).

Jilly Boyce Kay is Research Associate in Media and Communication, University of Leicester. Her key research focuses on the historically shifting gender politics of television talk shows. She has published in journals, including *Critical Studies in Television*, *Feminist Media Histories*, and *Journalism: Theory, Practice and Criticism*, and she is co-editor of *The Past in Visual Culture: Essays on Memory, Nostalgia and the Media* (2016). She is assistant editor of the *European Journal of Cultural Studies*.

Jo Littler is a reader in the Department of Sociology at City, University of London. She has written on a wide range of subjects including consumer culture, heritage, and celebrity. Her most recent book is *Against Meritocracy: Culture, Power and Myths of Mobility* (Routledge, 2017).

Sonia Livingstone, OBE, is a Professor in the Department of Media and Communications at The London School of Economics and Political Science. She researches children's and young people's risks and opportunities, media literacy, social mediations, and rights in the digital age. Her new book is *The Class: Living and Learning in the Digital Age* (NYU UP, 2016, with Julian Sefton-Green). A Fellow of the British Psychological Society, Royal Society for the Arts, and Fellow and past President of the International Communication Association, she leads the projects "Global Kids Online" and "Preparing for a Digital Future."

Aline Maia is a Brazillian journalist with a PhD in Communication from the Pontifical Catholic University of Rio de Janeiro. She teaches and coordinates coursework in Communication at the University Estácio Juiz de Fora, where she also leads a research agenda on communication, social media and media representations, media visibility, and youth.

Vicki Mayer is Professor of Communication at Tulane University, where she researches and teaches about media production and cultural industries. She has authored four books, edited three, and co-directed a variety of digital humanities projects, including ViaNolaVie: Talking Life and Culture in New Orleans (www.vianolavie.org).

Laurie Ouellette is Professor of Media and Cultural Studies at the University of Minnesota. She writes about television, social and political theory, governmentality, and neoliberal culture. She is author or editor of many books, including most recently *Lifestyle TV* (2016) and *Keywords for Media Studies* (2017, with Jonathan Gray).

Andrea Press is William R. Kenan, Jr. Professor of Media Studies and Sociology at the University of Virginia. She is the former Executive Editor of the Virginia Film Festival and Producer of the Roger Ebert Film Festival. She is the author or co-author of *The New Media Environment, Speaking of Abortion, Women Watching Television*, and the forthcoming volumes *Media-Ready Feminism and Everyday Sexism, Handbook of Contemporary Feminism,* and *Feminist Reception Studies in a Post-Audience Age.*

Marjorie Rosen is the author of three non-fiction books—*Boom Town: How Walmart Transformed an All-American Town into an International Community*; *Popcorn Venus: Women, Movies & the American Dream*; and *Mia & Woody: Love and Betrayal*—and one novel, *What Nigel Knew*, co-written under a pseudonym with another New York movie critic. A screenwriter and one-time senior writer at *People*, she is now an associate professor of film and journalism at Lehman College – CUNY.

Jen Schradie is a research fellow at the Institute for Advanced Study in Toulouse. She received an MPA from the Harvard Kennedy School and a PhD in Sociology and New Media at University of California, Berkeley. Her NSF-funded research interrogates digital democracy claims. She has published on the digital activism gap in *Social Problems* and the *International Journal of Communication* and is the author of a forthcoming Harvard University Press book on the topic. She has also written about digital production inequality in *Poetics* and *Information, Communication, and Society*.

Julian Sefton-Green is currently Professor of New Media Education at Deakin University, having previously worked as a schoolteacher, in teacher training, and in the informal education sector. He has researched and written widely on media education, digital culture, creativity, new technologies, and informal learning. Recent volumes include co-authoring *The Class: Living and Learning in the Digital*

Age (NYU Press, 2016) and *Learning Identities, Education & Community: Young Lives in the Cosmopolitan City* (CUP, 2016) (www.julianseftongreen.net).

Rob Wilkie is Associate Professor of Cultural and Digital Studies at the University of Wisconsin–La Crosse. He is the author of *The Digital Condition* and co-editor of *Human, All Too (Post)Human*. His work has appeared in such journals as *The Minnesota Review*, *International Critical Thought*, *JAC*, *Postmodern Culture*, and *Textual Practice*. He is currently working on a book on class and digital rhetoric.

Milly Williamson is a senior lecturer in Film and Television Studies at Brunel University. She has published widely on celebrity culture, promotional cultures, advertising and commercial media, television studies, and issues of gender representation. She is the author of *Celebrity: Capitalism and the Making of Fame* (2016).

Helen Wood is Professor of Media and Communication at the University of Leicester and has published widely on television, audiences, class, and gender. She is author of *Talking with Television* (2009) and *Reacting to Reality Television* (2012, with Beverley Skeggs); she has also edited *Reality Television and Class* with Beverley Skeggs (2011) and *Television for Women: New Directions* (2016) with Rachel Moseley and Helen Wheatley. She is editor of the *European Journal of Cultural Studies*.

INDEX

Lightning Source UK Ltd.
Milton Keynes UK
UKHW022203050520
362848UK00006B/78

9 781138 229792